THE CAMBRIDGE COMPANION TO
THE LITERATURE OF THE AMERICAN RENAISSANCE

The American Renaissance has been a foundational concept in American literary history for nearly a century. The phrase connotes a period as well as an event, an iconic turning point in the growth of a national literature and a canon of texts that would shape American fiction, poetry, and oratory for generations. F. O. Matthiessen coined the term in 1941 to describe the years 1850–1855, which saw the publications of major writings by Hawthorne, Melville, Emerson, Thoreau, and Whitman. This Companion takes up the concept of the American Renaissance and explores its origins, meaning, and longevity. Essays by distinguished scholars move chronologically from the formative reading of American Renaissance authors to the careers of major figures ignored by Matthiessen, including Stowe, Douglass, Harper, and Longfellow. The volume uses the best of current literary studies, from digital humanities to psychoanalytic theory, to illuminate an era that reaches far beyond the Civil War and continues to shape our understanding of American literature.

Christopher N. Phillips is the author of numerous articles and book chapters on American literature, published in venues such as *PMLA*, *Early American Literature*, and *Literature in the Early American Republic*. He is the author of *Epic in American Culture, Settlement to Reconstruction* (2012) and *The Hymnal: A Reading History* (2018). Among recent fellowships received are a National Endowment for the Humanities Postdoctoral Fellowship at the Library Company of Philadelphia and a Frederick Burkhardt Residential Fellowship from the American Council of Learned Societies in conjunction with the American Antiquarian Society.

A complete list of books in the series is at the back of this book.

THE CAMBRIDGE
COMPANION TO

THE LITERATURE
OF THE AMERICAN
RENAISSANCE

EDITED BY
CHRISTOPHER N. PHILLIPS
Lafayette College, Pennsylvania

CAMBRIDGE
UNIVERSITY PRESS

University Printing House, Cambridge CB2 8BS, United Kingdom

One Liberty Plaza, 20th Floor, New York, NY 10006, USA

477 Williamstown Road, Port Melbourne, VIC 3207, Australia

314–321, 3rd Floor, Plot 3, Splendor Forum, Jasola District Centre, New Delhi – 110025, India

79 Anson Road, #06-04/06, Singapore 079906

Cambridge University Press is part of the University of Cambridge.

It furthers the University's mission by disseminating knowledge in the pursuit of
education, learning, and research at the highest international levels of excellence.

www.cambridge.org
Information on this title: www.cambridge.org/9781108420914
DOI: 10.1017/9781108355643

First published 2018

Printed in the United States of America by Sheridan Books, Inc.

A catalogue record for this publication is available from the British Library.

ISBN 978-1-108-42091-4 Hardback
ISBN 978-1-108-43108-8 Paperback

CONTENTS

FIGURES

CONTRIBUTORS

DAVID HAVEN BLAKE is Professor of English at The College of New Jersey. He is the author of *Walt Whitman and the Culture of American Celebrity* (2006) and the co-editor of *Walt Whitman: Where the Future Becomes Present* (2008). His most recent book is *Liking Ike: Eisenhower, Advertising, and the Rise of Celebrity Politics*, winner of the 2017 PROSE award for Media & Cultural Studies.

MELBA JOYCE BOYD is a Distinguished Professor in African American Studies at Wayne State University in Detroit, and an Adjunct Professor in Afroamerican and African Studies at the University of Michigan – Ann Arbor. She is an award-winning author or editor of thirteen books, nine of which are poetry. Boyd's critically acclaimed and widely reviewed *Discarded Legacy: Politics and Poetics in the Life of Frances E. W. Harper, 1825–1911* (1994) was the first comprehensive study of Frances Ellen Watkins Harper. Boyd's poetry, essays, and creative nonfiction have appeared in anthologies, academic journals, cultural periodicals, and newspapers in the United States and Europe. She was a Fulbright Scholar at the University of Bremen, and has a Doctor of Arts in English from the University of Michigan, and B.A. and M.A. degrees in English from Western Michigan University.

JENNIFER L. BRADY is a lecturer and the Associate Director of Studies in the History & Literature program at Harvard University. Her work on sentimentality, anti-novel tracts, fan letters, and historical and imagined readers has appeared in *American Literature* and *Common-place*.

BARBARA HOCHMAN is Professor Emerita in the Department of Foreign Literatures and Linguisitcs at Ben-Gurion University. She has written widely on American fiction, reading practices, and interpretive norms. Her books include *Getting at the Author: Reimagining Books and Reading in the Age of American Realism* (2001) *and Uncle Tom's Cabin and the Reading Revolution: Race, Literacy, Childhood, and Fiction 1852–1911*, winner of the DeLong Book History Prize for 2012.

ZACHARY MCLEOD HUTCHINS is Assistant Professor of English at Colorado State University. He is the author of *Inventing Eden: Primitivism, Millennialism, and the Making of New England* (2014) and a dozen essays on American literature and culture, which have appeared in journals such as *ELH*, *Early American Literature*, *ESQ*, and *Nineteenth-Century Literature*.

CHRISTOPH IRMSCHER teaches at Indiana University Bloomington, where he is Provost Professor of English and George F. Getz Jr. Professor in the Wells Scholars Program, which he also directs. Among his books are *Longfellow Redux*, *Louis Agassiz: Creator of American Science* and, most recently, *Max Eastman: A Life*. The web version of his 2007 Bicentennial Exhibit on Longfellow won the Katherine Kyes Leab and Daniel J. Leab Exhibition Award of the American Library Association. His personal webpage is at www.christophirmscher.com.

GAVIN JONES is Professor of English at Stanford University, and has served as his department's Chair (2011–2015). He is the author of *Strange Talk: The Politics of Dialect Literature in Gilded Age America* (1999), *American Hungers: The Problem of Poverty in US Literature, 1840–1945* (2007), and *Failure and the American Writer: A Literary History* (2014). He is currently working on a study of John Steinbeck's visions of twentieth-century American history.

WYN KELLEY, Senior Lecturer in Literature at the Massachusetts Institute of Technology, is author of *Melville's City: Literary and Urban Form in Nineteenth-Century New York* (1996) and of *Herman Melville: An Introduction* (2008); and co-author, with Henry Jenkins, of *Reading in a Participatory Culture: Re-Mixing Moby-Dick in the English Classroom* (2013). Former Associate Editor of the Melville Society journal *Leviathan* and editor of the *Blackwell Companion to Herman Melville* (2006), she has published essays in a number of journals and collections. Associate Director of *MEL* (Melville Electronic Library), she also works to develop digital pedagogy with the HyperStudio, MIT's digital humanities lab, and is a founding member of the Melville Society Cultural Project.

CHRISTOPHER N. PHILLIPS is Associate Professor of English at Lafayette College. He is the author of *Epic in American Culture, Settlement to Reconstruction* (2012) and *The Hymnal: A Reading History* (2018). He is also the principal investigator on the Easton Library Company Database Project, a digital humanities collaboration between Lafayette College and the Easton Area Public Library in Easton, Pennsylvania.

JUDITH RICHARDSON is Senior Lecturer in the English Department at Stanford University, and Coordinator of the American Studies Program. She is the author of *Possessions: The History and Uses of Haunting in the Hudson Valley* (2003), and is currently at work on a book about nineteenth-century America's "plant-mindedness," its multivalent obsession with vegetable matters.

MARK RIFKIN is Director of Women's and Gender Studies and Professor of English at the University of North Carolina at Greensboro. He is the author of five books, including *Beyond Settler Time: Temporal Sovereignty and Indigenous Self-Determination* (2017), *Settler Common Sense: Queerness and Everyday Colonialism in the American Renaissance* (2014), and *When Did Indians Become Straight? Kinship, the History of Sexuality and Native Sovereignty* (2011) (winner of the John Hope Franklin Prize for Best Book in American Studies; winner of the Best Subsequent Book prize from the Native American and Indigenous Studies Association). He co-edited *Sexuality, Nationality, Indigeneity*, a special double-issue of *GLQ* (winner of the Best Special Issue award from the Councils of Editors of Learned Journals). He has served as president of the NAISA and on the editorial boards of *American Literature* and *J19*.

RUSSELL SBRIGLIA is Assistant Professor of English at Seton Hall University, where he teaches courses in eighteenth- and nineteenth-century American literature. He is the author of *American Romanticism and the Materiality of Transcendence: Five Hegelian Variations* (forthcoming), editor of *Everything You Always Wanted to Know about Literature but Were Afraid to Ask Žižek* (2017), and co-editor, with Slavoj Žižek, of *Subject Lessons: Hegel, Lacan, and the Future of Materialism* (forthcoming).

ALEXANDRA SOCARIDES is the author of *Dickinson Unbound: Paper, Process, Poetics* (2012) and the co-editor of *A History of Nineteenth-Century American Women's Poetry* (Cambridge University Press, 2016). Her essays have appeared in, among other publications, *Nineteenth-Century Literature, Legacy: A Journal of American Women Writers*, and *The Emily Dickinson Journal*. She is an Associate Professor of English at the University of Missouri.

ZOE TRODD is Professor of American Studies at the University of Nottingham and director of a university Research Priority Area on Rights and Justice. Her books include *American Protest Literature* (2006), *To Plead Our Cause* (2008), *The Tribunal: Responses to John Brown and the Harpers Ferry Raid* (2012), and *Picturing Frederick Douglass* (2015).

JEFFREY WALKER, Professor of English at Oklahoma State and former Fulbright lecturer in Norway and Belgium, authored a critical study of the Revolutionary poet and traitor Benjamin Church, edited collections of essays on Fenimore Cooper, co-edited Cooper's 1821 bestseller *The Spy* and the annual journal *Literature in the Early American Republic* (*LEAR*), and is completing an edition of Cooper's unpublished letters.

LAURA DASSOW WALLS teaches at the University of Notre Dame, where she is the William P. and Hazel B. White Professor of English and an affiliate of the History and Philosophy of Science Program. She has published widely on American

Transcendentalism, including her most recent book, the general-interest biography *Henry David Thoreau: A Life* (2017), which grew out of her first book, *Seeing New Worlds: Henry David Thoreau and Nineteenth-Century Natural Science* (1995). She is also the author of *Emerson's Life in Science: The Culture of Truth* (2003) and *Passage to Cosmos: Alexander von Humboldt and the Shaping of America* (2009), winner of the James Russell Lowell Prize from the Modern Language Association and the Merle Curti Award from the Organization of American Historians.

ACKNOWLEDGMENTS

Thanks as always to my wife, Emily, for sustaining so much of our life while this book took shape, and for our conversations that helped remind me of what fascinates me about the American Renaissance. For other conversations that helped to mold this project, my thanks to Ed Whitley, Claudia Stokes, Hal Bush, Brian Yothers, Hester Blum, Dana McClain, Faith Barrett, Ezra Greenspan, James Woolley, and Steve Belletto.

I voice my particular thanks to Ray Ryan, who believed in this project and its editor from the beginning and has seen it through the many ins and outs of producing a volume that can safely be said to "contain multitudes." Working with each of the contributors has also been a joy and an education of a high order, and I feel a much-enlarged scholar of the field in learning from and engaging with each of them. Thank you, one and all.

My work on this volume was supported by generous funding from a National Endowment for the Humanities Postdoctoral Fellowship at the Library Company of Philadelphia and a Frederick C. Burkhardt Fellowship from the American Council of Learned Societies, the latter while in residence at the American Antiquarian Society. My thanks to each of those institutions, both foundations and libraries, for fostering this contribution to the scholarship and teaching of American literary studies at a moment when the American Renaissance, with all its contradictory impulses and contested meanings, seems more relevant to our times than ever.

CHRONOLOGY

1803   Ralph Waldo Emerson born
         Louisiana Purchase

1804   Nathaniel Hawthorne (née Hathorne) born
         Haitian Revolution wins independence

1806   William Gilmore Simms born

1807   Henry Wadsworth Longfellow born

1808   Ban of American transatlantic slave trade

1809   Edgar Allan Poe born

1810   Margaret Fuller born

1811   Fanny Fern (née Sarah Payson Willis) born

1815   Napoleon defeated at Waterloo

1817   William Cullen Bryant, "Thanatopsis"
         Henry David (née David Henry) Thoreau born

1818   George Copway (Kah-Ge-Ga-Gah-Bowh) born
         Frederick Douglass (née Frederick Augustus Washington Bailey) born

1819   Washington Irving, *The Sketch Book of Geoffrey Crayon*
         Herman Melville (née Melvill) born
         Susan Warner born
         Walt Whitman born

1820   Missouri Compromise

1821   James Feminore Cooper, *The Spy*

1823   Cooper, *The Pioneers*

1825   Frances Ellen Watkins (Harper) born

1826   Cooper, *The Last of the Mohicans*
         South American independence from Spain

1830   Emily Dickinson born
       Simón Bolívar dies

1831   *Cherokee Nation v. Georgia*
       William Lloyd Garrison founds the anti-slavery newspaper *Liberator*

1833   Slavery abolished in British empire

1835   Simms, *The Yemassee* & *The Partisan*

1836   Emerson, *Nature*
       American artist Thomas Cole exhibits *Course of Empire* in New York
       Battle of the Alamo; Republic of Texas declares independence

1837   Hawthorne, *Twice-Told Tales* (volume 1)
       Financial Panic of 1837

1838   Poe, *Narrative of Arthur Gordon Pym of Nantucket*
       "Trail of Tears," part of decades-long Native removal policy

1839   Poe, *Tales of the Grotesque and Arabesque*

1840   Emerson, *Essays* (1st series)
       Fuller commences editing *The Dial*

1842   Hawthorne, *Twice-Told Tales* (volume 2)

1844   Emerson, *Essays* (2nd series)
       Anti-Catholic riots in Philadelphia
       Samuel F. B. Morse sends first American telegram

1845   Douglass, *Narrative of the Life of Frederick Douglass*
       Fuller, *Woman in the Nineteenth Century*
       Harper, *Forest Leaves*
       Poe, "The Raven"
       Texas admitted to the Union

1846   Hawthorne, *Mosses from an Old Manse*
       Melville, *Typee*
       Mexican War begins

1847   Copway, *Life, History, and Adventures of Kah-Ge-Ga-Gah-Bowh*
       Longfellow, *Evangeline*
       Melville, *Omoo*

1848   Melville, *Mardi*
       Poe, *Eureka*
       Mexican War ends
       Seneca Falls Convention, first women's rights convention
       Gold discovered in California
       Revolutions in France, Germany, Italy, Austria Empire
       Cole dies

1849   Irving, *Mahomet and His Successors*
       Longfellow, *The Seaside and the Fireside*
       Melville, *Redburn*
       Thoreau, "Resistance to Civil Government" (later *Civil Disobedience*)
       and *A Week*
       on the Concord and Merrimack Rivers
       Poe dies
       California Gold Rush

1850   Emerson, *Representative Men*
       Hawthorne, *The Scarlet Letter*
       Melville, *White-Jacket*
       Warner, *The Wide, Wide World*
       Margaret Fuller dies
       Compromise of 1850 – Fugitive Slave Act passes, California becomes
       a state

1851   Hawthorne, *The House of the Seven Gables*
       Longfellow, *The Golden Legend*
       Melville, *Moby-Dick*
       Cooper dies

1852   Douglass, "What to the Slave Is the Fourth of July?" and *The Heroic
       Slave*
       Hawthorne, *The Blithedale Romance*
       Melville, *Pierre*
       Stowe, *Uncle Tom's Cabin* (serialized in 1851)
       Warner, *Queechy*
       Franklin Pierce elected president

1853   Fern, *Fern Leaves from Fanny's Portfolio*
       Melville, "Bartleby"

1854   Fern, *Ruth Hall* and *Fern Leaves, 2nd series*
       Harper, *Poems on Miscellaneous Subjects*
       John Rollin Ridge, *The Life and Adventures of Joaquín Murieta*
       Thoreau, *Walden*
       Cummins, *The Lamplighter*

1855   Douglass, *My Bondage and My Freedom*
       Longfellow, *The Song of Hiawatha*
       Melville, "Benito Cereno"
       Whitman, *Leaves of Grass*, 1st ed.
       "Bleeding Kansas"

1856   Melville, *The Piazza Tales*
       Stowe, *Dred*
       Whitman, *Leaves of Grass*, 2nd ed.

CHRISTOPHER N. PHILLIPS

Introduction: The Very Idea of an American Renaissance

What was the American Renaissance? For F. O. Matthiessen, who coined the term in 1941, it was both a period and an event in American literary history. Focused on a narrow date range (1850–1855) and canon (five authors, all white males of the Northeast US), Matthiessen gave lengthy readings in his book *American Renaissance* of what he saw as the major texts of that period – Herman Melville's *Moby-Dick*, Nathaniel Hawthorne's *The Scarlet Letter*, Henry David Thoreau's *Walden*, among others. Yet at stake for Matthiessen was not simply identifying a watershed moment in the production of American literature; he aimed to show how "the possibilities of democracy" became powerfully central to American literature in those years and works.[1] In arguing that Melville, Hawthorne, Thoreau, Ralph Waldo Emerson, and Walt Whitman changed the national conversation about the ideal of democracy, Matthiessen changed the critical conversation about what we talk about when we talk about American literature. As Matthiessen himself argued, the idea of an American Renaissance is just as much about the present day's memories and aspirations as it is about anything unique to the 1850s or the antebellum period. This volume takes up the era and authors Matthiessen identified and places them in new contexts and company, those that speak more directly to the current state of American literary studies and the world that field inhabits. Before discussing the American Renaissance as a slice of nineteenth-century history, however, this introduction will provide a brief history of where the idea of an American Renaissance came from and where it has gone since the 1940s.

While Matthiessen holds the claim to coining the term "American Renaissance," the idea that a new era arrived in American literature with the rise of Emerson, Hawthorne, and their contemporaries is much older. Indeed, Dartmouth professor Charles F. Richardson referred to a

---

[1] F. O. Matthiessen, *American Renaissance: Art and Expression in the Age of Emerson and Whitman* (New York: Oxford University Press, 1941, repr. 1968), ix.

"New England Transcendental Renaissance" in his 1880s work *American Literature, 1607–1885*, a cue picked up by Matthiessen's forerunner at Harvard, Barrett Wendell, at the turn of the century.[2] In his *Literary History of America* (1900), Wendell identified what he called a "Renaissance of New England," led by Ralph Waldo Emerson, John Greenleaf Whittier, Henry Wadsworth Longfellow, James Russell Lowell, Oliver Wendell Holmes, and Nathaniel Hawthorne.[3] Other literary histories drew similar connections, from Vernon Parrington's *Main Currents in American Thought* (1927–1930) to Fred Lewis Pattee's *The First Century of American Literature* (1935) to Van Wyck Brooks's *The Flowering of New England* (1936). Lewis Mumford went so far as to refer to the generation before the Civil War as the "Golden Day" in a 1926 book by that name; one thing that set Mumford's work apart from the other studies mentioned above, and that made a major difference in Matthiessen's thinking when he read Mumford as a student, was a revision of the canon of authors involved in that crucial era. Instead of the poets Longfellow, Whittier, Lowell, and Holmes, who had become increasingly identified in twentieth-century American literary criticism as "the genteel school," Mumford championed "outsider" authors such as Melville, Whitman, and Thoreau. Matthiessen adopted Mumford's canon, and he used the New York roots of Melville and Whitman along with his democratic theme to make his account of American literature much more national in scope than previous accounts had been. Richardson's and Wendell's Renaissances were self-consciously regional; Matthiessen's rhetorically, if not geographically, encompassed the nation.

This new articulation of America's literary coming-of-age through its engagement with democracy, coming as it did on the heels of the United States's entry into World War II, was a powerful galvanizing force in the emergence of American Studies departments in the postwar years. R. W. B. Lewis's *The American Adam* (1955), Leo Marx's *The Machine in the Garden* (1964), and Leslie Fiedler's *Love and Death in the American Novel* (1960) all took the American Renaissance as a *locus classicus* for the themes and dynamics they each saw as central to American literature and culture. In an era dominated by New Criticism's commitment to close reading of individual works and the decidedly Anglophilic definitions of literary value that

---

[2] Charles F. Richardson, *American Literature, 1607–1885* (New York, 1886–1889), 1:427.
[3] This is the title of Book v in Barrett Wendell, *A Literary History of America* (New York: Scribners, 1900). On Richardson's and Wendell's influence on later directions in American literary historiography, see Claudia Stokes, *Writers in Retrospect: The Rise of American Literary History, 1875–1910* (Chapel Hill: University of North Carolina Press, 2007); Michael Boyden, *Predicting the Past: The Paradoxes of American Literary History* (Leuven: Leuven University Press, 2009).

shaped the close-reading-friendly canon, it was highly useful for scholars in the newly recognized field of American literature to follow Matthiessen's insistence on "read[ing] the best books first" (a line he took from Thoreau) and to have a method for identifying a set of American works as the best. David Bowers's statement in Robert Spiller's influential *Literary History of the United States* echoes Matthiessen succinctly: "In quality of style, and particularly in depth of philosophic insight, American literature has not yet surpassed the collective achievement of Emerson, Thoreau, Hawthorne, Melville, and Whitman."[4] That blend of stylistic mastery and philosophical weight was the magic formula for establishing these five authors as the heart of American literature for mid-twentieth-century critics.

This vital focus, both highly persuasive and eminently teachable – only five authors to cover, and focused on democracy – came at a price. Matthiessen celebrated the radical impulses of the abolition movement, citing *Uncle Tom's Cabin* as evidence of the abolition movement's energy, but he refused to do more than mention Stowe's book or treat her or her contemporaries, Frederick Douglass and Frances E. W. Harper, as literary authors. While focusing on authors who thought of themselves as outside or at least in tension with the American mainstream, this conception of the American Renaissance served to obscure women, minorities, and even writers like Longfellow and Whittier who engaged the mainstream while taking radical stances on abolition and celebrating American cultural and ethnic diversity. Michael Davitt Bell has pointed out that at nearly the same time that *The American Renaissance* was published, Fred Lewis Pattee published his study *The Feminine Fifties* (1940), which treated the same period but focused on a very different canon: the women whose engagement with sentimental discourse united them in a cultural moment and enabled their popular success. Stowe, Susan Warner, Maria Cummins, and Fanny Fern exemplified this moment for Pattee, but as Bell points out, Pattee's reading of these authors amounted to the same thing as Matthiessen's silence on them: an update of Hawthorne's notorious characterization of his competition as a "damned mob of scribbling women."[5] Not until after the foment of the Civil Rights Movement in the 1960s and 1970s would such women authors, along with black and Native authors, find anything like a secure place in the American Renaissance.

4 David Bowers, "Democratic Vistas," in *Literary History of the United States*, ed. Robert E. Spiller, Willard Thorp, Thomas H. Johnson, and Henry Seidel Canby (New York: Macmillan, 1948), 1:345–57, 345.
5 Michael Davitt Bell, "Conditions of Literary Vocation," in *The Cambridge History of American Literature: Volume 2, Prose Writing 1820–1865*, ed. Sacvan Bercovitch (New York: Cambridge University Press, 1995), 9–124, 74–6.

The Renaissance story began to change dramatically in the scholarly telling in the 1980s as paradigms of cultural studies and the New Historicism engaged with the recovery work that continued through the decade. Sacvan Bercovitch's *The Puritan Origins of the American Self* (1975) and *The American Jeremiad* (1978) had already begun to recast the American Renaissance not so much as a turning point as a new iteration of a long-running practice in American writing, which Bercovitch traced back to colonial New England; Richard Slotkin's *Regeneration Through Violence* (1973) also saw the American Renaissance as the culmination of an expansive myth-making project about the frontier stretching back to the Puritans. By the mid-1980s, several essay collections called for new concepts in considering the American Renaissance and American literary history more generally, including Bercovitch's *Reconstructing American Literary History* (1986), Bercovitch and Myra Jehlen's *Ideology and Classic American Literature* (1986), and Donald Pease and Walter Benn Michaels's *The American Renaissance Reconsidered* (1985). These collections urged the use of cultural studies, theoretical, and historicist methods in studying the American Renaissance, and three studies in particular helped to reshape scholarship in the field along these lines. Jane Tompkins's *Sensational Designs* (1985) offered a reassessment of the "cultural work" of sentimental fiction and a corollary rethinking of what counts as literary value and why; Pease's *Visionary Compacts* (1987) applied New Historicist contextualizations to American Renaissance texts highlighting the pressures of the impending Civil War, while also noting the pressures of the Cold War in the 1950s that made Matthiessen's American Renaissance so compelling to postwar English departments; and David S. Reynolds's *Beneath the American Renaissance* (1988) drew on extensive archival research to argue that what the New Critics most valued in Matthiessen's canon was in fact a result of authorial engagement with popular print – the very sentimental, sensationalist, and pulp materials that had earlier been rejected as unworthy of study. Eric Sundquist's *To Wake the Nations* (1993) put black writers such as Frederick Douglass alongside Melville and other Renaissance authors in bringing the dynamic new work in African-American literary scholarship into reconsiderations of American literary history, opening discussions of race and the American Renaissance at a new, much more holistic level. Before the so-called "culture wars" of the 1990s were challenging the hegemony of Western Civilization courses and the canons of European literature (including British literature), the American Renaissance was already a field in transition, a rich proving ground for new critical approaches and reconceived literary and cultural canons.

By the time Timothy Powell's *Ruthless Democracy* (2000) made the case for a multicultural understanding of the American Renaissance, a period that saw the rise of female and minority authorship no less dramatic than the production of white male New Englanders, it had become clear that the question of *what* the American Renaissance was had shifted to *who* the American Renaissance was. Growing interest in African-American writers from Douglass to Frances Harper to Harriet Jacobs made not just white commentary on race but the voices of slaves and free blacks more central to the period; white women from Stowe to Susan Warner to Lydia Sigourney to Frances Sargent Osgood have also expanded and diversified the authorial voices included in a typical course. While Native American voices from the period, such as George Copway and John Rollin Ridge, have begun entering anthologies and syllabi more frequently, the Vanishing Indian ideology espoused by Matthiessen and his canon has been more tenacious than the bracketing of black and female voices has been. Mark Rifkin argues in *Settler Common Sense: Queerness and Everyday Colonialism in the American Renaissance* (2014) that the erasure of the Native lies at the heart of the literature of the American Renaissance as well as the culture that grounded it – and that grounds us today. This volume explores ways that the American Renaissance canon has been expanded and offers reflections on the possibilities for further expansion and integration.

Additionally, the questions of *where* and *when* the American Renaissance have become much more prominent in the scholarship of the field. Barrett Wendell voiced his unease over the label "America" in the introduction to his study, as that term had such hemispheric reach it seemed to him inappropriate to apply it to the United States alone (he was dismissed as a pedant for making this argument in 1900); he also was careful to identify his renaissance as regional, though he saw it as leading the nation by example and influence. Scholars continued recovering writers from the South, West, and Mid-Atlantic regions, and beginning with Lawrence Buell's *New England Literary Culture* (1986) scholars asked how a single region had succeeded in making a claim to represent the nation in its cultural expression. The "hemispheric turn" proved especially helpful in challenging the New England focus of antebellum literary studies, exemplified by Kirsten Silva-Gruesz's *Ambassadors of Culture* (2002) and Anna Brickhouse's *Transamerican Literary Relations and the Nineteenth-Century Public Sphere* (2004), the latter in particular taking Matthiessen head-on in challenging both his choice of authors and his claims to national representation. The American Renaissance was going on in upstate New York, Sacramento, Cincinnati, Havana, Lima, and Concord simultaneously, as it turned out.

As the geography and demography of the American Renaissance has expanded in recent scholarship, so has the chronology. The now-standard inclusion of Poe (who died in 1849) hints at an expanded date range soon after Matthiessen's book first appeared. Bercovitch's earlier work already suggested a *longue durée* interpretation of the period, and recent works such as Jay Grossman's *Reconstituting the American Renaissance* (2003) have recast the period as one spanning many decades, even a century, as in Grossman's tracing of Emerson's and Whitman's 1850s writings back to divergent traditions of political discourse in the eighteenth century. Martin Kevorkian's *Writing Beyond Prophecy: Emerson, Hawthorne, and Melville After the American Renaissance* (2013) trailblazes what promises to be a fruitful line of scholarship in exploring what the Civil War and its aftermath changed in the writings of American Renaissance authors; Kevorkian argues that during and after the war, Emerson, Melville, and Hawthorne ceased to be American Renaissance authors, even though they kept writing.

Another productive way to pursue the *when* question recently has been looking not to the mid-nineteenth century but to the mid-twentieth century for the origins of the American Renaissance. Tellingly, Werner Sollors and Greil Marcus's *A New Literary History of America* (2009), a clear nod to Barrett Wendell's earlier work, discusses the American Renaissance not among the essays on the nineteenth century but in an essay on the twentieth, one that focuses on the motives and influences that shaped Matthiessen's study in his own historical moment.[6] Following the lead of Pease's work, Christopher Castiglia's study of Richard Chase and Grossman's study of Matthiessen (including a biography in progress as of this writing), have further brought Cold War studies to bear on understanding the meanings and combinations that have constituted the American Renaissance in postwar English and American Studies departments.[7] While the rich historical recoveries and reassessments of the mid-nineteenth-century United States are today more prolific than ever, we are at a moment in the history of the field when scholars are especially ready to take seriously Matthiessen's statement that his "double aim" in analyzing the literature he did was "to place

---

[6] Robert Polito, "1924: F. O. Matthiessen Meets Russell Cheney on the Ocean Liner Paris, and American Literary History Emerges from Skull and Bones: A Judgment of Art," in *A New Literary History of America*, ed. Werner Sollors and Greil Marcus (Cambridge, MA: Harvard University Press, 2009), 564–9.

[7] See Christopher Castiglia, "Cold War Allegories and the Politics of Criticism," in *The New Cambridge Companion to Herman Melville*, ed. Robert S. Levine (New York: Cambridge University Press, 2014), 219–32; Jay Grossman, "'Autobiography Even in the Loose Sense': F. O. Matthiessen and Melville," *Leviathan* 13.1 (2011): 45–57.

these works both in their age and in ours."[8] And at one of many moments in the history of literary studies – very much like Matthiessen's, in fact – when the relevance of the academic subject seems at issue, the question is a crucial one for us to ask.

This volume offers a rich range of engagements with the age of the American Renaissance, often circling back to the question of why we still study, teach, and learn from the writings of this era. Three main sections organize along lines of chronology and thematics. Part I, Into the Renaissance, looks at the origins and influences of 1850s American literature, focusing on foundational authors such as James Fenimore Cooper and Henry Wadsworth Longfellow as well as the pre-1850 works of figures like Emerson and Poe. It also considers several conceptual ways into the study of the period, from genre categories such as adventure fiction, the gothic, and transnational poetry to geographic frameworks of the local, the national, and the global, as well as balancing a focus on individual authors with considerations of "reader-based literary history," digital humanities, and psychoanalytic and reader-response theories. Part II, Rethinking the Renaissance, focuses on the 1850s, placing figures like Melville and Hawthorne alongside such dominant figures and emerging celebrities of the day as Fanny Fern, George Copway, Susan Warner, and Frances Sargent Osgood, highlighting issues of race and gender, writing and labor, child studies and spatial studies. This section takes Matthiessen's "age of Emerson and Whitman" into the latest "turns" of contemporary scholarship. And Part III, Beyond the Renaissance, stretches the era's temporal boundaries through the tracking of authorial careers – nearly all the most-studied figures of the American Renaissance wrote for years after the Civil War – as well as considering the place of the Civil War in demarcating the end of the period.

In Chapter 1, Christopher N. Phillips presents a case study of a subscription library in the small city of Easton, Pennsylvania, where surviving loan records and library catalogs from the 1850s indicate that much of the American Renaissance on the Easton Library Company's shelves appeared in magazines rather than in individual books, that sentimental writers gained an eager new audience toward the middle of the decade, and that the popularity of Hawthorne and Emerson was dwarfed by that of earlier writers like Walter Scott and, above all, Cooper. Jeffrey Walker explores the phenomenon of Cooper's wide popularity in Chapter 2, giving readings of key novels such as *The Spy* and *Last of the Mohicans* while contextualizing Cooper's career, as well as that of his Southern counterpart William

---

[8] Matthiessen, *American Renaissance*, viii.

Gilmore Simms, within the rise of youth culture, the rhythm of the school year, and the prominence of summer leisure reading as a space for absorbing the masculine adventure mythologies by which Cooper sought to narrate a new nation.

Turning from the nation to the self, Russell Sbriglia argues in Chapter 3 that the gothic, as seen in the writings of Poe and Philadelphia radical George Lippard, offered a critique of the optimism expressed by Transcendental thinkers such as Emerson and Bronson Alcott. Rather than contradicting or dismissing Emerson's ideas, Poe and Lippard showed that they are in fact grounded not in rational liberation from superstition but rather in the dark depths of the irrational itself in ways that, as Sbriglia argues, has considerable affinities with today's psychoanalytic theories, and offers a startling critique of the assumptions of American liberal democracy.

Chapters 4 and 5 place the careers of three of the nation's most influential authors – Emerson, Hawthorne, and Longfellow – in the context of their New England roots and their international aspirations. Gavin Jones and Judith Richardson use the literary landmarks of Hawthorne's and Emerson's Concord homes as springboards for exploring how dependent Emerson's cosmopolitan *Essays* were on the local climates of Harvard, Concord, and the lyceum stage, and how Hawthorne used New England's past and present to show the interconnectedness of locales, as sailors, Indians, French, British, and other far-flung characters intersect in the port towns and woods of Massachusetts. Christoph Irmscher's chapter finds a similar play between home and the globe at work in the writings of Longfellow, a poet fluent in over a dozen languages who used the trope of reading-as-travel to introduce his American readers to a global literary scene, while also bringing American places and stories to audiences worldwide. Irmscher closes Part I of the volume with a reflection on the importance of multilingual, translated literature – "world literature," as Goethe called it – for understanding how and why Longfellow's readers found him so appealing in his day.

Few topics were as central to the nineteenth-century United States as religion, and in Chapter 6 Zachary McLeod Hutchins highlights one of the central theological debates of the time: is the nation in spiritual decline, or will the rising generation lead America to a new age of virtue? Hutchins centers on a close analysis of Hawthorne's *Scarlet Letter* as a prime example of how a future-oriented embrace of youth culture led American Renaissance writers away from older religious orthodoxies to new possibilities of redemption. Debates over race were often just as heated and widespread as those over religion, and in Chapter 7 Barbara Hochman examines Stowe's ideas of race in *Uncle Tom's Cabin* as well as in the array of texts – children's stories, a collection of documentary sources on slavery, a playscript – she wrote in response to the misreadings of her complex view of American racial politics, and the sexual violence endemic to slavery, that began with the first enthusiastic responses to her work.

Mark Rifkin argues in Chapter 8 that misunderstandings of the realities of Native American authorship in antebellum America led Matthiessen and those following him to assume that Native writing was not sufficiently "literary" to study. In an extended close reading of Anashinaabe writer George Copway's *Life*, Rifkin shows that Copway's invoking of the language of diplomacy and of his status as a chief among the Mississauga of the Great Lakes region was his strategy for gaining a white audience: Copway could only be "heard" by non-Native readers if he posed as representing his nation.

The many women writers of the "feminine fifties" have perennially been dismissed as poetesses bound by verse convention or sentimental "scribbling women" whose need for income disqualified them from the pedestal of detached genius (never mind how much Hawthorne and Melville relied on their writing to support their families). In Chapter 9, Alexandra Socarides investigates the trope of the woman as natural poet in periodicals of the 1850s, noting how an ideal imposed on women by male critics and poets became a winning literary strategy for Osgood, Alice Cary, and others, even as Osgood and Cary spoke to the real, painstaking labor of authorship and the ways in which their gender rendered that labor invisible. Jennifer L. Brady in Chapter 10 focuses on prose writers Fanny Fern and Susan Warner, whose interactive relationships with their readers through the feedback loop of fan mail and the presentation of the authors' recognition of their readers created an economy of feeling that made such sentimental engagement an economic powerhouse for those skillful enough to master such writing.

Wyn Kelley closes Part II of the book with a reading of Melville, perhaps the era's most towering figure in popular culture today, in Chapter 11. Focusing on the spatial worlds of the ocean and the city, two equally generative zones in Melville's fiction, Kelley explains how the rise of spatial studies, geomapping, and related areas gives us new ways to understand Melville's social commentaries and formal innovations, even as his fluid notions of place, space, and mapping offer salutary critiques of the scientific assumptions in the digital mapping platforms we now use to track voyages and territories.

A similarly fluid figure opens the book's third part, as Walt Whitman's seemingly contradictory personae over the course of his career form the subject of Chapter 12. There David Haven Blake places the young vigorous Whitman, "one of the roughs," of the 1855 *Leaves of Grass* alongside the ailing "Good Gray Poet" that became Whitman's image in later life, pointing out that Whitman himself considered the years of the Civil War and following just as important to his poetic project as the antebellum years had been.

The changing needs, demands, and possibilities of authorship before and after the Civil War were perhaps most acutely felt by African-American authors, and Chapters 13 and 14 trace the remarkably polymathic careers of Frederick Douglass and Frances Ellen Watkins Harper, two of the most influential black writers of their day. Zoe Trodd shows that Douglass, born a slave in Maryland and a successful orator, author, journalist, and publisher in the decades after his escape to Massachusetts, harnessed the technologies of writing, print, and photography to continually remake himself in response to the needs of his abolition efforts, the Reconstruction, and the ongoing need to perform the fundamental humanity of African-Americans. Harper, born into Philadelphia's black middle class, used poetry in addition to oratory, fiction, and journalism to gain a hearing among abolitionists, women's rights activists, and others during her long career. In Chapter 14 Melba Joyce Boyd uses the biblical figure of Ishmael, so central to understandings of the American Renaissance thanks to the narrator of Melville's *Moby-Dick*, to present Harper as a self-conscious subject of resistance and exclusion, for whom writing and speaking became a way to confront painful realities and argue for a stronger collective will for good among Americans.

Laura Dassow Walls explores a very different kind of outsider figure in Chapter 15, as she focuses on Thoreau's career from the Walden period to his final years, during which time Thoreau came to understand himself as a scientist among poets, and vice versa. Walls argues that Thoreau's liminal status on the edges of several different communities – farmers, philosophers, naturalists, writers, orators – made him a vital ambassador between those communities, rather than a "mere" Transcendentalist.

A brief coda closes the volume, as Phillips considers the importance of war writing for American Renaissance writers. For Americans of the 1850s, their world was a postbellum one, shaped by the Mexican War of the late 1840s, and the horrors of the subsequent Civil War reshaped, and indeed launched, a number of literary careers, but it does not demarcate the transition from romanticism to realism nearly as neatly as Matthiessen, the *Norton Anthology*, or other shapers of American literary history have led us to believe. The American Renaissance, in a way, expands all the way to our present moment, and it is hoped that this volume will offer new ways to connect the world of the 1850s to ours today.

PART I

Into the Renaissance

I

CHRISTOPHER N. PHILLIPS

Reading the American Renaissance in a Pennsylvania Library

As many scholars have noted in the years since *American Renaissance* was first published, F. O. Matthiessen's claim for a maturing of national culture was deeply rooted in a remarkably local perspective on the nation. Of the five authors Matthiessen celebrated in his book – Hawthorne, Emerson, Thoreau, Melville, and Whitman – the first three were born in Massachusetts and attended New England colleges; Melville was born and died in Manhattan but lived in Massachusetts while writing *Moby-Dick* and much of his short fiction; Whitman, born on Long Island, spent most of his adult life living either in Brooklyn or Camden, New Jersey, though with a brief stint in New Orleans and a much longer one in Washington, DC, Whitman easily had the most southern experience among American Renaissance writers. At the same time, though Poe's aesthetic seriousness attracted Matthiessen's attention, Poe was too southern, and died too early in 1849, to truly share in the Renaissance that the Harvard professor envisioned. The American Renaissance was just as much about a place, and the cultural possibilities associated with that place, as it was about writing or art. And while Matthiessen's account of American literature in the 1850s has proved tenacious in college classrooms and scholarly frameworks across the United States and beyond, the manifestations of that account have necessarily been locally inflected.

To illustrate one localized American Renaissance, I begin this chapter with a brief history of the course that I teach on the period at Lafayette College. The college claims Francis A. March as the nation's first professor of English and March had taught American literature sporadically as early as the 1870s at Lafayette; the college followed the national trend of resisting American literature study at the college level, however, and only two courses on American literature were in the college catalog before World War II, a survey and a topics course.[1] The first American Renaissance course

---

[1] On Francis March's status as a pioneer of English studies, see Gerald Graff, *Professing*

entered the curriculum in 1947–1948, coinciding with the arrival of William A. Thomas, a recent graduate of the University of Pennsylvania and the first American literature specialist hired by the college. Thomas's catalog description was as follows:

> An intensive study of Emerson, Thoreau, Longfellow, Holmes, Lowell, Hawthorne, and Melville: the fulfillment of romanticism and the development of transcendental idealism in the middle of the nineteenth century.[2]

Matthiessen's influence is clear, though not total, and the celebratory tone of works such as the Spiller *Literary History of the United States* – which titled the section on the Renaissance authors "Literary Fulfillment" – comes through.[3] The addition of the "schoolroom poets," overwhelmingly popular but increasingly marginalized by academics and literary critics because of their popularity, suggests the uneasy balance Thomas sought to strike between public literary values and academic commitments to aesthetic genius; Whitman's notable absence also indicated how challenging the poet of the body and of the soul could be in classrooms, even as late as the 1940s.

Over the next several years Thomas brought his course description more in line with the emerging postwar canon: Poe and Whitman were added in 1951, while Longfellow, Holmes, and Lowell were dropped in 1953, leaving Matthiessen's five plus Poe. Upon Thomas's retirement in 1967, the description became more thematically neutral, though retaining the same list of authors. Remarkably, in 1977 the catalog reverted back to the celebratory 1953 description, and even as course numberings and curricular models changed over the next thirty years, the description remained until 2008. While it is an open question how representative this account is of the history of American literature courses nationally, two key elements emerge: the tenacity of the concept of an American Renaissance as an originary moment in American literature and the dueling canons of authors that underlie that concept. The latter point is this chapter's focus, as another local inflection

Literature: An Institutional History (Chicago: University of Chicago Press, 1987), 37–8. On the history of American literature curricula in higher education, see Elizabeth Renker, *The Origins of American Literature Studies: An Institutional History* (New York: Cambridge University Press, 2007). For Lafayette College's 1946 course offerings, see Lafayette College, *College Catalog, 1946–47* (Easton, PA, 1946), 43. Special Collections and College Archives, David Bishop Skillman Library, Lafayette College.

[2] Lafayette College, *College Catalog, 1947–49* (Easton, PA, 1947), 79. Special Collections and College Archives, David Bishop Skillman Library, Lafayette College.

[3] See Robert E. Spiller, Willard Thorp, Thomas H. Johnson, and Henry Seidel Canby, eds., *Literary History of the United States*, 3 vols. (New York: Macmillan, 1948).

gives us a new way to look at American literary history in the 1850s: the records of the Easton Library Company (ELC).

Founded in 1811 in the market town of Easton, Pennsylvania, the ELC was a shareholding library, initially funded by the sale of a hundred shares to local residents at $4 a share, with annual dues of $2 required to keep up one's membership. Before the Civil War, nearly all American libraries were run either on the shareholding model, run for profit by booksellers (these were generally known as circulating libraries), or provided as charitable institutions, as church and Sunday school libraries usually were.[4] As with shareholding libraries such as the Library Company of Philadelphia (LCP), whose example the ELC's founders consciously followed, the library's goal was to provide high-quality reading on a range of topics to those with sufficient interest and leisure to undertake "serious" reading, in areas such as politics, history, philosophy, and science. Yet early on the ELC departed from the LCP's approach by incorporating a significant fiction collection, intended as family entertainment since dependents of shareholders were allowed to check out books on their accounts. Many of Easton's leaders at the time had been educated in Philadelphia, and in a town of a few thousand about sixty miles up the Delaware River from Philadelphia, these men sought to bring some of the metropolis's refinement and cosmopolitan outlook to an area dominated by British and German immigrants.

The library saw increased growth in demand and in its collection size through the 1810s and 1820s, and in 1826 a group of local leaders organized by James Madison Porter called a town meeting to form a college, which opened in 1832 as Lafayette College. Porter and most of the local trustees were charter members of the ELC, and the commitment to reading as cultural and civic improvement was clearly linked to new efforts to improve educational opportunities in the Lehigh valley. Yet connections between the library and the college did not remain close, and by the 1840s, for reasons still not entirely clear, the library began to decline. One response from the board was to make shares available for rental six months at a time

---

[4] For an overview of the history of libraries in the nineteenth-century United States, see Kenneth E. Carpenter, "Libraries," in *A History of the Book in America, Volume 2: An Extensive Republic: Print, Culture, and Society in the New Nation, 1790–1840*, ed. Robert A. Gross and Mary Kelley (Chapel Hill: University of North Carolina Press/ American Antiquarian Society, 2010), 273–86; Carpenter, "Libraries," in *A History of the Book in America, Volume 3: The Industrial Book, 1840–1880*, ed. Scott E. Casper, Jeffrey D. Groves, Stephen W. Nissenbaum, and Michael Winship (Chapel Hill: University of North Carolina Press, 2007), 303–18. On the history of the ELC and its successor libraries, see Jane S. Moyer, "History of Library Services," in *Two Hundred Years of Life in Northampton County, Pa.* (11 vols., Easton, PA: Northampton County Bicentennial Commission, 1976) IV:1–18.

for a reduced fee, a policy that made library access available to a wider demographic, particularly women (only three women had their names on the original hundred shares). Another response was to continue offering a steady supply of new fiction and periodicals, which had always dominated the library's borrowing traffic. Even as membership and patron activity continued to decline in the 1850s, demand for novels and magazines, as well as travel writing, biographies, and histories, remained strong.

What kinds of books actually made it onto the ELC's shelves? In the 1810s, large multivolume sets of established authors were some of the first titles acquired and saw frequent use. The works of Shakespeare, Oliver Goldsmith, Alexander Pope, Jonathan Swift, and Tobias Smollett defined a canon of favorite authors that was decidedly British and eighteenth-century, if not earlier. These books were largely American reprints, but in the absence of international copyright such works were cheaper for American publishers to produce, and they were known quantities already market-tested for decades.

By the end of the decade, popular novelists such as Maria Edgeworth, Jane and Anna Maria Porter, and Sir Walter Scott had gained a considerable following among ELC patrons, and in the 1820s they met their first serious American competition in the dual phenomenon of Washington Irving and James Fenimore Cooper. Irving's *Sketch Book of Geoffrey Crayon*, where the iconic stories "Rip Van Winkle" and "The Legend of Sleepy Hollow" first appeared, was the hit of the decade, followed by Cooper's Revolution-era adventure novel *The Spy* and the various novels of wilderness and sea adventures that made Cooper the first American author to live entirely from the proceeds of his writing.[5] Catharine Maria Sedgwick's novels of manners and historical drama were close behind Cooper's and Irving's works in popularity. Beyond fiction, biographies of American figures such as George Washington shared shelf space with the rapidly growing cottage industry of memoirs of Napoleon, and accounts of explorations and travel around the globe gave Easton readers a window into a world that stretched far beyond Pennsylvania.

By the 1850s, Irving was less a sensation than he had been a generation earlier, but Cooper's popularity was still uncontested, and the ELC's acquisition of Stringer and Townsend's thirty-one-volume edition of Cooper's *Novels* seems to have shored up both supply and demand. Alongside

---

[5] For more detailed analysis of the reception of Irving and Cooper and their contemporaries in the ELC, see Christopher N. Phillips, "Reading on the Edge of the Atlantic: The Easton Library Company," in *Before the Public Library: Reading, Community, and Identity in the Atlantic World, 1650–1850*, ed. Mark Towsey and Kyle B. Roberts (Boston: Brill, 2018), 284–301.

Cooper was the long array of Harper Select Novels, a bargain series begun by New York's Harper & Brothers firm in 1842 that consisted exclusively of single-volume editions of European novels.[6] A great number of titles by adventure writers such as Edward Bulwer-Lytton, Charles Kingsley, and G. P. R. James came to the ELC as part of this series, as well as works such as Emily Brontë's *Wuthering Heights* and Jane Austen's *Sense and Sensibility*. Continental authors including Frederika Bremer, Alexandre Dumas, Eugène Sue, and Karl Spindler also found places on the ELC's shelves and in patrons' accounts. Dickens's novels did well at the ELC, and Scott remained popular in the 1850s.

These European luminaries were joined by American writers, though not largely from Matthiessen's list. Novelists such as John Pendleton Kennedy and Robert Montgomery Bird gained popularity in the 1830s, followed by the rise of American sentimentalist writers Susan Warner, Harriet Beecher Stowe, Fanny Fern, and Maria Susanna Cummins in the 1850s. William H. Prescott's *Conquest of Mexico*, Jared Sparks's biographies of Washington and Franklin, and Irving's historical accounts *Astoria* and *Mahomet and His Successors* were some of the most popular nonfiction works, and the library also acquired the first two volumes of John James Audubon's *Ornithological Biography*, the five-volume companion work to his more famous *Birds of North America* picture series. Audubon's works stood alongside Alexander von Humboldt's, whose travel accounts as well as his monument of ecological thought *Cosmos* made him the ELC's most popular science writer. Josiah Clark Nott's *Types of Mankind*, which notoriously arrayed illustrations and ethnographic accounts to argue for the inferiority of non-Caucasian races, was also added to the collection and received mild interest from ELC readers. The American Renaissance – which of course would not be named that until almost a century after the fact – was represented by Emerson's *Representative Men* and Hawthorne's *The Scarlet Letter* and *The House of the Seven Gables*. Hawthorne's most popular work in the ELC, his two-volume *Twice-Told Tales*, was published in 1837 and 1842, well before the 1850–1855 era that Matthiessen emphasized. No books by Thoreau, Melville, or Whitman ever appeared on the ELC's shelves.

That does not mean, however, that Thoreau and Melville were not present in the library. The ELC's most popular magazines in the 1840s and 1850s were the *Eclectic Magazine* and *Blackwood's Edinburgh Magazine*. The latter was a British publication, edited and published by William Blackwood, and was known for its feisty Tory politics; the former was a New York-based

---

[6] Eugene Exman, *The House of Harper: One Hundred and Fifty Years of Publishing* (New York: Harper & Row, 1967), 26.

magazine that drew exclusively from European sources. Their new challengers in the 1850s were *Harper's Monthly Magazine*, which offered a mix of European and American materials (including advance extracts from *Moby-Dick*), and *Putnam's Monthly*, a journal that focused exclusively on new American works and serialized writings by Melville and Thoreau. Part of the irony of *Putnam's* mission to promote American originality was that the editor kept a policy of leaving bylines out, meaning that readers could enjoy reading Melville and Thoreau without ever knowing whose works they had read. Magazines were highly popular at the ELC, often the most-borrowed titles in a given timespan, and the collection of magazines at the library indicate a continued interest in the best European literature alongside a growing interest in American offerings.

But just how can we know how popular these works were? The previous paragraph focused on acquisitions, which were shaped by shareholder requests but ultimately in the hands of the ELC's board of directors. The board's control over materials meant that they could respond to demand but also attempt to guide shareholders' tastes by choosing what they deemed worthy titles for the collection. What happened after the books and magazines went on the shelves comes into focus through the ELC's loan ledgers, which remarkably have survived intact from the library's opening day in 1811 to 1862, when the library ceased operating as an independent corporation. Using the loan records for Matthiessen's favored dates, 1850–1855, what follows is an essay in what Matthew Brown calls "reader-based literary history,"[7] an attempt to understand the literary culture of the 1850s not through what new works authors produced but through what readers actually took off the shelves. It is worth pointing out that in the case of library records, the loan of a book does not necessarily equal reading; as today, many readers in the ELC tried and failed to get through a book, and at times reading cover-to-cover was not even the goal. Library borrowings can be taken as a sign of a what I call *aspirational reading*, the awareness of and interest in a given book built to the level that would lead an individual to select this book, and not that one (at least this time), to try out.

It is also worth mentioning that, while I have been at work with a team of librarians and students to transcribe these records into a publicly accessible database, the records for the 1850s have been digitized as images but not transcribed.[8] My analysis here is based on a visual count from the two

---

[7] See Matthew P. Brown, *The Pilgrim and the Bee: Reading Rituals and Book Culture in Early New England* (Philadelphia: University of Pennsylvania Press, 2007).

[8] Scanned images for all the ledgers, and borrowing record transcriptions up to about 1830, are available at Christopher N. Phillips, *The Easton Library Company Database Project*, http://elc.lafayette.edu/.

loan ledgers covering the relevant years, and the counts are not as precise nor as contextualized as they would be as transcribed data in an electronic format. This analysis, while informed by digital humanities methods, thus reflects both older scholarly traditions of bibliography and library history and the material realities of the digital humanities – namely, that collaboration, project design, training, transcription, and analysis all take considerable investments of time and resources, and the work is thus much, much slower than the computation made possible by the painstaking creation of the data set and interface. The needs of digital scholarship, like all other forms of scholarship, share in the list of requisites Ishmael gives for writing: "Time, Strength, Cash, and Patience."[9]

Let us begin with Hawthorne. As the most-acquired and the most-read Matthiessen author in the ELC, Hawthorne saw his greatest success as a writer of short stories. This is not a great surprise, given Hawthorne's decades of work in that form beginning in the 1820s, which involved his stories' publication in magazines, gift books, and even newspapers across the United States. Even his *Scarlet Letter*, his first and today his most famous novel, began as a new collection of short stories and changed direction only after his publisher, James Fields, suggested that he expand his "Custom House" sketch into a book. *Scarlet Letter* and the next novel, *House of the Seven Gables*, combined for sixty-eight loans, with the latter book receiving a few more total loans (thirty-seven to thirty-one). *Twice-Told Tales*, Hawthorne's first book from a decade earlier, was borrowed fifty-one times, in one or both volumes, giving Hawthorne a grand total of 119 loans. By contrast, Emerson's *Representative Men* received a mere nine loans over the same period, indicating that philosophical reflection was much more palatable for ELC readers in a fictional form such as Hawthorne used. Hawthorne also seemed to be part of a new rising generation of popular authors; Sedgwick's four novels were borrowed seventy-three times in the same period, Irving's imaginative works had only thirty-three loans. *Uncle Tom's Cabin* had twenty loans, Dickens's *Oliver Twist* fifteen, and Cummins's *The Lamplighter*, an evangelical novel that epitomized for Hawthorne the productions of "scribbling women" with whom he found himself competing, had twenty-eight. Yet, while Hawthorne certainly enjoyed some popularity, it would be a stretch to grant him bestseller (or best-loaner?) status at the ELC. In the same period, Maryland writer John Pendleton Kennedy's *Swallow Barn* left the shelves forty-seven times, while *Wuthering Heights*

---

[9] Herman Melville, in *Moby-Dick; or, The Whale*, ed. Harrison Hayford, Hershel Parker, and G. Thomas Tanselle, Writings of Herman Melville 6 (Evanston/Chicago: Northwestern University Press/Newberry Library, 1988), 145.

was close behind with forty-five loans. Kennedy's novel portrayed an idyllic lifestyle in the grand plantation houses of antebellum Virginia – something of a pre-war *Gone With the Wind* – while Brontë's book offered a dramatic love story on the wild, windswept heaths of northern England. While it would be difficult to say whether these landscapes captured the imaginations of ELC readers more effectively than Hawthorne's New England locales, it is fair to say that Massachusetts, in either colonial or modern dress, did not dominate Easton's literary imagination.

Beyond these works, Walter Scott still loomed large, with a total 151 loans among over a dozen titles, including *Waverly*, *Ivanhoe*, *The Fair Maid of Perth*, and the *Tales of My Grandfather* series. Among the magazines, *Blackwood's* had a comparable 152 loans, while *Harper's* had 133 and *Putnam's* 104. But the clear favorites during the 1850s were the *Eclectic*, whose 376 loans topped its two nearest rival magazines combined, and Cooper's novels, with an astonishing 512 loans. Certainly, Cooper had quantity in his favor; the ELC had steadily acquired his novels as they appeared across the decades, and the Stringer and Townsend collected edition provided handy single-volume copies for Cooper fans. And "fan" is the appropriate word for a number of ELC patrons, whose interest in Cooper seems to have bordered on addiction at times. Easton newspaper publisher J. P. Hetrich tore through eight Cooper novels, primarily the Leather-Stocking novels and sea novels, in the summer of 1854. The following summer, merchant John Micke borrowed seven volumes of the collected edition in a row, favoring novels with Native American themes. Hiram Baldwin, one of the ELC's renters, had a similar streak of seven consecutive Cooper loans in the summer of 1854, with several more over the spring and summer of 1855, interspersed with selections from the works of Scott, Dickens, Kennedy, and South Carolina writer William Gilmore Simms, whose novels retained some of their earlier popularity with forty loans across a half-dozen titles in the early 1850s.[10] Following Jeffrey Walker's suggestion in this book's next chapter, the timing of these Cooper binges may reflect the presence of young readers in the home, particularly boys, filling their summer vacation by chain-reading adventure novels. Whoever the Cooper readers were in these homes, however, the loan ledgers make clear that the novelist provided, in great quantities, the kind of reading experience that ELC patrons craved.

One last element in the ELC's loan records discussed here raises anew the questions: what was different about the American Renaissance, and when

---

[10] Easton Library Company, *Shareholder and Borrowing Registers*, 5 vols., Records and Documents of the Easton Library Company, Easton Area Public Library, Easton, PA, IV:175, V:155, V:202. Scans for these records are available at http://elc.lafayette.edu/.

did the shift occur? The records for January 1850 to fall 1854 appear in the library's fourth ledger, while those for late 1854 and 1855 appear in the fifth and final ledger, and my visual count in those ledgers allowed for separate totals for each ledger. Two trends in the fifth ledger, while not conclusive, are quite intriguing. First, among the magazines, nearly all the *Eclectic* and *Blackwood* loans appeared in the fourth ledger; *Harper's* and *Putnam's*, on the other hand, saw very few loans in the fourth, with increases by orders of magnitude in the fifth.[11] Other popular titles, like the novels of Cooper and Scott, remained strong in the fifth ledger, each garnering at least 40 percent of their six-year totals in the final sixteen months, so a general decline in loans does not explain why *Eclectic* and *Blackwood* suddenly lost so much popularity. Was Easton finally beginning a new surge of interest in the latest American writing?

The second trend involves Hawthorne and the sentimental writers he resented. Of Hawthorne's 119 loans, 104 were in the fourth ledger; in the fifth, *Seven Gables* was borrowed fourteen times and *Twice-Told Tales* only once, while *Scarlet Letter* sat idle on the shelf. Fanny Fern's two series of *Fern Leaves* (her collected newspaper columns), as well as her novel *Ruth Hall*, combined for a mere twenty-six loans in the fourth ledger, but those titles plus her new *Life and Beauties of Fanny Fern* combined for forty-seven in the fifth. Susan Warner's *Wide, Wide World* and *Queechy* were borrowed only three times in the fourth ledger, but combined for fifty-one, the total number of loans for Hawthorne's most popular book, in the fifth. Similar surges of interest appeared in the fifth volume around Cummins's *Lamplighter*, and even actor-playwright Anna Cora Mowatt's new memoir, *Autobiography of an Actress*, outperformed Hawthorne's combined total in the fifth ledger. If 1855 was a pivot point in the relative popularity of American magazine writing, it also seems to have been a moment of rising interest in women's sentimental writing alongside declining demand for Hawthorne's penchant for darkness and ambiguity. Yet Rufus Griswold's four-volume edition of Poe's works entered the ELC's collection later in the 1850s, and without contextualizing data from the rest of the 1850s and 1860s, it is difficult to know how important these mid-decade shifts were in the ELC's history. The data do suggest, however, that the year Hawthorne wrote his (in)famous "scribbling women" letter to James Fields was a moment in which it did seem that his relative standing among the most successful women writers

---

[11] Ledger 4 totals for these magazines: *Eclectic*, 323; *Blackwood's*, 139; *Harper's*, 29; *Putnam's*, 12. Ledger 5 totals: *Harper's*, 104; *Putnam's*, 92; *Eclectic*, 53; *Blackwood's*, 13. Part of the explanation for the very low Ledger 4 total for *Putnam's* is the fact that the magazine began publication in 1853.

was open to question (if he worried during this time about the continued popularity of Cooper or Kennedy, he never said so).

The Civil War was the final nail in the declining ELC's coffin, as shareholders stopped paying dues while their attention and finances were called elsewhere. But the board did not want to see the library, with its own building and a collection of thousands of volumes – the largest in the Lehigh valley – simply disappear. Easton's first high school had recently opened across the street from the library, and an agreement in 1862 kept the ELC's doors open through support from the high school, in exchange for the students having access to the books one day a week. This arrangement continued for some thirty years, and among the few new acquisitions indicated in a late-century shelflist were copies of *Walden* and Emerson's *Essays*; apparently, Whitman was still too controversial, particularly for adolescent readers. The organization of the present-day Easton Area Public Library in 1903 brought a grand new Carnegie-funded building sited on a hill facing Lafayette College and the library's first professional director, Henry Marx. Marx was committed to preserving local history as part of the library's mission, and he carefully preserved the ELC's records and what remained of its original collection, one-sixth of which still survives today in the library's local history room named for him. What does not survive, however, is the considerable fiction collection. As the story has come down through library staff, Marx shared the belief that many of his colleagues at the American Library Association expressed that fiction, particularly popular and dated fiction, had no place in an institution committed to cultural uplift.[12] Heavily worn copies of Cooper's *Chainbearer* and Sedgwick's *Hope Leslie* are the sole survivors of a collection that once brought the latest, and for their purposes the greatest, literature to the culturally eclectic shareholders of the ELC.

The kind of evidence provided by the ELC loan ledgers is scarce in the pre-war period, as records routinely disappeared due to poor storage, damage from elements or pests, or simply a need for the space the records took up. More records are coming to light in the wake of digital methods providing new ways to gather, analyze, and present these nineteenth-century databases, and without comparison with other libraries' loan activity, it is difficult to say how representative the ELC was of national trends. Yet the reading patterns of this library bear a certain resemblance to what we know the writers of the American Renaissance read, enjoyed, and emulated. Cooper, Irving,

[12] Frank Felsenstein and James J. Connolly discuss similar tensions between librarians and patrons over the value of fiction in the Muncie Public Library; see *What Middletown Read: Print Culture in an American Small City* (Amherst and Boston: University of Massachusetts Press, 2015).

and Scott loomed large for Melville, Thoreau, Whitman, Hawthorne, Stowe, and Warner, among many others. In a review of Putnam's revised edition of Cooper's pirate novel *The Red Rover*, Melville paused from writing *Moby-Dick* to remark: "Long ago, and far inland, we read it in our uncritical days, and enjoyed it as much as thousands of the rising generation will." Melville in fact said little about the contents of the book in his review, focusing instead on his ideal book cover, dominated by a pirate flag, for the title; he could safely assume that the readers of the *Literary World*, where Melville's review appeared, would know Cooper's 1827 novel as well as he did.[13] The American Renaissance writers also knew Prescott's *Conquest of Mexico*, Humboldt's *Cosmos*, as well as the popular British novelists and poets. David Reynolds in his *Beneath the American Renaissance* demonstrated they also read widely in the popular print culture of the day, including periodicals, pamphlets, and cheap books focused on entertainment or reform politics that library boards like the ELC's generally did not deem serious enough to acquire for their collections.

Much more work needs to be done on the behavior of readers, or in this case borrowers, to fill in this hastily sketched picture of what the American Renaissance looked like to a public who lived through it. But if these preliminary findings from a small county seat in Pennsylvania are any indication of national trends, we might say the following: not only British writers but American writers from multiple regions drew at least as much readerly attention as those in Matthiessen's canon did; both books and magazines were key to driving popular taste, and the rise of new American-focused literary magazines may have begun to offset the dominance of cheap reprints of European works, at least among more affluent readers and institutions; and new interest in American women's writing built alongside a long-lived interest in the productions of earlier writers, even those before the nineteenth century, from Pope to Goldsmith to Shakespeare. And while in hindsight we might see the stirrings of a new era in the reception of American literature in the 1850s, that new era was complicated, variegated, and marked as much by continuity as by change. If we were to travel back in time and tell Matthiessen's favored authors that they were part of a powerful new movement that would be called the American Renaissance, they might believe us. But if we were to tell the mid-century patrons of the ELC the same thing, we would be fortunate to only receive polite skepticism in return.

[13] Herman Melville, "A Thought on Book-Binding," *Literary World* 6 (March 16, 1850): 276–7.

2

JEFFREY WALKER

Cooper, Simms, and the Boys of Summer

Throughout the history of the book in nineteenth-century America, James Fenimore Cooper and William Gilmore Simms, each in his own way, led the charge in educating a nascent American reading public and helping to invent an American literature. Before the arrival of the American Renaissance and the cadre of writers who would reshape the American literary identity in their own image, Cooper and Simms developed for an audience of fledgling readers a new historical fiction of their own that emphasized and recounted the exciting adventures of young men in both North and South. Few of their books landed on the reading lists of schoolrooms in their lifetime, but their ideas spoke to the everyday reader. And their populist fiction would soon flood the market with books written for adults, but consumed more greedily by schoolboys as summer reading. Readily available editions of Cooper's and Simms's works eventually appeared everywhere.[1]

The American novel made its first appearance on stage in 1789 when William Hill Brown's epistolary *The Power of Sympathy* and Olaudah Equiano's *The Interesting Narrative of the Life* surfaced; the 1790s also saw popular works such as Susanna Rowson's *Charlotte: A Tale of Truth* (1791) and Hannah Foster's *The Coquette* (1797). But no one, not even the readers of *Charlotte Temple*, whose popularity in the new Republic made it a national bestseller, could have anticipated the notoriety of Cooper's tales in nineteenth-century America and Europe. Because none of these earlier

---

[1] Once their copyrights expired, the number of single and collected editions grew quickly. See Robert E. Spiller and Philip C. Blackburn, *A Descriptive Bibliography of the Writings of James Fenimore Cooper* (New York: R. R. Bowker Company, 1934) and Keen Butterworth, "William Gilmore Simms," in *First Printings of American Authors: Contributions toward Descriptive Checklists*, ed. Matthew J. Bruccoli and C. E. Frazer Clark, Jr., vol. 1 (New York: Gale, 1977) for descriptions of collections of Cooper's and Simms's works available to the American public in the nineteenth and early twentieth centuries here and abroad, most prominently in England, France, and Germany.

American bestsellers made the journey across the pond to become transatlantic bestsellers, someone had to step up if American novels expected to find a place on anyone's bookshelf. And in the early nineteenth century, only Cooper, with Irving and later Simms, caught the imagination of the American reading public, a public whose growth as reader paralleled the author's growth as writer.

So when Kay Seymour House once asked whether Fenimore Cooper was obsolete for contemporary readers, she answered her own question with alacrity.

> Students having difficulty with Cooper's prose often ask why the average reader of his time had no problem. The answer points to the fact that in the typical American home, the Entertainment Center used to be the bookcase, and it usually contained at least the Bible, Shakespeare, Milton's *Paradise Lost*, or Homer. Beyond these minimal holdings, readers relied on reprints of British books cheaply pirated in those days before international copyrights. Generations raised before electric lights ... passed the evenings writing letters, playing board games, or listening to someone read aloud. The last was the choice of the Cooper family and Fenimore read routinely from the latest import or from his current writing.[2]

Cooper connected to his reading public and entertained them by celebrating the history of the nation and its heroes and by turning those tales into rollicking adventures. While his four Revolutionary novels used the War of Independence as its venue and its American players to help entice more native readers, his introduction of Leather-Stocking in *The Pioneers* in 1823 and the scout's reappearance in four other tales in the next eighteen years cemented Cooper's reputation at home and abroad as America's "foremost in that band of Pioneers, who are opening the way for the march of the nation [and its native writers] across the continent [and the world]."[3] Soon Cooper, with Irving and Simms, would become standard American fixtures: Americanizing adventure, luring a generation of new readers, and creating a national literature later American authors could take for granted.

With the rise of public education and the rise of the book, Cooper's tales of young men's adventures in the burgeoning nation were a hit. Leonard Tennenhouse argued a decade ago, "Cooper's frontier fiction lends itself to

---

[2] Kay Seymour House, "Is Fenimore Cooper Obsolete?," in *Reading Cooper, Teaching Cooper*, ed. Jeffrey Walker (New York: AMS Press, 2007), 20.

[3] James Fenimore Cooper, *The Pioneers, or the Sources of the Susquehanna; A Descriptive Tale*. Historical introduction and explanatory notes by James Franklin Beard, text established by Lance Schachterle and Kenneth M. Andersen, Jr. (Albany: State University of New York Press, 1980), 456.

allegorical readings about the founding of a nation at once masculine and American in origin."[4] Cooper created *American* characters who inhabited a storybook world where everything seemed possible; he forged his reputation as a writer whose *version* of America was the home of his pioneers, and he fattened his pocketbook in ways most young native writers in the early years of the American Renaissance had not yet imagined possible.

And Cooper's books continuously captured a large readership.[5] While little extant evidence as yet collected or published shows Cooper's novels finding their niche in the majority of public libraries nationwide, libraries whose histories have recorded their purchases or inventoried their books suggest his works did fill the stacks of many athenaeums. Because historical romances were popular with readers, librarians saw them as vehicles for increasing circulation and generating library income. The Concord (Massachusetts) Social Library, eager "for the revenue generated by loans of its books to the townspeople, the library managers regularly acquired 'new and popular books' for the collection, ... [and] crucial to this success were the many current novels, British and American alike, the library ordered annually; in the 1820s and early 1830s, the latest works ... by Scott, Cooper, Irving, Sedgwick, and others accounted for nearly half of all purchases."[6] These new books occupied library shelves and kept them warm for Horatio Alger's tales of boys that would flood the market a generation later and attract the same readers. Alger's late-century "brand of Christian paternalism," an "essential tool for moral improvement," appealed to Cooper's readers who saw his adventures as a guidebook to the development of American character. And while Cooper's stories were often "tinged with a flavor of biblical

---

[4] Leonard Tennenhouse, "Is There an Early American Novel?," *NOVEL: A Forum on Fiction* 40.1 (Fall 2006): 5. As a young man Cooper himself was "so 'extravagantly fond' of 'novels and amusing tales' ... he read them 'incessantly,' " as Wayne Franklin explains in *James Fenimore Cooper: The Early Years* (New Haven: Yale University Press, 2007), 66. In fact, "the boy's pleasure in reading fiction was so great that he even began imagining himself as an author" (67).

[5] For example, Cooper sold as many as 40,000 volumes a year and earned $6,500 annually from his fiction. See John Tebbel, *A History of Book Publishing in the United States* (New York: R. R. Bowker, 1972), 1:210, 222. Books were also available in other venues and in multiple shapes and sizes, ready for the young American reader to buy. On the child as reader, see Patricia Crain's *Reading Children: Literacy, Property, and the Dilemmas of Childhood in Nineteenth-Century America* (Philadelphia: University of Pennsylvania Press, 2016).

[6] Kenneth E. Carpenter, "Libraries," in *A History of the Book in America: Volume 2: An Extensive Republic: Print, Culture, and Society in the New Nation, 1790–1840*, ed. Robert A. Gross and Mary Kelley (Chapel Hill: University of North Carolina Press, 2010), 273–86, 281. For further discussion of American libraries in Cooper's time, and of Cooper's popularity in those libraries, see Chapter 1 in this volume.

humility," they did not always appeal to the same "middle-class meritorious instincts and to the unrealized aspirations of working-class readers"[7] Alger captured in the postwar years. Cooper spoke to a larger strain of the reading public. One of his young late nineteenth-century readers wanted a hero "who upheld his country and who would not step out of his way because it was hard or because he had to meet a quarrel" and an author "who would not let another run over him" and "would support an argument to the last."[8] He got what he wanted from Cooper. In his review of Sedgwick's first novel, *A New England Tale* (1822), Cooper described a good novel as "address[ing] itself very powerfully to our moral nature and conscience ... constantly to remind us that 'we have all of us, one human heart'." He also worked to make his readers to educate their imaginations – "to increase our knowledge, correct our false opinions, and, what is more powerful than all, appeal to our sympathies." Cooper wanted *American* novelists to write *American* fiction, stories recording "our domestic manners, the social and moral influences ... and the multitude of local peculiarities, which form our distinctive features."[9] And mid-century American novelists such as Melville filled most of Cooper's prescriptions.[10] Cooper became America's first "professional" novelist, and many of the writers in the American Renaissance not only read but followed his example.[11]

---

[7] Frank Felsenstein and James J. Connolly, *What Middletown Read: Print Culture in an American Small City* (Amherst and Boston: University of Massachusetts Press, 2015), 141.

[8] Harry Truman's notebooks are found in the Harry S. Truman Library in the Papers of Harry S. Truman, Pertaining to Family, Business, and Personal Affairs. Truman's essay on Cooper is found in his "English note Book First Year Kept by Harry Truman," dated 1899, and found on pages 7–9 and reprinted by permission.

[9] James Fenimore Cooper, *Early Critical Essays*, ed. James Franklin Beard (Gainesville: Scholars' Facsimiles & Reprints, 1955), 99, 98–9, 97.

[10] Franklin, *Cooper: The Early Years*, xxi. "Born just when Cooper started writing his first books," Melville "quite literally had grown up on them. He especially devoured the sea tales." Margaret Cohen in *The Novel and the Sea* (Princeton: Princeton University Press, 2010) praises Cooper for his sea fiction, especially *The Pilot* (1824) and notes Melville's use of organizing "*Moby-Dick's* adventures as a chase, in the use of the ship's movement through space-time as a technique of dramatization [was] pioneered by Cooper" (184).

[11] William Charvat, *The Profession of Authorship in America, 1800–1870* (Columbus: Ohio State University Press, 1968), 68. Poe, too, worked hard to become a professional author, and he kept up with Cooper's works, including his travel books, reviewing "Cooper's Switzerland" in the *Southern Literary Messenger* 2 (1836): 401. In *Adventure, Mystery, and, Romance: Formula Stories as Art and Popular Culture* (Chicago: University of Chicago Press, 1976), John C. Cawelti suggests "Cooper invented the western" and "not only became the founder of this major popular tradition but the influence of his Leatherstocking [*sic*] is equally inescapable in major American writers and forms part of the background of Thoreau, Melville, Hawthorne, Twain, Faulkner, and Hemingway" (194).

The *book* soon became the vehicle for engagement and excitement in the nation's evolving cultural and literary history, providing glimpses into the lives of Americans most readers had never met or even imagined. The results illustrate Wolfgang Iser's phenomenological approach to the history of the book. For Iser, the act of "reading causes the literary work to unfold its inherently dynamic character," and he sees a literary text as "something like an arena in which reader and author participate in a game of the imagination … [and] must therefore be conceived in such a way that it will engage the reader's imagination in the task of working things out for himself, for reading is only a pleasure when it is active and creative." Although Cooper's stories were formulaic (a comfort to many readers) and represented his borrowing from the Scott model, by Americanizing many of Scott's tropes, Cooper made them feel contemporary in the reader's mind. "This is why," Iser explains, "the reader often feels involved in events which, at the time of the reading, seem real to him, even though in fact they are very far from his own reality."[12] House's argument for Cooper's popularity extends Iser's analysis of the reading process. The ability of people "to imagine scenery described only in words accounts for the instant popularity of Cooper's Leather-Stocking Tales not only among city dwellers in the United States but readers in Europe and Asia." So, "Cooper's descriptions," she concludes, "were also responsible for starting something like a mystique of the American west. Even in staid Boston, a reader wrote of Natty Bumppo as he disappeared into the forest with his hounds at the end of *The Pioneers*, 'I longed to go with him.' "[13]

For readers to participate in their reading experiences requires an ability to understand the story. "The need to decipher," Iser explains, "gives us the chance to formulate our own deciphering capacity … we bring to the fore an element of our being of which we are not directly conscious."[14] Longing to travel with the Leather-Stocking, and imagining what such travel might entail in terms of dangers and hardships, helps the reader embrace the adventure. So Cooper did whatever necessary to capture his reader's imagination, engage them in sensing a wider panorama of the American scene, and unfold America's history.

[12] Wolfgang Iser, "The Reading Process," in *Reader-Response Criticism: From Formalism to Post-Structuralism*, ed. Jane P. Tompkins (Baltimore: Johns Hopkins University Press, 1980), 51, 54. See also David D. Hall, "Readers and Reading in America: Historical and Critical Perspectives," in his *Cultures of Print: Essays in the History of the Book*, ed. David D. Hall (Amherst: University of Massachusetts Press, 1996), 169–87, for variations in the history of reading.
[13] House, "Cooper Obsolete," 18.
[14] Iser, "Reading Process," 67–8.

To merge history with fiction and to appoint "himself the historian of an unfolding history,"[15] Cooper turned to the Revolution for stories designed to thrill his panoply of readers. From his family friend John Jay, he had heard tales "of the patriot spy [and George Washington] which inspired Cooper's first successful, though as yet uncompleted romance."[16] Harvey Birch, double agent, and his relationship with Mr. Harper (Washington incognito) was the stuff of romance, ideal for his second, bestselling novel, *The Spy* (1821), a breakthrough for Cooper and a model (along with his sea novels) for later emulation. Jay provided Cooper with the source for a larger ensemble of regional characters and plotlines for his adventure stories. As an "adopted" member of the Westchester County DeLancey family (he married Susan in 1811), Cooper knew much of its myth and folklore, "familiarizing himself with the Westchester past: its terrain, people, manners, language, custom, folklore, and military history." This "neutral ground" was a "simmering cauldron of conflicts between British and American forces. Westchester's fertile fields and picturesque farms were constantly invaded for plunder by brigands of renegade Americans known as 'Cow-Boys,' whose leader James DeLancey, the 'Outlaw of the Bronx,' was the cousin of Susan Cooper's father." And once he began the novel, James P. Elliott explains, "Cooper apparently cultivated the memories of survivors of the Revolution, inviting them to Angevine [the Cooper cottage] to spin their yarns."[17] Cooper's arrangement of these memories, combined with his own inventions, resulted in his first Revolutionary War romance.

These yarns used such sources and models for the perilous adventures of the spy and his consort Mr. Harper (both donning various disguises for counterespionage, reminiscent of the popular Andre and Arnold stories), as well as the renegade Cow-Boys and Skinners. The tales reveal the clash of loyalties in the Wharton tribe. British Captain Henry Wharton, son of the family patriarch, finds himself arrested as a spy when he visits his kin behind British lines. His sister Sarah, a Tory sympathizer, battles his older sibling Frances, a patriot-lover. This conflict represents the schism between public and private duty to country and self, and this tale of the Westchester social

[15] House, "Cooper Obsolete," 18.

[16] James Fenimore Cooper, *The Letters and Journals and Journals of James Fenimore Cooper*, ed. James Franklin Beard (Cambridge, MA: The Belknap Press, 1960–1968), 1:71. Subsequent paginal references to this edition, cited as *L&J*, will appear parenthetically in the text.

[17] James P. Elliott, "Historical Introduction," in James Fenimore Cooper, *The Spy: A Tale of the Neutral Ground*, ed. James Fenimore Cooper. Historical introduction by James P. Elliott; explanatory notes by James H. Pickering; text established by James P. Elliott, Lance Schachterle, and Jeffrey Walker (New York: AMS Press, 2002), xxi.

and political world generated good American press for young Cooper. The *New York Commercial Advertiser*, for example, on December 28, 1821, applauded the young author by suggesting "the first work ... must, and will, be highly popular, and will secure to the author a reputation in the republic of letters, of which he may be justly proud." The *New York American* admitted on January 3, 1822, "the charm of it is yet, strong upon our minds, and our feelings still bear witness to the deep interest of its story." Philadelphia's *National Gazette and Literary Register*, on January 20, 1822, touted Cooper as displaying "talents for this walk of literature, from which the country may anticipate much credit and entertainment." Boston's *North American Review* said of Harvey Birch, "better known by the name of the Spy of the Neutral Ground ... that the American revolution is an admirable basis, on which to found fictions of the highest order of romantic interest."[18] And finally William Gilmore Simms, Cooper's admirer and imitator, declared "The publication of the Spy ... was ... the first practical reply to a sarcasm," a reference to Sydney Smith's glib question in 1820 in the *Edinburgh Review* when he asked "In the four corners of the globe, who reads an American book?"[19] Cooper's *Spy* and its American readers provided the answer, and Simms deftly concluded, "To Mr. Cooper the merit is due, of having first awakened us to this self-reference – to this consciousness of mental resources, of which our provincialism dealt, not only in constant doubts, but in constant denials. The first step is half the march."[20]

Cooper's colorful dramatis persona explains part of his popularity. House talks about Cooper creating "a coherent fictional world containing hundreds of characters that represented the possibilities of American life."[21] They featured young women adrift in a world dominated by men, whose only function was to serve as the romantic interests of a male hero or as a plot device. In *The Spy*, the Wharton sisters represent two sides of the young American ingénue. Frances, pro-American, marries sensibly; Sarah, pro-British, disgraces herself in her affairs. Cooper's other "females," intentionally humorous women, include Katy Haynes, Birch's housekeeper; Isabella Singleton, the idealistic femme fatale who accidentally dies from a bullet

---

[18] Contemporary nineteenth-century reviews of Cooper's novels can be found on microfilm at the American Antiquarian Society. See also George Dekker and John P. McWilliams, eds., *Fenimore Cooper: The Critical Heritage* (London/Boston: Routledge/Kegan Paul, 1973).

[19] Sydney Smith, "Review of Seybert's *Annals of the United States*," *Edinburgh Review* 33 (January 1820): 79.

[20] William Gilmore Simms, "Cooper, His Genius and Writings," in *Views and Reviews*, ed. C. Hugh Holman (Cambridge, MA: The Belknap Press, 1962), 258–62.

[21] Kay Seymour House, *Cooper's Americans* (Columbus: Ohio State University Press, 1965), 3.

intended for the man she nurses; and Betty Flanagan, the Irish "petticoat doctor." As James Wallace explains, "The other characters in *The Spy* constitute a gallery of character types: Captain Lawton, the Virginia horseman; Dr. Sitgreaves, the philosophical pragmatist ... [and they are] the beginning of Cooper's extensive exploration of regional types in fiction ... In these regional characters Cooper's readers could find something familiar and accessible."[22] By adding Harvey Birch, double agent hero, and Mr. Harper, father- and Washington-figure, *The Spy* serves as a springboard for novels featuring adventure, mystery, and heroism, attractive to regional, national, *and* international audiences.

Simms's own Revolutionary romances and tales of the forest borrow much of formula Cooper invented, but they also use what Sir Walter Scott began. While Cooper improved Scott by simplifying his plots, making his young lovers less important to the story, reducing the role of historical events, placing most of his historical characters outside the historical action, and centering the action most often on a single character, Simms preferred Scott's method. C. Hugh Holman explains Scott's and Cooper's influence on Simms and how Simms responded to each. Simms thought Scott to be "the perfect example of an ideal romancer," finding flaws in Cooper's use of Scott. Simms felt shifting focus from a set of lovers to "massive characters relatively independent of both the young-lover plot and the historical situation" a mistake. As Simms wrote in his *Views and Reviews in American Literature, History, and Fiction* (1845), Cooper's major heroes were usually the same character throughout his work: "Hawk[-]eye, the land sailor of Mr. Cooper is, with certain suitable modifications, the same personage [as the Pilot] ... It would not be difficult to trace Cooper's one ideal through all his novels. Even in the Bravo ... we find the Pilot and Natty Bumppo, where we should least look for them, in the person of Jacopo, the assassin of Venice."[23] For Cooper this was not an issue for debate. "In most of his romances," George Dekker explains, "Cooper solved this problem by virtually dispensing with the kind of famous historical personages and events that figure so prominently in most of the Waverly novels. As a result Cooper's cast of characters could be smaller, his plot simpler, and his natural settings could bulk larger than was usual in Scott's romances."[24] And, as James Grossman reports, Cooper's adventure novels are not about "social complication ... [almost] everything

[22] James D. Wallace, *Early Cooper and His Audience* (New York: Columbia University Press, 1986), 104–5.

[23] C. Hugh Holman, "The Influence of Scott and Cooper on Simms," *American Literature* 23.2 (May 1951): 208, 208–9.

[24] George Dekker, *The American Historical Romance* (Cambridge, MA: Cambridge University Press, 1987), 58.

happens for the sake of the excitement of the action."[25] And excitement was the stuff of bestselling fiction for young readers. For Cooper, "the power of invention, apparently, never failed him … His tank was always full; he always had more novels in his head than he had time to write."[26]

This does not mean Simms was unpopular or unproductive or his contributions to the American historical romance minimal. Often called the "southern Cooper" for good reason, his novels devoted to the Revolution in South Carolina were designed "not to add new facts to historical records, but to interpret and to illustrate the impact of events upon men and society."[27] In his introduction to *The Partisan* (1835), the first of these Revolutionary War romances, he says:

> While the persons of the Drama, many of them, are names of the nation, familiar to our daily reading … The individual must be made an example for the benefit of the race … a nation gains only in glory and in greatness, as it is resolute to behold and pursue the truth. I would paint the disasters of my country, where they arose from the obvious errors of their sons, in the strongest possible colours. We should then know – our sons and servants, alike, should then know how best to avoid them.[28]

For Simms, the historical romance far more resembled the historical novel, one more expository than dramatic. Simms uses historical figures, such as Francis Marion (the "swamp fox"), who harassed the British in South Carolinian marshes, as representatives of real people with strengths and weaknesses, virtues and vices. For him, most of the historical events of his romances are true to the regions where the action takes place. Cooper also records regional events and people, too, but he captured more fully the imagination of his readers because his stories seemed more accessible to the growing nation. For both writers, the historical characters they celebrated promoted regional and national fame, and both made names for

[25] James Grossman, *James Fenimore Cooper* (New York: W. Sloane, 1949), 215–16.

[26] Matthew J. Bruccoli, ed., *The Profession of Authorship in America, 1800–1870: The Papers of William Charvat* (Columbus: Ohio State University Press, 1968), 68.
David Leverenz, "Men Writing in the Early Republic," in *A History of the Book in America: Volume 2: An Extensive Republic: Print, Culture, and Society in the New Nation, 1790–1840*, ed. Robert A. Gross and Mary Kelley (Chapel Hill: University of North Carolina Press, 2010), 359. Until the 1840s, Cooper was one of only three authors who supported themselves primarily by their publications, Irving and Sigourney, the other two.

[27] C. Hugh Holman, "William Gilmore Simms' Picture of the Revolution as a Civil Conflict," *The Journal of Southern History* 15.4 (November 1949): 442.

[28] William Gilmore Simms, *The Partisan: A Romance of Revolution*, ed. Stephen E. Meats (Fayetteville: University of Arkansas Press, 2011), 7.

themselves by penning adventure stories the public purchased and turned into bestsellers.[29]

Cooper made his moral adventures especially exciting with *The Last of the Mohicans* (1826). In this second of the Leather-Stocking Tales, he enables his readers to "go with" Natty Bumppo, the young Hawk-eye, on his journey to rescue the Munro girls from Magua and his band of Hurons by creating a vivid *word picture* to help his reader's imagination "enter the field" and recreate, as Iser argues, "the world [the novel] presents." Decades after *Mohicans* appeared, Cooper, in a letter to Louis Legrand Noble, dated January 6, 1848, praised the artist Thomas Cole as "one of the very first geniuses of the age. The March of Empire [*The Course of Empire*], his best work I think, ought to make the reputation of any man ... The series are a great epic poem ... that has already deeply affected me" (*L&J*, V:397). That Cooper admired Cole's work is certain, and that he employed analogous techniques to portray his own version of the heroic has been amply demonstrated.[30] Both were moralists "who, not content merely with the accurate presentation of the external scene, sought to convey through the use of landscape a moral theme of universal application."[31] Cooper, like Cole, was "every bit aware of volcanic disturbances within American mass culture as were writers such as Melville and Hawthorne, but, unlike them, he did

---

[29] Cooper's books, such as *Mohicans* (six times), *Spy* (twice), *Pilot*, and *Red Rover*, retained their shine for young twentieth-century readers in comic book form between 1944 and 1992, while Simms's historical character, Francis Marion, appeared in eight one-hour episodes ("The Swamp Fox") on *Walt Disney Presents* between October 1959 and January 1961. Both were "principal contributors" to *Graham's American Monthly Magazine*. See Susan Belasco, "The Cultural Work of National Magazines," in *The History of the Book in America: Volume 3: The Industrial Book, 1840–1880*, ed. Scott E. Casper, Jeffrey D. Groves, Stephen W. Nissenbaum, and Michael Winship (Chapel Hill: University of North Carolina Press, 2007), 258–70, for more information on the role magazines played in nineteenth-century America. David Reynolds explains their popularity in *Beneath the American Renaissance: The Subversive Imagination in the Age of Emerson and Melville* (New York: Alfred A. Knopf, 1988) by arguing each wrote "Romantic Adventure" fiction, either exploring the "turbulence and linguistic violence of frontier or city life ... through ... a central hero [such as Leather-Stocking]" or "a totally secular world of social outcasts [such as *Yemassee*] whose often criminal adventures are explained without explicit moralizing and with obvious fascination with the villainous or tabooed" (183).

[30] For example, see James Franklin Beard, "Cooper and His Artistic Contemporaries," *New York History* 35 (October 1954): 480–95; Howard Mumford Jones, "Prose and Pictures: James Fenimore Cooper," *Tulane Studies in English* 3 (1952): 133–54; and Donald A. Ringe, "James Fenimore Cooper and Thomas Cole: An Analogous Technique," *American Literature* 30 (March 1958): 26–36, for an analysis of the relationship between Cooper and Cole.

[31] Ringe, "Cooper and Cole," 27.

not permit these disturbances to infiltrate his consciousness, shake loose settled beliefs, and thus prepare the way for ambiguous literature."[32] This concept appears with certainty in the four landscapes Thomas Cole painted in depicting scenes from Cooper's *Mohicans*. The first two canvases surfaced in 1826 and the second pair in 1827.[33] The 1827 paintings – both labeled *Landscape Scene from* The Last of the Mohicans: *Cora Kneeling at the Feet of Tamenund* – portray the same scene, with some subtle differences in landscape and symbolic vision. Both capture the moment when Cora throws herself at the feet of Tamenund, the Delaware chief, and begs for her life; both depict a ring of Native Americans surrounding Cora and her fellow prisoners in a rocky clearing at the edge of the mountain.

But in the two 1826 paintings, the first, *Landscape, Scene from* The Last of the Mohicans: *The Death of Cora*, Cole portrays Cora's plight following her unsuccessful plea for her freedom in scenes from the 1827 duo. In the final chase, Magua absconds with Cora, but finds himself followed closely by Duncan, Uncas, and Hawk-eye, and the pursuit ends with dramatic action. Dragged up the mountain, Cora finally stops "unexpectedly on a ledge of rocks, that overhung a deeper precipice" and cries to her captor "I will go no further … Kill me if thou wilt, detestable Huron, I will go no further."[34] Magua demands Cora "choose the wigwam or the knife," but before Cora answers, Uncas appears, and Magua, nonplussed at his Mohican rival and distracted from his catch, suddenly discovers one of his minions knifing Cora. She dies, and after Uncas kills Cora's assassin, Magua passes his own knife into the Mohican. Frightening and dramatic, the scene by author and painter draws parallels between the characters and the physical American landscape. Rendered dark and ominous – much like the scene in Cooper's novel – Cole's landscape and his use of color suggest impending doom. Wearing a "white robe … seen fluttering" (335) in the novel and in Cole's painting, Cora stands in contrast to the savages, awash in dark colors and red tunics. The civilized meets the savage, and this time the savage wins.

---

[32] Reynolds, *Beneath*, 187.

[33] Many thanks to Rebecca Ayres Schwartz, "Historicism and Nostalgia in Thomas Cole's *Last of the Mohicans*," *James Fenimore Cooper Society Miscellaneous Papers* 25 (May 2008): 22–4, for an incisive description and discussion of the four paintings.

[34] James Fenimore Cooper, *The Last of the Mohicans; A Narrative of 1757*. Historical introduction by James Franklin Beard; text established with explanatory notes by James A. Sappenfield and E. N. Feltskog (Albany: State University of New York Press, 1983), 338. Subsequent references to this edition will appear parenthetically.

In the other 1826 painting, *Landscape with Figures: A Scene from* The Last of the Mohicans, Cole's landscape articulates his initial response to chapter 32 of the novel, the climax to the second chase and the most exciting chapter in the novel. Cooper's narrative, like Cole's interpretation, is provocative. Following the action in the penultimate chapter of the novel Cole portrays in *The Death of Cora*, Magua flees after killing Uncas. But the ever-keen eye of Hawk-eye sees Magua as he

> made a desperate leap, and fell short of his mark; though his hands grasped a shrub ... The form of Hawk-eye had crouched like a beast about to take its spring, and the muzzle of the half raised rifle played like a leaf fluttering in the wind ... it poured out its contents. The arms of the Huron relaxed, and his body fell back ... Turning a relentless look on his enemy, he shook his hand in grim defiance. But his hold loosened, and his dark person ... glided past the fringe of shrubbery which clung to the mountain, in its rapid flight to destruction. (338)

Cole's depiction, like Cooper's word painting, is exacting, exciting, and dramatic, and he shows us the same narrative sequence of Cooper's scene, imitating Cooper's words by bathing the central figures in light, rendering the landscape in shadows and in rich, dark hues, and framing the scene with decayed trees, jagged rocks, and a threatening and stormy sky. Coloring the wilderness scarlet and filling the scene with the kind of wild, rushing streams Cooper describes earlier in his novel, Cole implies that civilization cannot exert control over the savage wilderness. And even though Hawk-eye, much like Twain's Huck Finn, lights out for another territory at story's end, Cole paints smoke rising in the background of the painting, a detail suggesting the march westward as inexorable and the American environment just as threatening as the savages.

Thomas Cole and Fenimore Cooper used the landscape to frame and to create a national American identity, one rich in conflicts and contrasts. And if, as Cooper had written in his letter about the artist, Cole raised landscape painting to the level of the heroic and the epic, then so, too, did Cooper fashion a new kind of epic literature – the American epic – in his historical romances.[35] Observer and reader see Cole and Cooper develop methods

---

[35] See John P. McWilliams's chapter "Red Achilles, Red Satan" in his *The American Epic: Transforming a Genre 1770–1860* (New York: Cambridge University Press, 1989), 123–57. It is also fruitful to explore other attempts at shaping the American epic for different generations. Christopher N. Phillips, in his *Epic in American Culture: Settlement to Reconstruction* (Baltimore: Johns Hopkins University Press, 2012) notes that Benjamin West, whose work preceded Cole's, also painted a version

for landscape and word paintings almost identical in their logic. The minu-
tiae of nature were sketched on the spot and recombined in the studios of
painter and novelist into massive views. These separate natural elements –
elaborately detailed close-ups of leaves, branches, rock forms – were spliced
together somewhat in the spirit of a film editor, except that the editing took
place in the painter's eye and the writer's mind. Observer and reader see a
technique enlarge the notion America was vast beyond exhaustion, a place
of adventure and horizon without limit. This epic confrontation of such
forces represents that moment when the protagonist confronts his antago-
nist and delivers a choice to the reader of what kind of world seems most
suited to an American: an open, often lawless, world or one representing a
settled society. Most of Cooper's heroes try to shape that new world, but
they often find the dialectic between civilization and nature hard to settle.

That same dialectic would not be solved any more easily by the writers
of the American Renaissance, in part because they eventually found themselves removed from the need for assertions of patriotism. They could, and
they did, form yet another new kind of epic literature, one that could satirize sacred cultural values and at the same time generate new forms. They
had read Cooper avidly as boys, and while they often followed his lead in
turning out their own tales, they ultimately left home and forged their own
path. In *Walden* (1854), Thoreau observes the battle of his ants using a
mixture of epic and mock epic, heroic and burlesque, but "Like Melville and
Whitman, [he] can neither discard such rhetoric nor refrain from parodying
it. Such an inseparable mixing ... becomes a distinctive trait of the literature of the 1850s."[36] Then, too, Hawthorne unveils the history of young
Robin Molineux, but the level of irony he employs to report the sequence
of Robin's "nighttime confrontations, rendered in a superb modulation of
tones – from callow confidence, to violent frustration, to honest uncertainty,
and on to the verge of some mature toleration of self-contradiction – seems
regulated by some absolutely law of growing up,"[37] is well beyond the pay
grade of Cooper's Deerslayer. Melville uses irony to review Cooper's *Red
Rover* (1826) and to suggest the book needs "a flaming suit of flame-colored
morocco, as evanescently thin and gauze-like as possible, so that the binding

---

of the epic "not for adult consumption, but ... to have at least as much of an influence
on the young." West, however, discovered when epic paintings became popular, the
"slippery boundary between prestige and popularity, a common dilemma for authors
from Cooper to Longfellow" (104) became problematic.

[36] Michael Colacurcio, *The Province of Piety: Moral History in Hawthorne's Early Tales*
(Durham, NC: Duke University Press, 1995), 131.

[37] *Ibid.*, 131.

might happily correspond with the sanguinary, fugitive title of the book."[38] And even Whitman invents a self and turns his *Leaves of Grass* into an epic of democracy in free verse. Cooper and Simms may have authored the playbook, but the young writers of the American Renaissance played their own game and offered American readers a sense of the evolution of heroic, national literature, too.

[38] Herman Melville, "A Thought on Book-Binding," *Literary World* 6 (March 16, 1850): 276–7.

3

RUSSELL SBRIGLIA

The Trouble with the Gothic: Poe, Lippard, and the Poetics of Critique

Both inside and outside of the canon, simultaneously central and peripheral, the gothic has long occupied a liminal position among the literature of the American Renaissance. Though F. O. Matthiessen included Hawthorne and Melville among the five Mount Rushmore-like profiles that comprise his *American Renaissance* (the other three being Emerson, Thoreau, and Whitman), he seldom used the term "gothic" to characterize their writings, categorizing them instead under the genre of tragedy.[1] Such a marginalization of the gothic, as Teresa Goddu points out, is not an exception but the rule. Often overshadowed by more ostensibly "respectable" generic categories such as the "romance" and frequently displaced by broader generic terms like "melodrama" and "dark," the gothic has remained "almost fully repressed" in Americanist literary scholarship.[2]

For Goddu, this "desire to quarantine the gothic from higher literary forms" is due in large part to its "seemingly antagonistic relationship to America's ... identity" as "a nation of hope and harmony."[3] Again, the example of Matthiessen appears to bear this out. Matthiessen could countenance Hawthorne and Melville's "reaffirmation of tragedy" in the face of "the optimistic strain from Emerson to Whitman" because, like classic tragedians, they tempered their belief that man was "radically imperfect" with "a recognition that man, pitiful as he may be in his finite weakness, is still capable of apprehending perfection, and of becoming transfigured by that vision."[4] He could not, however, countenance Poe's "bitter[ ] hostil[ity] to democracy" – a hostility no better exemplified than by the following

---

[1] See F. O. Matthiessen, *American Renaissance: Art and Expression in the Age of Emerson and Whitman* (New York: Oxford University Press, 1941).
[2] Teresa Goddu, *Gothic America: Narrative, History, and Nation* (New York: Columbia University Press, 1997), 6.
[3] *Ibid.*, 6, 4.
[4] Matthiessen, *American Renaissance*, 179–80.

line from one of his later tales, the thinly veiled political satire "Mellonta Tauta": "democracy is a very admirable form of government – for dogs."[5]

Yet, tempting though it is to attribute the gothic's quarantining to its seemingly inherent skepticism of the American experiment, the ascendant reputation of the works of Poe's friend and contemporary George Lippard in recent years suggests that this isn't necessarily the case. Lippard's gothic novels, in particular his runaway bestseller *The Quaker City; or, The Monks of Monk Hall* (1845), have garnered an increasing amount of attention from scholars of antebellum American literature of late precisely *because* they bespeak an even greater "devotion to the possibilities of democracy," an even greater desire to "give fulfilment to the potentialities freed by the Revolution," than many of the writings of Matthiessen's monumental five.[6] D. Berton Emerson, for instance, asserts that in *The Quaker City* Lippard aims at nothing short of "reclaiming the radical democratic energy of the Revolutionary moment" by "resuscitati[ng] ... Revolutionary democratic ideals."[7] Much like Melville's fiction, then, Lippard's demonstrates that the radical energies of the gothic could just as easily be put in advancement of the American jeremiad.[8]

Such being the case, what I want to suggest in what follows is that the trouble with the gothic has less to do with its politics, which can range anywhere from reactionary (Poe) to revolutionary (Lippard), than its poetics of critique – a poetics which enlists a lowbrow, popular form in the service of performing highbrow philosophical and psychoanalytic thinking. In the case of Poe, though it is easy to write off his tales, especially his "tales of perversity," as I call them, as "factitious" grotesqueries that exist "Out of Space – out of Time," in actuality they are complex philosophical meditations on and critiques of the Emersonian concept of self-reliance.[9] Likewise, though it is easy to write off *The Quaker City* as a tasteless dime novel whose "penny-dreadful plots of sensational sex and sensational violence"

[5] *Ibid.*, xii, ix; Edgar Allan Poe, *Poetry and Tales*, ed. Patrick F. Quinn (New York: Library of America, 1984), 880.
[6] Matthiessen, *American Renaissance*, ix, xv. As Matthiessen explains in the book's preface, this devotion to the possibilities of democracy is the "one common denominator" (ix) uniting his five authors.
[7] D. Berton Emerson, "George Lippard's *The Quaker City*: Disjointed Text, Dismembered Bodies, Regenerated Democracy," *Nineteenth-Century Literature* 70.1 (2015): 106, 105.
[8] See Sacvan Bercovitch, *The American Jeremiad* (Madison: University of Wisconsin Press, 1978).
[9] The dismissal of Poe's tales as "factitious" is from Matthiessen, *American Renaissance*, xii; the line "Out of Space – out of Time" is from Poe's poem "Dream-Land," in *Poetry and Tales*, 79.

perpetuate the very ills Lippard pretends to protest, in actuality it is a complex, proto-psychoanalytic critique of the problematic nature of pleasure.[10]

The Trouble with Genius: Poe, Transcendentalism, and the Perversity of Self-Reliance

Though Matthiessen's exclusion of Poe from the American Renaissance canon would set the precedent for his exclusion from the majority of "myth and symbol" paradigms that dominated the classic period of American literary studies (the 1950s and 1960s), the groundwork for this exclusion was first laid by Vernon Louis Parrington, who in his Pulitzer Prize winning *Main Currents in American Thought* (1927) proclaimed that "the problem of Poe, fascinating as it is, lies altogether outside the main current of American thought."[11] A practitioner of "quite another kind" of romanticism than that of his contemporaries, Poe, Parrington maintained, held aesthetic and political ideals that "ran counter to every major interest of the New England renaissance," above all "the mystical, optimistic element in transcendentalism."[12] Though more recent scholarship on Poe has sought to give him a more "American face," the "problem of Poe" remains much the same today as it did for Parrington.[13] Colin Dayan, for instance, asserts that Poe "remained outside the community of noble sentiments" represented by "the Emersonian strain of American literary history." Whereas authors like Emerson, Thoreau, and Whitman preached "a grandiose American nature" and "unlimited self-expansion," Poe, unable to follow Emerson's "belie[f] in the deification of the human race through the medium of a nature seen as 'a version of a moral sentence,'" sought to instead "delimit the American dream."[14]

While accounts like Dayan's are absolutely correct to retain Parrington's emphasis on Poe's antagonistic relationship to the Emersonian tradition and the visions of the American dream represented therein, what the majority of them continue to miss is that the true problem of Poe is not that he lies altogether outside the main current of American thought – its

---

[10] Larzer Ziff, *Literary Democracy: The Declaration of Cultural Independence in America* (New York: Viking, 1981), 92.

[11] Vernon Louis Parrington, *Main Currents in American Thought: An Interpretation of American Literature from the Beginnings to 1920*, 3 vols. (New York: Harcourt, Brace, and World, 1927), II:58.

[12] *Ibid.*, 58, 57.

[13] See Shawn Rosenheim and Stephen Rachman, eds., *The American Face of Edgar Allan Poe* (Baltimore: Johns Hopkins University Press, 1995).

[14] Joan Dayan, *Fables of Mind: An Inquiry into Poe's Fiction* (New York: Oxford University Press, 1987), 5.

Transcendentalist vein in particular – but that he constitutes its dark undercurrent. Less the aloof, proto-modernist practitioner of "art for art's sake" than he has long been made out to be, Poe was instead an astute, if caustic, critic of his culture, a figure who frequently engaged the thought of his contemporaries, including the idealist "cant," as he typically regarded it, of the Transcendentalists.[15] Yet Poe went about critiquing the "noble sentiments" of the Transcendentalists parasitically, using his gothic tales as vehicles for undermining them from within by seeing their unintended or unacknowledged consequences to fruition. Such parasitism is no better exemplified than in what I have elsewhere termed Poe's "tales of perversity."[16] Though other works of Poe's challenge Emerson and company more directly, it is his tales of perversity that constitute his most trenchant critique of the Emersonian tradition, in particular its doctrine of self-reliance.

Among the most memorable moments in Emerson's "Self-Reliance" is that in which he proclaims, "I shun father and mother and wife and brother, when my genius calls me. I would write on the lintels of the door-post, *Whim*. I hope it is somewhat better than whim at last, but we cannot spend the day in explanation."[17] Heeding his own Orphic proclamation from the conclusion of *Nature* that "A man is a god in ruins," Emerson here seeks to (re-)establish "the kingdom of man over nature" by placing himself in the position of both Old and New Testament God, invoking not only Jesus's demand that the apostles leave their families to follow him (Matthew 10:37–38), but also God's commands that the Jews place the blood of the lamb and sacred scripture on their doorjambs in order to secure divine protection (Exodus 12:23, Deuteronomy 6:9).[18] As Joel Porte and Saundra Morris explain, the implication of these lines is that "Emerson replaces sacred scripture and the blood of the lamb with his own inclinations or intuitions" – intuition being another term for the whimsical call of genius.[19] Important to note here is that while these lines have deservedly garnered a good deal of critical attention, they are in fact the culmination of a larger discussion regarding self-reliance and human divinity. Earlier in the same paragraph, Emerson recounts the following conversation between himself

---

[15] Poe frequently assailed what, in a review of Elizabeth Barrett Browning's poetry, he referred to as "the cant of the transcendentalists." See Poe, *Essays and Reviews*, ed. G. R. Thompson (New York: Library of America, 1984), 119.

[16] See my essay, "Feeling Right, Doing Wrong: Poe, Perversity, and the Cunning of Unreason," *Poe Studies* 46 (2013): 4–31.

[17] Ralph Waldo Emerson, *Essays and Lectures*, ed. Joel Porte (New York: Library of America, 1983), 262.

[18] *Ibid.*, 45, 49.

[19] Joel Porte and Saundra Morris, *Emerson's Poetry and Prose*, ed. Joel Porte and Saundra Morris (New York: Norton, 2001), 123n9.

and a "valued adviser" who was "wont to importune" him with "the dear old doctrines of the church": "On my saying, What have I to do with the sacredness of traditions, if I live wholly from within? my friend suggested, – 'But these impulses may be from below, not from above.' I replied, 'They do not seem to me to be such; but if I am the Devil's child, I will live then from the Devil.' "[20] As he does in the "*Whim*" passage, Emerson here practices what he preaches in *Nature*, answering his own plea for "a religion by revelation to us" rather than via the "biographies, histories, and criticism" of "foregoing generations" – a plea that goes hand in hand with his plea for "a poetry and philosophy of insight and not of tradition."[21]

Poe was all too familiar with such Emersonian instances of "ecstatic intuition."[22] In "Never Bet the Devil Your Head," he lampooned them as symptoms of "the transcendentals," a "disease" whose "austere Merry-Andrewism" causes those "beset" by it to make "Tom-Fool[s]" of themselves. The afflicted in this particular tale is one Toby Dammit, a character who, in spite of his name, has absolutely no concept of damnation. Coming across an archway on an "uncomfortably dark" and "gloom[y]" bridge, the perpetually "good humor[ed]" and "excessively lively" Dammit cavalierly "bets the Devil his head" that he can leap over the bridge's turnstile and "cut a pigeon-wing over it in the air."[23] No sooner does he utter this eponymous phrase, his "favor[ite]" for "all … forms of wager," than an avatar of the Devil ("a little lame old gentleman of venerable aspect" with "a black silk apron over his small-clothes") arrives on the scene and forces him to make good on his bet.[24] Upon attempting the leap, Toby is decapitated by an iron bar obscured by the darkness of the scene, and the old man promptly

[20] Emerson, *Essays and Lectures*, 261–2.
[21] *Ibid.*, 7.
[22] The term "ecstatic intuition" comes from "The Philosophy of Composition," wherein Poe uses it to characterize the romantic notion that poetry is "compose[d] by a species of fine frenzy." Emerson advances just such a romantic theory in "The Poet," in which he insists that the "true poet" is not merely a "m[a]n of poetical talents, or of industry and skill in metre," one whose head is "a music-box of delicate tunes and rhythms," but rather one who composes by the "insight" (the "very high sort of seeing") bestowed by the "Imagination," the "nectar" of which "inebriate[s]" and "intoxicates" the poet. Poe, *Essays and Reviews*, 14; Emerson, *Essays and Lectures*, 450, 459–60, 461. When juxtaposed with Poe's mechanistic account of "The Raven" as having been composed "step by step … with the precision and rigid consequence of a mathematical problem" (15), these lines from "The Poet" go a long way toward accounting for Emerson's dismissal of Poe as "the jingle-man," a remark he purportedly made to William Dean Howells. See Howells, *Literary Friends and Acquaintance: A Personal Retrospect of American Authorship*, ed. David F. Hiatt and Edwin H. Cady (Bloomington: Indiana University Press, 1968), 58.
[23] Poe, *Poetry and Tales*, 463.
[24] *Ibid.*, 461, 464.

runs off with his head. When the narrator of the tale attempts to get "the transcendentalists" to foot the "very moderate bill" for Toby's funeral, not believing in the Devil, they refuse to do so.[25]

Such a tale goes a long way toward contextualizing the derisive appellation with which Poe branded the Transcendentalists: the "Frogpondians," a moniker which suggests that Poe viewed the Transcendentalists' pronouncements regarding human divinity as a type of croaking cant that goaded them into taking foolhardy leaps of faith regarding the supposed moral and intellectual perfectibility of man.[26] Indeed, given that the name explicitly references the Frog Pond of Boston Common, Poe may have also had in mind the iconic passage from *Nature* in which, crossing Boston Common, Emerson imagines himself becoming a "transparent eye-ball" through which "the currents of the Universal Being circulate," making him "part or particle of God."[27]

Yet, satirize the Transcendentalists as he would, Poe was ultimately just as much a prophet of transcendence himself. The trajectory of Poe's transcendence, however, to invoke a concept of Kenneth Burke's, was downward rather than upward.[28] Richard Kopley steers us in the right direction when he suggests that Poe's scorn for the Transcendentalists was due not only to their "seeming credulity" regarding human progress and perfectibility, but also their "inadequate recognition of the power of guilt," a power for which Poe, as any number of his tales suggest, had a great "appreciation."[29] While I agree with Kopley on both counts, a tale like "Never Bet the Devil Your Head" suggests that Poe would have ultimately viewed these issues as symptoms of a far greater failure on the part of the Transcendentalists to adequately recognize the power, let alone the existence, of evil.

It is Poe's tales of perversity, however, that feature his most damning indictments of this failure, Emerson's in particular. Attending to "the spiritual danger [of] putting 'Whim' in the place of the name of God," Poe, in these tales, takes seriously what Emerson all too cavalierly rejects, or, more precisely, all too blithely accepts: namely, the possibility that the whims of

---

[25] *Ibid.*, 467.
[26] For Poe's application of the moniker "Frogpondians" to the Transcendentalists, see, for instance, his editorial in the November 22, 1845 edition of the *Broadway Journal*, reprinted in *Essays and Reviews*, 1096–9.
[27] Emerson, *Essays and Lectures*, 10.
[28] For Burke's concept of "transcendence downward," see his *Language as Symbolic Action: Essays on Life, Literature, and Method* (Berkeley: University of California Press, 1946), 244.
[29] Richard Kopley, "Naysayers: Poe, Hawthorne, and Melville," in *The Oxford Handbook of Transcendentalism*, ed. Sandra Harbert Petrulionis, Laura Dassow Walls, and Joel Myerson (New York: Oxford University Press, 2010), 599, 604.

one's genius come from below, not above, that the "impulses" of genius against which Emerson's adviser cautioned him are actually imps of the perverse, "direct instigation[s] of the Arch-Fiend," as the narrator of "The Imp of the Perverse" dubs such "fits of perversity."[30] As the old man does to Dammit, Poe calls Emerson's bluff by examining the consequences of being the Devil's child, of discovering that in following the imp(ulse)s of one's genius, one is living from, or for, the Devil.

Here it is crucial to note that Poe's tales of perversity retain the Emersonian language of genius. Consider, for instance, the following passage from "The Imp of the Perverse," a tale which, insofar as it bears greater resemblance to a philosophical essay than a short story, constitutes a perfect parallel for Emerson's writings:

> We stand upon the brink of a precipice. We peer into the abyss – we grow sick and dizzy. Our first impulse is to shrink from the danger. Unaccountably we remain. By slow degrees our sickness, and dizziness, and horror, become merged in a cloud of unnameable feeling. By gradations, still more imperceptible, this cloud assumes shape, as did the vapor from the bottle out of which arose the genius in the Arabian Nights. But out of this *our* cloud upon the precipice's edge, there grows into palpability, a shape, far more terrible than any genius, or any demon of a tale, and yet it is but a thought, although a fearful one, and one which chills the very marrow of our bones with the fierceness of the delight of its horror. It is merely the idea of what would be our sensations during the sweeping precipitancy of a fall from such a height ... There is no passion in nature so demoniacally impatient, as that of him, who shuddering upon the edge of a precipice, thus meditates a plunge. To indulge for a moment, in any attempt at *thought*, is to be inevitably lost; for reflection but urges us to forbear, and *therefore* it is, I say, that we *cannot*.[31]

Troping on the Cartesian figure of the "evil genius" (*malin génie*), Poe here transforms the call of genius that Emerson associates with self-reliance into a demonic call for self-annihilation. In this paradigmatic instance of perversity, a similar incidence of which appears in *The Narrative of Arthur Gordon Pym*, following the whim of one's genius – a genius which, like Emersonian intuition, lies somewhere between affect ("a cloud of unnameable feeling," a "passion") and cognition (a "thought," an "idea") – leads not to the ascension of man to the godly throne from which, Emerson laments, we have wandered, but rather to the descent of man into the realm of the Arch-Fiend.

[30] Stanley Cavell, *Emerson's Transcendental Etudes*, ed. David Justin Hodge (Stanford: Stanford University Press, 2003), 29; Poe, *Poetry and Tales*, 829, 831.
[31] Poe, *Poetry and Tales*, 829.

And yet, contrary to his philosophy of composition, which is utterly inimical to Emerson's, Poe's philosophy of perversity is the unacknowledged – or, more precisely, the underacknowledged – underside of Emerson's philosophy of self-reliance. In rendering manifest the diabolic potential latent in the impulsive, whimsical call of genius, Poe's imp of the perverse constitutes what philosophers would characterize as an "immanent" critique of self-reliance, one that undermines Emerson's most favored concept on its own grounds, sabotaging it from within by exposing its blind spots and internal contradictions. As Donald Pease has recently pointed out with regard to the aforementioned "*Whim*" passage, insofar as the Emersonian call of genius represents an "influx[ ] of creative power that [can] neither be fully generated by, nor wholly assimilated to, subjective consciousness," it "introduce[s] a constitutive division into [Emerson's] subjectivity that disallow[s] the possibility of any unified identity," thereby "compromis[ing] the autonomy of [his] will."[32] Fully aware that the call of genius utterly undermines any pretentions the Emersonian subject may have to a unified, "imperial self," Poe exposes and exploits this self-division, focusing not on its creative or constitutive power, but its destructive power.[33] Emerson's doctrine of self-reliance prompts him to boast that "no law can be sacred to me but that of my nature" and that "the only right is what is after my constitution; the only wrong what is against it," but Poe's doctrine of perversity – "one of the indivisible primary faculties ... which give direction to the character of Man," as he defines it in "The Black Cat" – prompts readers to ask, What if our nature, our constitution, is itself wrong, is inherently malignant instead of benign?[34] What if, by "living wholly from within," we are living according to the whims of an evil genius, one whose demoniacal impulses steer us not toward self-elevation (let alone self-preservation) but self-annihilation?

To thus return to the issue with which we began, Poe's gothic tales do indeed delimit the American dream of which the Emersonian tradition remains the primary literary purveyor, presenting us instead with (to adopt a turn of phrase from "The Imp of the Perverse") "the nightmare of the soul."[35] Such tales advance not an affirmative message of unlimited self-expansion but a skeptical message of compulsive self-erasure. Yet, just as

---

[32] Donald E. Pease, "'Experience,' Antislavery, and the Crisis of Emersonianism," in *The Other Emerson*, ed. Branka Arsić and Cary Wolfe (Minneapolis: University of Minnesota Press, 2010), 137.

[33] Quentin Anderson famously used the term "imperial self" to characterize the Emersonian subject. See Anderson, *The Imperial Self: An Essay in American Literary and Cultural History* (New York: Knopf, 1971).

[34] Emerson, *Essays and Lectures*, 262; Poe, *Poetry and Tales*, 599.

[35] Poe, *Poetry and Tales*, 831.

a nightmare is nonetheless a type of dream, so too is the downward transcendence depicted in these tales nonetheless a type of transcendence – a transcendence that, though not of the optative Emersonian variety, is ultimately of the same mint, the underside of the same Transcendental coin.

The Trouble with Pleasure: *Jouissance* in Lippard's *The Quaker City*

In his wide-ranging *Beneath the American Renaissance*, a book that helped put popular authors like George Lippard back on the map, David Reynolds notes how, like other "city mystery" novels modeled after French author Eugène Sue's *The Mysteries of Paris* (1842–1843), Lippard's *The Quaker City* (1845) provides a blistering exposé of "depravity among the urban elite."[36] Indeed, Reynolds deems it "the quintessential radical-democrat sensation novel."[37] Yet it is also "the quintessential American Subversive text," a novel whose social critique is often overshadowed – or, more precisely, undercut – by a "hyperbolic sensationalism" that, "time and again," threatens to become "an end in itself."[38] As Reynolds explains, though the ostensible aim of *The Quaker City* is "to stamp out various behavioral sins and social iniquities" such as "intemperance, licentiousness, and urban poverty," both the frequency and the fervor with which it returns to subversive themes and stages sensationalist scenes suggests that Lippard, like other "immoral or dark reformers," was ultimately less interested in scouring "foul moral sewers" clean than in "exploring dark forces of the human psyche, in venting subrational fantasies, and even in airing misanthropic or skeptical ideas."[39]

Critics of *The Quaker City* who have followed in Reynolds's wake have tended to focus far less on its gothic elements than on the cultural work achieved by the "popular reform impulse" motivating its radical-democratic political vision.[40] Yet Reynolds is surely correct to emphasize both, for the novel's radicalism is ultimately inseparable from those elements of it often dismissed as mere gothic claptrap. Indeed, if, as Louis Harap alleges, *The*

---

[36] David S. Reynolds, *Beneath the American Renaissance: The Subversive Imagination in the Age of Emerson and Melville* (New York: Knopf, 1988), 83.

[37] *Ibid.*, 301.

[38] *Ibid.*, 207, 206, 207.

[39] *Ibid.*, 55.

[40] *Ibid.*, 85. For examples of the type of cultural historicist work done on *The Quaker City* since Reynolds, see Dana D. Nelson, *National Manhood: Capitalist Citizenship and the Imagined Fraternity of White Men* (Durham, NC: Duke University Press, 1998), 135–75; Shelley Streeby, *American Sensations: Class, Empire, and the Production of Popular Culture* (Berkeley: University of California Press, 2002), 38–77; and Samuel Otter, *Philadelphia Stories: America's Literature of Race and Freedom* (New York: Oxford University Press, 2010), *passim*.

Quaker City is "a reductio ad absurdum of the Gothic novel,"[41] this is not because Lippard set out to parody the gothic, but, on the contrary, because he, like Poe, took the gothic deadly seriously. In the absurdities of the gothic, Lippard, again following Poe's lead, discovered a literary form equal to the task of not merely representing but also reflecting on and wrestling with the absurdities of modern psychic life – absurdities that, in Lippard's prescient diagnosis of modern subjectivity, are driven, above all, by a (sado)masochistic economy of pleasure.

Though a number of critics have addressed the novel's problematic relation to the issue of pleasure, the majority have done so almost exclusively from the perspective of its potential prurient effect on (and appeal to) readers. Leslie Fiedler, for instance, in his classic study of the American gothic, *Love and Death in the American Novel*, esteemed the novel a work of "horror pornography … justified as muckraking."[42] Though earlier American novelists likewise boasted of having "torn the veils of delicacy aside" in the interest of exposing sex scandals, Lippard went far beyond his predecessors in "let[ting] us look our fill … behind the veil," "lingering … lasciviously over" and "encourag[ing] the reader to relish" the steamy and sordid details of such affairs along with him.[43] Yet however accurate such assessments may ultimately be about the "pornographic" pleasure the novel has been wont to stir in its readers, they overlook the deeper, more pressing trouble with pleasure that exists at the level of the text itself. *The Quaker City* may indeed be a work of "porno-gothic" that "serves up a sexual smorgasbord" to its readers, but its main characters, for all that has been made of their gross sensualism, are scarcely ever allowed to enjoy such sexual pleasures themselves.[44] On the contrary, the type of pleasure Lippard's characters enjoy is far from enjoyment.

This problematic pleasure is no better exemplified than by the novel's archetypal figure of the libertine, the arch-seducer Gus Lorrimer. Here it is crucial to note that *The Quaker City*'s frame narrative harkens back to the seduction novel of the eighteenth century. As Lippard proclaimed in his preface to the 1849 edition – a preface in which he defends the book against charges of being "the most immoral work of the age" – the novel is "founded upon" the "idea" that "*the seduction of a poor and innocent girl, is a deed*

[41] Louis Harap, *The Image of the Jew in American Literature: From Early Republic to Mass Immigration*, 2nd ed. (Syracuse: Syracuse University Press, 2003), 48.

[42] Leslie Fiedler, *Love and Death in the American Novel* (New York: Stein and Day, 1966), 245, 244.

[43] *Ibid.*, 246.

[44] Joseph V. Ridgely, "George Lippard's *The Quaker City*: The World of the American Porno-Gothic," *Studies in the Literary Imagination* 7.1 (1974): 88.

altogether as criminal as deliberate murder" and that "*the assassin of chastity and maidenhood is worthy of death by the hands of any man, and in any place.*"[45] True to his word, Lippard suffers Lorrimer to be killed at the hands of one of his victims' brothers, the hero of the novel, Byrnewood Arlington. Yet at the novel's outset, prior to Byrnewood's knowledge that it is his own sister, Mary, whom Lorrimer intends to make his next conquest (as well as Lorrimer's knowledge that Byrnewood is Mary's brother), the two engage in a wager over whether or not Lorrimer's intended target is indeed "the flower of one of the first families in the city" or a mere "common lady of the sidewalk."[46] In fact, Byrnewood begins the novel as Lorrimer's protégé of sorts, as the latter promises to instruct the former in the ethos of libertinism by sneaking him into the novel's subtitular gothic mansion, Monk Hall – a house, he teases Byrnewood, "where the very devil is played under a cloak, and sin grows fat within the shelter of quiet rooms and impenetrable walls." When, in response to this pledge to familiarize him with "the nature of the *secret life* of this good Quaker City," Byrnewood remarks that Lorrimer "seem[s] to have a pretty good idea of life in general," Lorrimer replies as follows: "Life? What is it? As brilliant and as brief as a champagne bubble! To day a jolly carouse in an oyster cellar, to-morrow a nice little pic nic party in a grave-yard. One moment you gather the apple, the next it is ashes. Every thing is fleeting and nothing stable, every thing shifting and changing, and nothing substantial! A bundle of hopes and fears, deceits and confidences, joys and miseries, strapped to a fellow's back like Pedlar's wares." When Byrnewood asks "the *Reverend* Gus Lorrimer" what "moral" is to be deduced from this sermon, Lorrimer replies, "One word, my fellow – ENJOY! Enjoy till the last nerve loses its delicacy of sense; enjoy till the last sinew is unstrung; enjoy till the eye flings out its last glance, till the voice cracks and the blood stagnates; *enjoy*, always *enjoy*."[47]

Despite his invocations of champagne bubbles and jolly carouses in oyster cellars, the enjoyment that Lorrimer here describes is not the type of spontaneous debauchery it may at first appear to be. On the contrary, it is a highly structured enjoyment, an enjoyment that, insofar as it appears in the guise of a monstrous duty, lies, as Freud would put it, altogether "beyond the pleasure principle" (hence Lippard's use of caps,

[45] George Lippard, in *The Quaker City; or, The Monks of Monk Hall: A Romance of Philadelphia Life, Mystery, and Crime*, ed. David S. Reynolds (Amherst: University of Massachusetts Press, 1995), 1–2.
[46] *Ibid.*, 15.
[47] *Ibid.*, 23.

italics, and exclamation points).[48] Lorrimer isn't so much the carefree pleasure seeker he presents himself to be but is, rather, the dutiful subject desperately trying to comply with a hedonistic command that, paradoxically, assumes the form of a moral imperative: *ENJOY!* Here we have a perfect illustration of what Freud's successor Jacques Lacan termed "*jouissance*": enjoyment not as sheer, unmediated pleasure, but as a traumatic pleasure-in-pain.

This split between spontaneous and structured, obligatory enjoyment is reinforced throughout Lorrimer's seduction of Mary Arlington. In the scenes leading up to what is ultimately Lorrimer's rape of Mary, the narrator informs us that, in truth, "there were *two* Lorrimers in *one*": on the one hand, "the magnificent Gus Lorrimer," the "careless, dashing, handsome fellow who could kill a basket of champagne with any body, drive the neatest 'turn out' in the way of horse flesh that the town ever saw, [and] carry a 'frolic' so far that the watchman would feel bound to take it up and carry it a little farther"; on the other hand, Lorrimer "the libertine," the man for whom "Woman – the means of securing her affection, of compassing her ruin, of enjoying her beauty, has been [his] book, [his] study, [his] science, nay [his] *profession* from boyhood."[49] That enjoyment, in particular the enjoyment of "woman," is Lorrimer's "profession" is a point introduced early on in the novel. When, upon first meeting each other, Byrnewood informs Lorrimer that he is a junior partner in the importing house of Livingston, Harvey, & Co., Lorrimer replies by proclaiming himself both "junior and senior partner in a snug little wholesale business" of his own: "The firm is Lorrimer, & Co. – the place of business is everywhere about town – and the business itself is enjoyment, nothing but enjoyment."[50] In both instances, we have enjoyment not as leisure or pastime but as "business" or "profession," and, as it turns out, enjoyment is hard work. One is never off the clock when it comes to the monstrous imperative to enjoy, and all the frivolous pleasures of Lorrimer the magnificent are nothing but masks intended to cover up the terrifying *jouissance* that lies at the core of Lorrimer the libertine. As he exclaims to Byrnewood upon the latter's discovery that it is his own sister whom he intends to seduce: "Know me as I am! Not the mere man-about-town, not the wine-drinking companion, not the fashionable addle-head you think me, but the *Man of Pleasure!*"[51] To know Lorrimer "as he

[48] See Sigmund Freud, *Beyond the Pleasure Principle*, trans. James Strachey (New York: Norton, 1961).

[49] Lippard, *The Quaker City*, 89, 97, 101.

[50] *Ibid.*, 24.

[51] *Ibid.*, 101.

is" is to know him as, in the words of Lacan, "*le sujet de la jouissance*," the subject of *jouissance*.[52]

As Lacan's greatest ambassador, Slavoj Žižek, stresses, to be the subject of *jouissance* is not to experience perpetual pleasure or satisfaction. On the contrary, if anything, the primary characteristic of the subject of *jouissance* is perpetual *dissatisfaction*, for, as Žižek explains, the reversal of "*permitted* enjoyment," of the "freedom-to-enjoy," into the "*obligation* to enjoy" has the effect of "block[ing] access to enjoyment."[53] This is precisely the case with Lorrimer in the two scenes directly following his rape of Mary. In the first, "[s]tricken with remorse," Lorrimer "fle[es] with a madman's haste from the scene of his crime," "endeavor[ing] to drown the voice within him, and crush the memory of the nameless wrong." But it is "all in vain." Like one of Poe's characters when struck by a fit of perversity, Lorrimer finds himself "[i]mpelled by an irresistible desire, to look again upon the victim of his crime." Upon reentering the chamber, he is instantly struck by a "fearful agitation," as his face, "so lately flushed with passion, in its vilest hues," becomes "palest and livid," his "white lips" tremble "with a nervous mo[ve] ment," and his hands "clutch[ ] vacantly at the air" as though "wrestl[ing] with an unseen foe."[54] In a hallucination that turns out to be a presentiment of his actual death at the conclusion of the novel, this unseen foe becomes an "invisible hand" that guides him to a "merry death" in a "wide river" whose "waves turn to blood, red and ghastly blood."[55]

The second scene following Lorrimer's rape of Mary begins with his exclamation of words that echo those from his earlier "sermon": "I have gathered the fruit, and it is ashes!" Sitting "for hours" with "arms crossed over his breast," a "wan and pallid face" that "droop[s] low on his clasped hands," and eyes that "glance[ ] vacantly ... beneath the shadow of ... corrugated brows," Lorrimer finds himself "stricken with a strange apathy his very soul impressed with a fear, whose nature he might not analyze" and a heart "imbued with a terrible remorse for the irreparable wrong":

> I have gathered the fruit and it is ashes! ... Oh, would to heaven, that before the commission of this wrong, I had known my heart! Would that I had felt, twelve hours ago, how dear this girl would have been to me as a wife! How

[52] Jacques Lacan, "Of Structure as an Inmixing of an Otherness Prerequisite to Any Subject Whatever," in *The Structuralist Controversy: The Languages of Criticism and the Sciences of Man*, ed. Richard Macksay and Eugenio Donato (Baltimore: Johns Hopkins University Press, 1970), 194.

[53] Slavoj Žižek, *For They Know Not What They Do: Enjoyment as a Political Factor*, 2nd ed. (New York: Verso, 2002), 237.

[54] Lippard, *The Quaker City*, 146.

[55] *Ibid.*, 148.

she would have wound herself into my heart, and grown into my very existence; the life of my life, and of my soul, a better and a purer soul! Curses, eternal curses upon the creed of the heart-cankered worldling which has dragged Mary to ruin, and which will ... within a few brief days, hasten her wronger to an untimely and unwept death.[56]

Fear, remorse, apathy: these, not satisfaction, are the effects that result from attempting to comply with the "creed" of enjoyment. The greater Lorrimer's sacrifice to this creed – a sacrifice not merely of his future happiness were he to wed Mary (something which, prior to raping her, he briefly considers) but of his very life – the greater his guilt, the greater his dissatisfaction.

From this perspective, the true trouble with pleasure in *The Quaker City* lay not in its unequal distribution, its theft from the proletarian masses and its exclusive, excessive enjoyment by the aristocratic few, but in the very nature of pleasure itself.[57] Herein lies the true radicalism of *The Quaker City*'s gothic vision, a radicalism that renders its author less the "American Sue," as Lippard styled himself, than the American Sade. For like Sade's (and Poe's) dark romanticism, Lippard's underscores the uncanny resemblances not only between pleasure and pain, but, more fundamentally, between morality and monstrosity, ethics and excrescence.[58] This, above all, is why Lippard is the quintessential immoral/dark reformer: not because he was "inventing moral disguises for notably immoral, sometimes even sacrilegious ponderings," but because, like Sade and Poe, he had discovered the immoral, sacrilegious core of morality itself, had discovered that the *jouissance* his characters suffer to enjoy and enjoy to suffer does not stand in opposition to the moral law but is instead the moral law's monstrous kernel.[59]

---

[56] *Ibid.*, 215.

[57] See, for instance, Ziff, whose reading of *The Quaker City* as the outgrowth of a proto-Marxian "vision of social injustice as the historical result of the deliberate conspiracy of the powerful few" is representative of most scholarship on the novel. Ziff, *Literary Democracy*, 92.

[58] For the classic formulation of the overlap/coincidence of sadism and morality – Kantian morality in particular – see Jacques Lacan, "Kant with Sade," in *Écrits: The First Complete Edition in English*, trans. Bruce Fink (New York: Norton, 2006), 645–68.

[59] Reynolds, *Beneath*, 91.

4

GAVIN JONES AND JUDITH RICHARDSON

Emerson and Hawthorne; or, Locating the American Renaissance

To locate the epicenter of the New England Renaissance, we might look no farther than the Old Manse. Nestled beside the Concord River, within eyeshot of the Old North Bridge – legendary battle site of the American Revolution – the house was built for Ralph Waldo Emerson's grandfather, Reverend William Emerson, in 1770. After his death it became the long-time abode of Reverend Ezra Ripley, who married William's widow Phebe in 1780. Emerson himself lived at the Old Manse, as a guest of Ripley's, in 1834–1835: there, in an upstairs room, he would draft *Nature* (1836), the earliest significant statement of his Transcendentalist thinking. The same room would become the study of another young writer, Nathaniel Hawthorne, who rented the Old Manse after Ripley's death, moving in on the day of his wedding to Sophia Peabody in 1842, and living there until 1845. Here Hawthorne would write many of the tales subsequently collected in *Mosses from an Old Manse* (1846), tales that would inspire one of the era's most explicit calls for American literary independence: Herman Melville's essay-review, "Hawthorne and His Mosses" (1850).

Melville makes an implicit case for an American Renaissance by comparing Hawthorne to writers of the English Renaissance – Shakespeare most centrally – in an essay that ranges from nationalistic praise of American originality over foreign imports to recognition of a burgeoning literary field on American soil. Published anonymously in the persona of a Virginian plantation-owner spending July in Vermont, "Hawthorne and His Mosses" also registers sectional tensions in a republic moving rapidly toward war over slavery. National space is not a given but a problem, one that Hawthorne's New England raciness might solve, thinks Melville, by shooting its strong roots into the hot soil of his "southern" soul: "So all that day, half-buried in the new clover, I watched this Hawthorne's 'Assyrian dawn, and Paphian sunset and moonrise, from the summit of our Eastern Hill.' "[1]

---

[1] Herman Melville, "Hawthorne and His Mosses," *The Literary World* 7 (August 17,

Quoting from Hawthorne's introductory sketch to *Mosses*, "The Old Manse," Melville was surely aware that this exotic dawn and sunset were not originally Hawthorne's, but rather Hawthorne's paraphrase of Emerson's experience as he absorbs the day's passage from a hilltop by the Manse: "The dawn is my Assyria; the sun-set and moon-rise my Paphos, and unimaginable realms of faerie; broad noon shall be my England of the senses and the understanding; the night shall be my Germany of mystic philosophy and dreams" (*Nature*, 15).[2] Emerson's vision of nature refuses to stay put, charting instead a process of spiritual growth that is equally a move across time and space, from the birth of power in a near-Eastern kingdom, through the realm of classical myth (Paphos on Cyprus is home to the worship of Aphrodite), toward the intellectual visions of European philosophical tradition. If Emerson looks outward, Hawthorne's vision of the Manse turns inward toward the grim portraits of Puritan ministers on the walls, or to the old newspapers and almanacs whose ephemera teach lessons of local history. At stake in Hawthorne's "Old Manse" sketch is the very nature of literary location, whether it should be mined for the sources of local identity, or else harbor the international journeys of troubled pilgrims who seek in Emerson's "intellectual fire, as a beacon burning on a hill-top" an answer to the riddle of the universe ("Old Manse," 1146).[3]

The location of the American Renaissance – in terms of its historical parameters, geographical borders, and representative writers – has been a perennially controversial subject, particularly as scholars have questioned the concept of the nation and pressured the exclusionary ideologies underscoring literary canons and major movements. The critical fortunes of Emerson and Hawthorne have accordingly fluctuated. Hawthorne has been variously described as a literary historian of the origins of national experience; a writer who, to the contrary, undermines the ideologies of official national identity; or else a distinctly non-national writer more interested in the traumas of a provincial past. Emerson has been viewed as pioneer of a peculiarly American philosophical vision (Pragmatism); a religious thinker in the tradition of New England Puritanism and Antinomianism; or else a figure to be understood beyond the nation altogether, a writer interested in deep time and unbounded space. In a sense, all these views are valid because Emerson and Hawthorne engage in a dynamic debate over the *idea* of location as the ground of literary creation and identity. If we find in Emerson a kind of cosmopolitan thinker

1850): 1.
[2] Unless otherwise noted, all references to Emerson are from Ralph Waldo Emerson, *Essays and Lectures*, ed. Joel Porte (New York: Library of America, 1983).
[3] All references to Hawthorne's short pieces are from Nathaniel Hawthorne, *Tales and Sketches*, ed. Roy Harvey Pearce (New York: Library of America, 1982).

who explores the routes of international reference, and in Hawthorne a writer tangled in the roots of New England history, then we should note too the contradictions in any distinction between local and global. After all, while Hawthorne was at the Old Manse penning tales clad in Concord moss, he was also editing the *Journal of an African Cruiser* (1845) for his friend and patron Horatio Bridge – an account of a US man-of-war's adventures suppressing the slave trade on the West African coast, published by Wiley and Putnam as the inaugural volume of its "Library of American Books."

Emerson's *Essays* (First Series, 1841; Second Series, 1844) culminates not with another chapter in the series but with a piece set off from the rest: "New England Reformers." Told by his publisher that the manuscript was too short, Emerson added an essay that countered what early reviewers found wanting: a sense of place, an essential Americanness or strong New England flavor to the work. An exercise in local color, "New England Reformers" distills the ferment of reform sweeping New England, with its dizzying array of ultraists and militant dissenters, its phrenologists and mesmerists, its activists for "the protection of ground-worms, slugs, and mosquitos" (592). The essay ends with a call to accept our true "leadings" that will move us from such monomania and surface customs, toward the reception and communication of higher powers. Connected to yet disconnected from the whole, just as it both describes and transcends regional space, "New England Reformers" suggests the difficulty of locating place in Emerson's work. If Transcendentalism is more an angle of vision than a philosophical doctrine, as Emerson once described it, then where does it look *from*?

"New England Reformers" connects Emerson's *Essays* back to his earlier addresses and lectures. Addressing a collective group or ad hoc community, often of young, white, American men, these are works in which Emerson's awareness of location – and of national space – is strongest, if already complex. In "The American Scholar" (1837), for example, Emerson addresses two audiences simultaneously: the members of the Phi Beta Kappa Society in Cambridge, at the "re-commencement of our literary year," and implicitly a broader audience capable of reading this story of local education as a narrative of progression in national culture with the American scholar at the fore. As the piece describes an arc of movement from doubt, to exhortation, to a performative enactment of prospective greatness, place gives birth to process – an emergence into action that moves beyond a celebration of national life through poetry's power to grapple with cosmic themes. In "The American Scholar," as with other addresses and lectures, Emerson's nationalism is both prospective and fraught. The embrace of the local – "the familiar, the low" – is merely a threshold to "antique and future worlds" (69).

When awareness of occasion breaks into the address, Emerson's ecstatic call to convert the world ironically becomes a negation of the nation, with its indolent scholars, low mind, and disgusting avarice. Emerson's entire mindset is finally pitched against emplacement, against having "our opinion predicted geographically, as the north, or the south" (71). Location is there to be transcended.

Yet Emerson's addresses and lectures still reveal his position in a New England literary and religious culture, centered historically on the Puritans, and on various traditions of anti-authoritarian dissent. His lectures on reform and on "the times" in particular show the influence of the jeremiad, a New England sermonic mode that combined self-condemnation, in the face of failure, with an exhortation to future spiritual fulfillment. Emerson's lay sermons, as he called his lectures, preserve the ambiguity of the jeremiad, though often with a loud criticism of the national culture and its system of trade. When essays do sustain more optimistic national ideology, as in "The Young American" (1844), they flag America's growing system of transportation, whereby the locomotive and the steamboat, "like enormous shuttles," weave and bind a thousand national threads into one vast web. Opposing social conventions, transportation here allows a vision of the national space as pure process, movement, and futurity. It enables Emerson to convert a sense of location as *periphery* (being on the edge of European culture) into one of *emergence*, sustained by the boundless resources of the Western land, and by what Emerson calls an "hourly assimilation," a new "celerity" and homogeneity to time that enables the imagination of national identity (213).

This concern with process, so key to Emerson's philosophical vision, is captured in a line from "Self-Reliance" (1841): "I would write on the lintels of the door-post, *Whim*" (262). The need to trust individual intuition is expressed in an image of moving on, from the conventionalism of a domestic space, toward an ongoing process of becoming in the world. The threshold (like the hyphen in the title of the essay) is a transitional space, a boundary at which something enters another state through an outward power of movement. Emerson's idea of Whim is not free-floating, idealized sentiment. It comes framed in "Self-Reliance" by the sociopolitical realities of Emerson's time and place, by abolitionism and the presence of slavery on the one hand, and by the philanthropic societies that respond to the persistence of poverty on the other. Emerson might reject the touristic worship of foreign places and the restless imitation of foreign models. But his principle of self-reliance is formed in denial of the social problems and instituted limitations of the national space. This is why the nation becomes indistinct in the other essays, coming into view only as a staged performance in "The Poet" (1844), in which we can almost hear the creak of the rolling panorama: "Our logrolling, our stumps and their politics, our fisheries, our Negroes and Indians, our boats ..." (465). It would take one of Emerson's disciples, Walt Whitman, to discover in such catalogs that "The United States themselves are essentially the greatest poem."[4]

Emerson's great friend, Thomas Carlyle, quipped that Emerson was like a Hindu holy man talking to himself on a mountain, capturing in a phrase Emerson's tendency toward solipsism, his desire for ascendance, and his interconnection with world literature – his deep influence by writers beyond a Eurocentric circle. Coined by Goethe, "world literature" was a term Emerson would have encountered in his neighbor Margaret Fuller's translation of Johann Peter Eckermann's *Conversations with Goethe in the Last Years of His Life* (1838). Marx and Engels would expand on the idea in *The Communist Manifesto* (1848): the rise of a global economy will create the conditions for a literature beyond national narrow-mindedness. Emerson's essay "History," which opens the First Series, seems to put such theories into practice. To read aright is to participate in cultural universality, to be transported to realms of power by experiencing and incorporating a "train of images" drawn from a vast mosaic of world literature (243). Emerson's theory prefigures ideals of detached engagement that recent scholars have termed cosmopolitanism: excessive "intellectual nomadism" bankrupts the mind but staying too much at home "has its own perils of monotony and deterioration" ("History," 247). And it is not unlike the "distant reading" prophesized by the literary critic Franco Moretti, as scholars seek to understand the historical waves of literary change through wide-scale collation of others' research. Emerson's multitemporal and multicultural idea of history moves progressively toward America, and toward democracy, though "History" ends with doubt that the glories of the classical past will be appreciated by "the Esquimaux seal-hunter ... the Kanàka in his canoe ... the fisherman, the stevedore, the porter" (256). Cosmopolitanism can easily seem a new imperialism, just as Emerson compares the roads leading from Rome into Persia, Spain, and Britain to the power of the human heart to trace highways into every natural object.

Scholars of world literature have viewed it as a mode of reading and circulation rather than as a canon of works. For Emerson, it is both. Books gain a specific gravity by how they are received, phenomenologically, by the wandering mind. In "Experience" (1844), Emerson quotes without attribution a mystifying line from a book of sacred writings by ancient Persian

4 Preface to *Leaves of Grass* (1855) in Walt Whitman, *Complete Poetry and Collected Prose*, ed. Justin Kaplan (New York: Library of America, 1982), 5.

prophets, *The Desatir*: "There is now no longer any right course of action, nor any self-devotion left among the Iranis" (478). Emerson's source was a complex, trilingual work, itself potentially a forgery that claimed to be a translation from a translation of a lost ancient language, supposedly brought from Isfahan in Iran to Mumbai, India in 1773 by the father of the mullah who translates it together with the governor of Bombay – a book that lands on Emerson's desk after Bronson Alcott brings it to Concord from London in 1842. Transcending its content, the quotation seems to flag the crucial process of literary transmission itself, the romance or drama of transnational textual journeys.

If texts travel to Emerson through his personal connections (an Emerson work is always a kind of network), many of his essays also traveled extensively before they made it into print, sent to friends and family or delivered as lectures. The lectures that would become *Representative Men* (1850), for example, were delivered to various British audiences during Emerson's 1847 tour. In "Uses of Great Men" – the introductory lecture of *Representative Men* – Emerson expands his theory of the receptive self rising from the masses by intellectual travel into foreign parts to receive communications of primary power. Emerson's example of the great man whose presence raises the value of all citizens, is the "man who invented the railroad" (615). And indeed, the representative men Emerson chooses are defined by their capacity to travel (Plato in Egypt and perhaps farther east), to enable the travel of others (Napoleon the builder of roads), to draw readers into adventurous journeys (to see Montaigne's inscriptions on his library walls), or to influence other national literatures with their "world-books" (Shakespeare in German translation). Goethe becomes the prophet of an emergent global modernity, the writer most able to comprehend the "rolling miscellany of facts and sciences" in a world that "extends itself like American trade" (751). Not only do works gain in translation, according to Emerson's understanding of world literature; translation is the *only* process by which works gain their life, as we take liberties with world-books, turning them to our purposes, just as world-books – ranging from the Vedas to Robin Hood – are themselves the products of folk compilation in an ongoing process of accession into higher forms (716). If Emerson's ultimate world-books are romances that communicate a spirit of quest and hope, then his essays have their own adventurous quality in their global comparativism. Emerson's friend Theodore Parker criticized this quality as inconsistent, overly intuitive, obscure, and even reckless in its use of Oriental sources. But for another contemporary reviewer, Emerson was "a sort of intellectual Sam Patch" – a famous American daredevil of the time – going about the world in ever greater leaps and bounds.

Despite his ideals of intellectual nomadism, Emerson would be drawn to the concrete qualities of place in his racy travel narrative, *English Traits* (1856). Emerson knew his etymology, and the choice of *traits* in his title suggests a new interest in the restrictions of place (etymologically, a "trait" is a drawn line, related to the word *tract*). The land Emerson describes in such detail is defined by its *finished* quality: "the fields have been combed and rolled till they appear to have been finished with a pencil" (784). Limitation can be seen too in Emerson's range of reference, far narrower than usual. *English Traits* is Emerson's effort to understand a people of commerce for whom the spiritual sense, the idealism, the universalism of the soul – all of the transcendent forces underscoring Emerson's world literacy – were dead. In their stead emerges a lower category, in between place and soul, something not immortal but, according to Emerson, capable of being transferred: the category of race. Emerson's understanding of race was complicated, not unlike that of the great English critic Matthew Arnold whose ideal of culture as a higher, spiritual principle would emerge from an understanding of Englishness as a dialectical fusion of Celt and Saxon. At its center, Emerson understood Englishness as a resilient, Saxon racial essence, which explains the nation's physical vigor and its mechanized tendencies, "as if they had oil also for their mental wheels" (842). Balancing praise with criticism that was harsher still in his Notebooks, Emerson felt that the nation's Saxon materialism had made a ground "where nothing will grow." "The voice of their modern muse," he wrote in typically strong style, "has a slight hint of the steam-whistle" (*English Traits*, 903).

Of course, Emerson admired steam-whistles and the transportation revolution that enabled them; George Stephenson, the father of the railway system, was perhaps his hero above all others. The extent to which Emerson's idea of Englishness contains contradictions allows him finally to locate himself in a special way, less as a New England sage or purveyor of world literature, and more as a *transatlantic* writer. Emerson's growing interest in race would fuel his late philosophy of power – in *The Conduct of Life* (1860) the will to power is very much a Saxon force overcoming the fated limitations of other races – just as it would resolve the problems of place that saw Emerson vacillate between Concord and the globe. Emerson described New Englanders as "doubled distilled English" in an 1843 lecture,[5] with the United States becoming the "seat and centre of the British race," a place for its powers of conscience and freedom – the "ideal or metaphysical

---

5 Ralph Waldo Emerson, "New England: Genius, Manners, and Customs," in *The Later Lectures of Ralph Waldo Emerson*, ed. Ronald A. Bosco and Joel Meyerson, vol. 1 (Athens: University of Georgia Press, 2001), 40.

necessity" of race that Emerson saw wanting in other racial theories – that would continue growing beyond "an old and exhausted island" (*English Traits*, 790, 916). If Emerson believed that English idealism had died in the Elizabethan age,[6] then he locates a new Renaissance on American soil, in a heightened power of the spiritual and the ideal, with which Emerson himself was already closely identified. Seeing England in commercial crisis, he ends *English Traits* with a journey home, to "the capes of Massachusetts and my own Indian stream," where "the elasticity and hope of mankind must henceforth remain on the Alleghany ranges, or nowhere" (936). Emerson's interest in race allows him finally to resituate American commercialism, not as part of the global system of trade betokening the emergence of world literature, but as a continuation of a racial destiny that is difficult to read as anything less than a narrowing of vision. As a temporal location, Emerson's American Renaissance was always in the future, the only place where its contradictions could be sustained.

Hawthorne was in his third year as United States Consul at Liverpool when *English Traits* appeared. He wrote his erstwhile Concord neighbor that it represented the truest criticism yet written about England. Hawthorne's agreement is evident in his last finished work, *Our Old Home* (1863), distilled from notebooks kept in England from 1853 to 1860. Comparing maps in his Liverpool office, Hawthorne finds Great Britain "so provokingly compact that we may expect it to sink" (7).[7] The character of John Bull had likewise become narrow and stolid, fossilized by the heavy air of industrialization and long settlement in one spot. If the book's title suggests continuity in the possessive *Our*, its *Old* confirms what Emerson argues: the spirit of the Anglo-Saxon race had crossed the Atlantic. Yet that third word, *Home*, sets Hawthorne apart from Emerson in his magnetic attraction to the domestic, in both geopolitical and localized senses, while his accounts of the varied English scenes he tours show an obsession with the particularity of place. We thus find Hawthorne flustered in Uttoxeter at his inability to locate *exactly* where Samuel Johnson stood in the rain to do penance for some fifty-year-old fault against his father: "How strange and stupid it is, that tradition should not have marked and kept in mind the very place!" (136–7).

Hawthorne's place-consciousness surfaces in numerous ways: in the language he uses to characterize his favored literary mode, the Romance, as

---

[6] *Journals and Miscellaneous Notebooks of Ralph Waldo Emerson*, ed. Merton M. Sealts, Jr., vol. x (Cambridge, MA: Belknap Press of Harvard University Press, 1973), 511.

[7] Nathaniel Hawthorne, *Our Old Home: A Series of English Sketches*, ed. Fredson Bowers (Columbus: Ohio State University Press, 1970).

a "neutral territory" (149) in *The Scarlet Letter* (1850),[8] for example; or in the recurrent pity he feels toward individuals who have not found their place; or in the general importance locations have throughout his writing. In his novel *The House of the Seven Gables* (1851), there simply is no story without the Pyncheon house, with its ancestral curse emerging from contentious ground. So much had happened there, writes Hawthorne, that "the very timbers were oozy, as with the moisture of a heart" (374).

Hawthorne's locational imperative is perhaps most pronounced in his tales and sketches, even as these shorter pieces were his most mobile commodities, often getting plucked from their original sites of publication – frequently in local periodicals – to be reprinted elsewhere, including his own major collections *Twice-Told Tales* (1837, 1842), *Mosses from an Old Manse* (1846), and *The Snow-Image* (1852). Drawing from the reminiscences of housekeepers and stashes of journalistic ephemera, from obscure annals and local legends, Hawthorne works, in tale after tale, to evoke a sense of spirit and story unique to his New England. (Many of Hawthorne's stories can be classed as "treasure tales," centered on uncovering value within their specific locations.) "Alice Doane's Appeal" (1835)[9] captures Hawthorne's larger designs on his readers in a visit to Salem's Gallows Hill, a desire to tell the local with such eloquence that his companions will "See!," really see and feel the history that happened there (215). We find numerous sketches that, eschewing story altogether, seem more like exercises in micro-travel writing, situated reverie, even a kind of ethnography. Anticipating Thoreau's quip in *Walden* (1854), Hawthorne, we might say, traveled a great deal in New England. His narrators repeatedly lead readers down unfashionable by-streets, on walks along the New England sea-shore, on rambles around Salem town or visits to the town pump, to show just how much there is to contemplate in microcosm. "How various are the situations of the people covered by the roofs beneath me," he writes in "Sights from a Steeple" (1831), "how diversified are the events at this moment befalling them!" (46). At moments – typically self-ironizing ones – Hawthorne's fixation on place can seem a fish-eyed myopia as the local assumes absurdly outsized importance. When the incoming and outgoing years meet on the steps of Salem's City Hall in "The Sister Years" (1839), the elder gives her younger sister the ultimate gift: back-issues of the *Salem Gazette* to read!

For all his localism, though, Hawthorne was not completely isolationist. His New England, hinterland as it may seem, is really a borderland

---

[8] All references to Hawthorne's novels are from Nathaniel Hawthorne, *Novels*, ed. Millicent Bell (New York: Library of America, 1983).

[9] Hawthorne stories are dated by year of initial publication.

adjoining other cultures in a North American patchwork of European colonialism. Hence the "iron tongue" that calls Salemites to worship and that tolled the news of the Revolution, started life in France, is made from a melted Spanish cannon, and was captured from a Catholic mission near Lake Champlain ("A Bell's Biography" [1837], 480). Hawthorne's tales are inflected too by New England's historical relationship to the whole maritime world. Most of the locals who gather around the stove in the shop of "The Village Uncle" (1836) have sailed farther than the "Middle Banks" – not a few to the East Indies. And it was not terribly uncommon, Hawthorne recounts in "Chippings with a Chisel" (1838), for a Martha's Vineyard boy to make his grave on the other side of the world. Hawthorne's own father, a sea captain, died in 1808 in Suriname.

Like Emerson, then, Hawthorne approaches a global sense in relation to trade and traffic. If Emerson envisions this commerce as prophetic, for Hawthorne it is a historical fact of place. Scattered throughout Hawthorne's stories is evidence of literal transnational exchange; "curiosities from beyond the sea" (61) decorate the modest home in "The Wives of the Dead" (1832). Populating Hawthorne's everyday New England are a French Protestant tavern keeper, in "My Kinsman, Major Molineux" (1835); a Quaker boy, adopted by Puritans, whose outlandish name, Ilbrahim, reflects his birth among the Muslims of Turkey, in "The Gentle Boy" (1832); a foreign young couple of indeterminate nationality, traveling with a box that displays world scenes, in "The Seven Vagabonds" (1833); sailors with the air of Spanish creoles, in "The White Old Maid" (1835); and various Irish, English, and Native American figures, along with persons of African ancestry – a reminder of New England's connection to the transatlantic history of the slave trade.

Hawthorne's writings demonstrate a transnational commerce that is intellectual and cultural as much as material. Lodged in his study, Hawthorne, like Emerson, had a whole literary world at his fingertips (even though, before leaving for Liverpool in 1853, he had traveled little outside New England). Through wide reading, his small chamber becomes "space enough to contain the ocean-like circumference of an Arabian desert" and "the mountains of Central Asia"; even with his "humble means" he can imaginatively import "the magnificent merchandise of an Oriental bazaar" ("Night Sketches" [1838], 549). "A Virtuoso's Collection" (1842) imagines an itinerant showman exhibiting his impossible collection at a local museum; it also provides an opportunity for Hawthorne to display his own power of reference, with over two hundred allusions ranging among classical mythology, Arthurian literature, Egyptian legend, Christian allegory, and more. The mix-and-match quality of the virtuoso's display, its "tendency to whimsical combinations and ludicrous analogies" (711), allegorizes Hawthorne's own integration of American culture and history into a transferable, transnational, and transhistorical catalogue that disrupts linearity or spatial boundary. Hawthorne's allusive athleticism registers not just influence: it marks his sense of rightful heirship to world literature. *A Wonder-Book for Boys and Girls* (1852) enacts exactly this taking of possession, claiming equal birthright (and copyright) by reframing tales from classical mythology for American children. And we find Hawthorne adapting the form as well as the content of foreign models, just as the itinerant narrator of "The Seven Vagabonds" pursues a design "to imitate the story tellers of whom Oriental travellers have told us" (152). Several of Hawthorne's tales, meanwhile, are set in Canterbury, including "The Canterbury Pilgrims" (1833), which echoes Chaucer's technique of serial tale-telling by a motley assemblage.

But Hawthorne's Canterbury is not after all in Chaucer's medieval England. It is Canterbury, New Hampshire – a real town known for its Shaker community. Despite tapping widely into the transnational, Hawthorne never fully shares Emerson's privileging of dislocation. He returns to fertile possibilities *within* locality, closing the 1842 edition of *Twice-Told Tales* with "The Threefold Destiny: A Faery Legend" (1838), a story all about finding on your own native doorstep what you have searched for the world over. If Emerson's global comparativism outweighs his nationalism, then Hawthorne pushes back more firmly on slavish deference to foreign models. Hawthorne may hold inviolate a certain pantheon of world authors, but his tales self-consciously satirize Eurocentric alter-egos who try to boost American literature with Tennysonian stanzas and German mysticism ("The Antique Ring" [1843]). In "The Devil in Manuscript" (1835), he accordingly indicts American publishers for perpetuating a transatlantic imbalance in literary trade through an indifference to American work. Many of the foreign-born or trained artists and scientists who move through Hawthorne's pages are suspicious, if not villainous, characters. The foreign is not infrequently associated with corruption and disease, whether in the poisonous Italian plants of "Rappaccini's Daughter" (1838), or in "Lady Eleanore's Mantle" (1844), where a haughty English dame introduces a smallpox epidemic to colonial New England, brought in on her fashionable foreign finery.

Emerson embraced the perpetual motion and homogenizing power of transportation. For Hawthorne, there is something unsavory, even demonic, in dislocating rapid transit. After all, it is ostensibly the devil in "Young Goodman Brown" (1835) who can travel from Boston to Salem in fifteen minutes. "The Celestial Railroad" (1843) promises effortless progress to salvation, in Hawthorne's *Pilgrim's Progress*-like spoof on technological faith, but it turns out to be a devilish con. The true path, Hawthorne suggests, lies in footwork that keeps pace with human experience and touch with the ground. "The Hall of Fantasy" (1843) follows Emerson in its satire of America's airy dreamers and monomaniacal reformers (including Hawthorne's one-time companions at the utopian Brook Farm), but even the Great Men whom Emerson celebrates – Swedenborg and Goethe – come in for sly undercutting here.

Emerson's horror was that of being locked in place, Hawthorne's of unrooted abstraction. Thus even at his most allegorical and fanciful – as in the supra-terrestrial zones that feature in a cluster of tales in *Mosses from an Old Manse* – Hawthorne's aim was always one of integration; he sought to locate moral truths in finite, humanized spaces. As Hawthorne describes it in *The Scarlet Letter*, Romance resides in the effect of moonlight on the familiar floor of his own room, spiritualizing the mundane so that "Ghosts might enter here" (149). If Emerson's crucial idea of Whim is inscribed on a threshold that leads out, then Hawthorne's situated portals tend to be sites of *ingress*, where spiritual and historical shadows can enter, just as we can accordingly enter into contact with them.

There are apparent exceptions to this rule of ingress. For example, the prophetic procession out from the Boston Province-House of all former royal governors, as the Revolution approaches, in "Howe's Masquerade" (1838), returns us to the complex relationship between the local, transnational, and national in Hawthorne's work, found in a fraught love triangle between old England, New England, and America. Like Emerson's transatlanticism, Hawthorne's writings testify, on multiple levels, to just how "entangled" old English roots remain with "our heart-strings" (*Our Old Home*, 33). Despite his distaste for the English, Hawthorne himself feels the tug surfacing not least in uncanny moments of déjà vu when on British soil. Closer to home, we might even say that Hawthorne's tales work to keep the English in New England, as ousted royal governors, and other British figures, remain to haunt the new nation. Yet transplantation yields differentiation in New World conditions. In particular, Hawthorne attributes the rise of a distinct New England character to a staunch dedication to liberty, sprouted in England's seedbed but growing riotously in Puritan settlements to become the basis of a new patria. Not for nothing does *Twice-Told Tales* open with "The Gray Champion" (1835), in which a spectral figure, in the garb of the original settlers – the very "type of New-England's hereditary spirit" – materializes whenever a threat to "our liberties" emerges (236, 242). Hawthorne's ambivalence toward the Puritan past notwithstanding, we see in such moments a regional pride, growing from a sense that American independence started here. Of all the objects in "A Virtuoso's Collection," Hawthorne's narrator is most excited by "Major

Pitcairn's pistol, the discharge of which, at Lexington, began the war of the revolution" (703).

But the insistence on location here (at *Lexington*) – not to mention that Pitcairn was a Scot fighting for the British – begs the question: Does Hawthorne fully cross that bridge from the local to the national? In "A Book of Autographs" (1844), Samuel Adams is described as never so much a citizen of the United States as he was "a son of the Old Bay Province" (965). The same might be said of Hawthorne himself. If Hawthornian Romance proves a slippery category, its binaries rarely holding together, so too can the nation seem, for Hawthorne, an unstable territory lying somewhere between concept and location, always threatening to split into placeless abstraction on the one hand, and obdurate regional difference on the other. And when the nation does literally split into sections, during the Civil War, Hawthorne's ability to write a Romance likewise collapses into "the fragments of a shattered dream" (*Our Old Home*, 4). Ironically, the places where a national identity comes into view with most coherence can be found in Hawthorne's late, if frequently ambivalent, writings from overseas. In *Our Old Home*, we find Hawthorne speaking in more pronounced and positive terms about his countrymen than in his earlier, domestic writings. But Hawthorne still seems reluctant to *represent* them, diplomatically as well as textually: he is unnerved by a sense "of having somehow lost the property of my own person" when his countrymen call him "my Consul!" (11). And when the Mayor of London calls on Hawthorne to speak in the role of American representative, the book ends abruptly.

The Marble Faun (1860), Hawthorne's last published novel, might be considered another failure of voice. The story of a group of young American artists who become involved in a mysterious murder in Rome, *The Marble Faun* was ostensibly an attempt to discover in Italy the historical latitude for Romance that its preface alleges is absent from the American scene. But the result reads more like Hawthorne's attempt to describe the alchemy by which Romance might emerge, rather than actually performing it. The problem is that these American characters do not fit their environment. At a basic level, they do not understand the events surrounding them, just as the murder at the heart of the novel remains unexplained. More profoundly, European encounters have corrosive effects, not least on the artist-characters' aesthetic originality (Hilda, one of the naive Americans, becomes a mere copyist in Rome). If the spirit of that first Renaissance began in Italy, ran through England, and came to reside in America as forward-looking idealism, then it ironically disables these American Adams and Eves from understanding a fallen world that lives *in* rather than above history. The Roman ruins refuse to echo aright American voices; the domestic spaces the characters encounter are failed ones; and the sheer heaps of history lying around become so much obscuring dirt. Steeped in Romantic poetry and classical myth, the American characters seem unable to take Rome and its people as fully real (does Donatello, they wonder to the end, have the ears of a faun?). Philosophically speaking, America represents, for both Hawthorne and Emerson, a spiritual mecca for the world's homeless seekers of liberty. But in a final irony, Americans themselves seem ultimately innocents abroad, neither here nor there, far from at home in the world.

Just after *The Marble Faun*'s publication in 1860, Hawthorne returned to the United States, to Concord, to a house he had purchased in 1852 from the Alcotts. Hawthorne had rechristened it The Wayside, a typically two-faced name that bespoke a desire for retreat from modern life even as it reduced the place to a trivial stopover along a route to elsewhere. Looking back from the 1860s, the ambiguous name seems prophetic of those questions of place and dislocation that came to haunt Hawthorne's late life and work. Unable to feel settled at The Wayside, deeply rattled by the Civil War, and finding himself incapable of finishing a growing pile of promised Romances, the author sought solace in walks atop the hill behind The Wayside. Perhaps he desired to capture again some glimpse of that Assyrian sunrise, those romantic global horizons that Emerson once espied from his optimistic vantage beside the Old Manse, barely two miles up the road. But by other measures, the distance was vast. To a gloomy Hawthorne, amid a world grown full of irreconcilable divisions and impending postwar realities, it seemed more likely that he, and the whole cultural age centered on Concord, were soon to be tossed by the wayside of history.

5

CHRISTOPH IRMSCHER

Cosmopolite at Home: Global Longfellow

Among the photographs on my study wall is a portrait of my great-grandmother, Ida von Pechmann, a woman of some refinement and, by the standards of her time, more than ordinary education. Born in 1860 in the picturesque medieval town of Memmingen, Bavaria, she later followed a man she barely knew, the merchant Wilhelm Alexander Mueller, to Alexandria, Egypt. There she would bear him five children during a long and, by all accounts, happy marriage. I have always wondered what would have induced Ida to leave everything behind and to embrace an uncertain future at the side of a virtual stranger. A small part of the mystery unraveled when I came across a beautiful notebook, bound in green marble boards, with Ida's name engraved on a small label pasted on the front cover. When Ida was about sixteen, she began to use that book to write down and preserve her favorite poems. Not unexpectedly, many of them are by German writers (Friedrich Rückert, Johann Wolfgang von Goethe, Friedrich Schiller, and Heinrich Heine). In one of the first poems she copied, Ferdinand Freiligrath's "Die Auswanderer" ("The Emigrants"), the speaker somewhat smugly warns a band of would-be exiles that they will regret their decision: "Ah! in strange forests how ye'll yearn / For the green mountains of your home."[1] Ida, of course, didn't yet know that one day she too would leave the green mountains of her home country behind. But, in a way, she was prepared; the poems she collected allowed her mind to travel even though she herself hadn't yet.

For alongside the German works she anthologized were also plenty of poems by foreign writers, among them Byron, Béranger, and Lermontov. The foreign poet with the most entries was Henry Wadsworth Longfellow. Ida's Longfellow selections included "Regentag" ("The Rainy Day"), in a

---

[1] "Gedichte," c. 1876–1882, author's collection; Freiligrath, "The Emigrants," translated by C. T. Brooks, in Longfellow, *The Poets and Poetry of Europe. With Introductions and Biographical Notices* (1845; New York: C. S. Francis and Co., 1877), 361.

translation by Freiligrath; "Das Licht der Sterne" ("The Light of Stars"); "Nachtglocke" ("Curfew"); "Am Abend" ("The Day Is Done"); and "Tagesanbruch" ("Daybreak"). Longfellow's most famous poem, "The Psalm of Life," appears too, later in the volume, in English, as part of a handful of other poems Ida copied in their original language, by Robert Burns, Elizabeth Barrett Browning, Felicia Hemans, and Amelia Opie. The group also includes, again in English, "The Rainy Day." Remarkably, right among these supposedly original (i.e. untranslated) poems we find Goethe's "Erlkönig," in both English and French ("The Erl-King"; "Le roi des aunes"), which suggests Ida had a refreshingly unconventional understanding of what constitutes an original language.

Longfellow would have approved of her view, as will become clearer in the course of this chapter. The Longfellow poems Ida had chosen to copy into her book, familiar to contemporary readers everywhere, are all concerned with simple things – life, the weather, the beginning of the day, the coming on of night. Seeing them again, in Ida's collection, I was struck how several of them share a concern with the experience of reading, either as an ongoing process or as something that has been already completed. In "The Light of Stars," the poet voices the hope that his "brief psalm" might soothe his reader, while in "The Day Is Done" he asks her more directly to read to him "some simple and heartfelt lay," presumably a poem very much like a Longfellow poem. "The book is completed," he sighs in "Curfew," adding later in the poem: "The story is told."[2]

Modern efforts to rehabilitate Longfellow – as a cultural mediator, a craftsman, or a scholar-poet – have largely left such simpler poems aside, as if they were a continuing source of embarrassment.[3] But these were the products of his pen that were most widely known; they spoke the international lingua franca of poetry, recognized nationally and especially internationally. The Longfellow poems admired by Ida and her contemporaries work to validate the ordinary experiences of life – the cares and worries of the day, the desire for rest at night – while at the same time heightening them, dignifying them with the ubiquitous power of literature, present in whatever language and culture you happen to be born into. In F. O. Matthiessen's foundational *American Renaissance*, Longfellow is described mostly in terms of what he lacked and what his peers such as Emerson, Hawthorne, Thoreau, and Whitman possessed in abundance – insight into

---

[2] *The Complete Poetical Works of Henry Wadsworth Longfellow*, ed. H. E. Scudder (Cambridge, MA: Houghton, Mifflin and Company, 1893), 4, 64–5, 70.

[3] A good example is poet Howard Nemerov's edition of Longfellow poems for the Laurel Poetry series, in which not even one of Ida's favorites appears (*Longfellow* (New York: Dell, 1960)).

the deeper patterns of human behavior, authenticity, vigor, and solidity of feeling.[4] Matthiessen's verdict set the tone for the scholarly consensus on Longfellow, which, despite a recent spate of more appreciative studies, has survived almost intact.[5] Longfellow's contribution to American literature, if it is considered at all, is usually perceived to exist at an odd angle to the more solidly innovative work of writers associated with the American Renaissance. But Longfellow disappoints us only if we continue to expect the wrong things from him and if we try to fit him into a narrowly national-ist framework. He was, for a considerable period of time, one of the world's most widely read poets, equally familiar to the nine-year-old Bertha Shaffer in Ohio, Ida von Pechmann in Memmingen, Germany, and Syud Hossein, a young man from Calcutta in India, to name just three of his thousands of admirers, and this is precisely where any new discussion of his importance needs to start.[6] This chapter focuses on the ways in which Longfellow's life-long interests in travel, translation, and the genre of anthology – interests that appealed to international readers such as my great-grandmother – have shaped his poetry and allowed him to do work none of his literary contem-poraries was similarly equipped to do.

Longfellow would have appreciated the multilingual character of Ida's private anthology. We know that he spoke nine languages fluently and that he was likely able to read at least eight others.[7] Foreign visitors confirmed he sounded like a native to them – praise that mattered a great deal to him. When he was in Venice in 1828, he reported delightedly that everyone at his hotel had mistaken him for an Italian.[8]

However, it was precisely his linguistic versatility that made Longfellow an instant suspect in the eyes of his literary peers. While writers associ-ated with the American Renaissance were clamoring for a nation that was not only politically but culturally and intellectually independent,[9]

[4] F. O. Matthiessen, *American Renaissance: Art and Expression in the Age of Emerson and Whitman* (1941; New York: Oxford University Press, 1968), 13, 173–4, 567.
[5] See Charles Calhoun, *Longfellow: A Rediscovered Life* (Boston: Beacon, 2004); Christoph Irmscher, *Longfellow Redux* (2006; Urbana: University of Illinois Press, 2008); Stephen Burt, "Longfellow's Ambivalence," *The Cambridge Companion to Nineteenth-Century American Poetry*, ed. Kerry Larson (New York: Cambridge University Press, 2011), 157–71.
[6] See Christoph Irmscher, *Longfellow Redux*, 23–4, 93, 96.
[7] See Christoph Irmscher, *Public Poet, Private Man: Henry Wadsworth Longfellow at 200* (Amherst: University of Massachusetts Press, 2009), 153.
[8] Henry Wadsworth Longfellow to Stephen Longfellow, December 19, 1828, in *The Letters of Henry Wadsworth Longfellow*, ed. Andrew Hilen, 6 vols. (Cambridge, MA: Belknap, 1966–1982), 1:287.
[9] See the beginning of Emerson's *Nature* (1836) and Oliver Wendell Holmes's characterization of Emerson's address "The American Scholar" (1837) as America's

Longfellow appeared to be hankering for an even closer relationship with the faded muses of European literature. Herman Melville, in his now famous adulatory review of *Mosses from an Old Manse* by Longfellow's Bowdoin College classmate, Nathaniel Hawthorne, laid down the law: "No American writer should write like an Englishman, or a Frenchman; let him write like a man, for then he will be sure to write like an American."[10] A similar nationalist impulse fueled Emerson's professed aversion to traveling as a "fool's paradise," a form of self-delusion that absolves us from working on our self-improvement at home. Equally forceful was Emerson's disciple, Henry David Thoreau, when, at the end of *Walden*, he encouraged his readers to explore their own inner "streams and oceans" rather than go abroad to find the sources of the Nile or the Niger. Thoreau not only talked the talk but walked the walk, even if only for the distance of a mile: his travel destination, Walden Pond, was a hop, skip, and a jump from Emerson's home.[11]

Longfellow's admiration for all things foreign might seem quaint to modern readers today, a nineteenth-century version of ethnocentrism made palatable by a form of eclectic literary tourism. But we need to remember the context in which he was doing his work. In 1852, for example, when Longfellow was seeking signatures on a petition for cheaper international postage, his own boss, President James Walker of Harvard, proudly announced "he had never had but one letter from Europe" and was hopeful he'd never receive another one.[12] And we also need to understand that Longfellow, in constant conversation with writers from other countries (Freiligrath serves as my example in this chapter), wasn't advocating travel as a recreational activity but as a way of rethinking the role other cultures play in our lives, a way in which the "foreign" is always already a part of "home" and vice versa.[13]

Longfellow's obsessive interest in other languages and cultures flies in the face of injunctions like President Walker's to stay put. He had traveled all over the world even when he had stayed mostly inside his library. Over fifty

"intellectual Declaration of Independence"; Oliver Wendell Holmes, *Ralph Waldo Emerson* (New York: Chelsea, 1980), 88.

[10] Melville, "Hawthorne and His Mosses," *Moby-Dick*, ed. Harrison Hayford and Hershel Parker (New York: Norton, 1968), 535–55, 546.

[11] Emerson, "Self-Reliance" (1841), in Emerson, *Essays and Lectures*, ed. Joel Porte (New York: Library of America, 1983), 278; Thoreau, *Walden or Life in the Woods* (Boston: Houghton Mifflin, 1893), 495.

[12] Longfellow to Charles Sumner, March 27, 1852, *Letters*, III: 336–7.

[13] For Longfellow's role in fostering a network of Spanish-language activity, see Kirsten Silva Gruesz, *Ambassadors of Culture: The Transamerican Origins of Latino Writing* (Princeton: Princeton University Press, 2001). A wider intellectual context is sketched out in Amin Paul Frank and Christel-Maria Maas, *Transnational Longfellow: A Project of American National Poetry* (Frankfurt am Main: Peter Lang, 2005).

languages are represented among the approximately 14,000 books still kept at Craigie House in Cambridge, Longfellow's former residence. They include, apart from the usual suspects such as French, German, Italian, and Spanish, some more exotic candidates, namely Armenian, Danish, Celtic, Chinese, Cornish, Dutch, Flemish, Finnish, Greek, Hawaiian, Hindi, Japanese, Latin, Persian, Provençal, Russian, and Welsh. The topics and genres of books range from foreign language dictionaries and grammars to poetry and children's books.[14]

Of course, Longfellow's job required him to take a more than casual interest in foreign languages. But he did so with a zeal that put his colleagues (who likely didn't even speak the languages they professed to teach) to shame.[15] During the six years he taught languages at Bowdoin College, Longfellow published no less than five textbooks. When he assumed his Harvard professorship, he hired native speakers to provide his students with what we would now call an "immersive" experience. In his own courses, he pioneered the modern concept of "comparative literature," teaching Dante, Molière, and, especially, Goethe.[16] To him, the United States was a "composite" nation, fused of so many different languages and cultural experiences that it needed a "composite" American literature. And American literature simply had to be *Weltliteratur*, to use Goethe's phrase, literature *of* and *for* the world.[17]

The richness of the world's literary traditions, which Longfellow felt American literature was admirably suited to distill and transform, found its natural expression in the half-dozen anthologies he edited during his career. Nineteenth-century readers like Ida von Pechmann loved putting together their own private collections. But Longfellow took the genre to new heights, publishing a collection of Italian short stories; a selection of short French plays; two anthologies of poetry, *The Waif* (1844) and *The Estray* (1847); the mega-anthology *The Poets and Poetry of Europe* (1845); and, during the last decade of his life, the multivolume *Poems of Places* (1876–1879). One striking feature of Ida von Pechmann's homemade poetry book was the care she took to note, at the end of each translated poem, the name of the translator if known. She might have been inspired by Longfellow's *Poets and Poetry*, a gigantic tribute to the importance of literary translation in

[14] Irmscher, *Public Poet*, 169–70.
[15] Henry Wadsworth Longfellow to Stephen Longfellow, February 27, 1829; *Letters*, I: 297.
[16] Irmscher, *Public Poet*, 51–2 and chapter 8.
[17] Longfellow, Journal, January 6, 1847, Houghton Library, Harvard University, bMs Am 1340. See also Christoph Irmscher, *Longfellow Redux*, 188–9.

selections drawn from ten different languages and national traditions, ranging from the Anglo-Saxon to the Portuguese. Each chapter of Longfellow's anthology presented poems in roughly chronological order, and individual authors were introduced by headnotes of varying length that often transcended the purposes of mere information.

A good example is the headnote for the section featuring a series of poems by Ferdinand Freiligrath, one of the writers featured in Ida's collection. Longfellow's approval of Freiligrath's embeddedness in the German river town of St. Goar – the way Longfellow himself had made his home on the banks of the Charles River in Cambridge, Massachusetts – turns into effusive praise for his friend's literary qualities: "He has the richest imagination and the greatest power of language. His writings are filled with the most vivid pictures, sketched with a bold hand and a brilliant coloring." Remarkably, this confirmed homebody had a distinct penchant for travel. But Freiligrath's trips were strictly literary ones, nurtured from childhood with books about adventures and travel. He had, as Longfellow noted with palpable delight, "beheld these scenes with the eye of the mind only."[18]

The selection of Freiligrath poems that follows takes the reader from Persia ("The Moorish Prince") to the moonlit plains of Africa, where a lion pounces upon a drinking giraffe ("The Lion's Ride"), to the rocky shores of Iceland, where the speaker partakes of moss-tea, "the chalice of my future life" ("Iceland Moss Tea") to, finally, a poem that plays on the origins of the Alexandrine verse, suggesting this "desert-barb from Alexandria" has provided the poet with a faster and wilder means of travel than any horse ever ridden by an emir or sheik ("The Alexandrine Metre").[19] Like Ida von Pechmann, Longfellow also included "The Emigrants." But, framed by the other poems that evoke the steppes, deserts, and oases of the world, Freiligrath's poem seems less like a critique of those who leave home than an encouragement to think of travel differently: through poems or translations of poetry you may, Freiligrath seems to be telling his readers, own the world without ever leaving your hometown.

Of course, that is an easy view to take when one's life isn't threatened, as Freiligrath's eventually was, thanks to his active involvement in the 1848 revolution. When that happened, he made sure that he got out of St. Goar, heading first for Belgium and Switzerland, eventually settling in London.

---

[18] *Letters*, 11:476; *Poets*, 359. For more on Freiligrath, see Irmscher, "*Westwärts, Westwärts!*," in *Reconsidering Longfellow*, ed. Irmscher and Robert Arbour (Madison: Fairleigh Dickinson University Press, 2014), 101–19.

[19] According to Longfellow's table of contents, the translations are by C. T. Brooks and James Clarence Mangan (the latter reprinted from the *Dublin University Magazine*).

But the principle that is at stake in Freiligrath's poetry is not rendered invalid by political exigency. For Longfellow and Freiligrath, travel was a state of mind. If Pascal once lamented that all our unhappiness came from our inability to stay quietly inside our own rooms, Freiligrath and Longfellow would claim the opposite, though with the important concession that it is okay to stay inside one's chamber as long as we allow our imaginations to roam free.[20]

Such roaming was, in fact, the topic of the two bestselling long poems Longfellow wrote, *Evangeline: A Tale of Acadie* (1847) and *The Song of Hiawatha* (1855). In each of them, travel and translation are again closely connected. Consider *Evangeline*, for a considerable period of time the most popular epic poem of the nineteenth century: a free rewriting, in classical hexameter, of the old story of Romeo and Juliet, but in a multilingual and multicultural setting. Longfellow's protagonist Evangeline, brutally expelled from her homeland along with her fellow Acadians, is a native speaker of French and Longfellow's poem is saturated with references to Acadian culture, their customs and their stories. Thus, even if *Evangeline* is not an actual translation, the casual reader gets the feeling that it could be one.

Searching desperately for her lost lover Gabriel, Evangeline traverses the continent until she finds him, almost by accident, in yellow-fever-ridden Philadelphia, too late for a happy ending. Most of the locations evoked in the poem, from the Acadian village of Grand-Pré to the Atchafalaya basin to the Ozark Mountains, Longfellow had never visited himself. What is often regarded as Longfellow's attempt to write a specifically American epic is in fact a tribute to the power of stories to travel across national, cultural, and linguistic boundaries. The emotional high point in the poem comes when Evangeline shares her life story with a Shawnee woman who has suffered a similar loss, "another / Hapless heart like her own" (*Works*, 93). The ending of the poem, describing the graves of the reunited Catholic lovers in the heart of Protestant Philadelphia, implies provocatively that American audiences weren't yet ready for such narratives of cross-cultural travel: "In the heart of the city, they lie, unknown and unnoticed. / Daily the tides of life go ebbing and flowing beside them, / Thousands of throbbing hearts, where theirs are at rest and forever" (*Works*, 98).

The theme of lost stories, collected by the poet-translator, reappears in *The Song of Hiawatha*, a kind of mythic biography of an Ojibway messiah who reconciled warring tribes and created a universal pictographic language in which they could express their shared histories. But although

---

[20] Blaise Pascal, *Pensées and Other Writings*, ed. Anthony Levi, trans. Honor Levi (Oxford: Oxford University Press, 1995), 44.

Hiawatha, like any epic hero, fulfills a number of tasks, ranging from being swallowed by a giant fish to fighting an evil shape-shifting trickster, his mission eventually fails. The Black Robes, harbingers of Western domination, arrive and Hiawatha vanishes into the sunset. Significantly, the leader of the Black Robes stumbles when he tries to speak Hiawatha's language, struggling to pronounce the "words yet unfamiliar" (*Works*, 163). In the mellifluous poetic universe of Hiawatha's world, given to us in another one of Longfellow's quasi-translations, which came equipped with a glossary of Ojibway words, the white conquerors are the linguistically challenged outsiders.

Emerson, when Longfellow sent him a copy of *Hiawatha*, was surprised that his colleague had found so much poetic material in Native American myths. "Indians" had, he wrote to Longfellow, "poor small sterile heads" and no imagination.[21] Years later, Emerson was even more dismayed when he found out that Longfellow was devoting his creative efforts to a mega-anthology of *Poems of Places*, a "Poetic Guide-Book" that eventually ran to thirty-one volumes.[22] "The world is expecting better things of you than this," Emerson admonished him. "You are wasting time that should be bestowed upon original production."[23] Emerson's comment highlights the odd place Longfellow held just outside the loosely defined framework of writers associated with the American Renaissance: as one who touted the values of a truly American literature without fetishizing the importance of being "original." Being truly American, to Longfellow, meant a willingness to give oneself up to travel "the World over," if not literally, then at least mentally, he rejoiced in a letter to his friend George Washington Greene.[24] In each of the volumes of *Poems of Places*, pocket-sized like Baedekers, the individual entries (many of them translations) were sorted according to the places and not the authors that had produced them. And the names of those places appeared in strictly alphabetical order, a refreshingly democratic approach.

As an editor, Longfellow, despite his political views, was not without his cultural blind spots. The Africa volume, for example, opens with a rather ethnocentric poem by his friend Freiligrath, dreaming, from his home on the Rhine, about the continent as a murderous queen demanding bloody tributes from her suitors, whom she then kills anyway. The next poem, "Under the Palm-Trees,"

---

[21] Emerson to Longfellow, November 25, 1855, *The Selected Letters of Ralph Waldo Emerson*, ed. Joel Myerson (New York: Columbia University Press, 1997), 386.

[22] See Longfellow, Journal, May 29, 1874, Houghton Library, Harvard University, bMS Am 1340.

[23] W. Sloane Kennedy, *Henry W. Longfellow: Biography, Anecdote, Letters, Criticism* (Cambridge, MA: Moses King, 1882), 116.

[24] May 31, 1878; Longfellow, *Letters*, VI: 364.

also by Freiligrath, describes the systematic mangling of a white man's body by a leopard and a tiger, who fight over their gruesome, profusely bleeding prey. "Woe, white man!" exclaims the speaker, watching the proceedings with perverse delight. "On thee thy mother nevermore shall glad her eyes!" The moral of the poem transcends Freiligrath's lurid text: Africa belongs to the Africans, he states, or perhaps also to the giant snake that emerges at the end of the poem, devouring them all, tiger, leopard, and dead white man.[25]

The point of this blood-soaked fantasy – the white man imagining a place where white men don't belong, in a German poem translated into English so it can be included in an American anthology – is restated a bit more ably in Longfellow's own contribution to the volume, the poem "Egypt." Here the speaker, as if flying on Aladdin's magic carpet, follows the course of the river Nile (precisely what Thoreau said we shouldn't do), heading for the magical city of Cairo.[26] Longfellow's eye for narrative detail is remarkable. We see the huge water-wheels along the Nile, "belted with jars and dripping weeds," that deliver much-needed relief to the parched lands on the shore. After he has flown into Cairo, the poet admires the jars for sale in the bazaars. They are, like the water-wheels, enormous, "huge as were those wherein the maid / Morgiana found the Forty Thieves / Concealed in midnight ambuscade." Ali Baba has risen again from a past that probably never even happened in the first place.[27]

Somewhat ironically, Longfellow uses one literary fantasy (his speaker's imaginary voyage) to validate another one (Scheherazade's tale in *Arabian Nights*). Having seen the giant vessels of Cairo with his own dreaming eyes, his speaker now "more than half believes" the story of Ali Baba and the Forty Thieves. But it isn't really necessary that he or the reader *fully* believes that Aladdin ever existed. Longfellow's American poem about Egypt confirms, on a level not defined by any irritable reaching after fact and reason, the universal truth of Scheherazade's storytelling. Phrased more abstractly, the overall lesson of *Poems of Places* is not that one shouldn't travel but that one doesn't even *need* to travel, at least as long as there is literature capable of imagining an elsewhere that is *here*. Longfellow's readers may certainly continue to travel for the sake of travel. But for Longfellow it was important that we keep our minds nimble at home. In his world, there was no excuse

---

[25] Freiligrath, "Africa"; "Under the Palm-Trees," *Poems of Places: Africa*, vol. XXIV of *Poems of Places*, ed. Longfellow, 31 vols. (Boston: Houghton, Osgood and Co., 1873), 7–8.

[26] See the same motif in Longfellow's "Kéramos" (1877), where Longfellow takes his readers around the world in search of examples of the potter's craft; see Irmscher, *Public Poet*, 180–2.

[27] Longfellow, "Egypt," *Poems of Places: Africa*, 62–4.

for parochialism and bigotry, or for a poetry that defiantly closes, as the soul does in an Emily Dickinson poem, "the Valves of her attention."[28]

When my great-grandmother Ida von Pechmann, compiling her mini-anthology, decided to include Goethe's "The Erlkönig" first in German and then in two translations, she wasn't simply flaunting her foreign language skills. Poetry, for her, was transportable, not tied to any one language, free to reach across continents (as it turns out, she herself was too when she moved to Egypt in 1889). An impressive extension of this principle was Longfellow's first collection, *Voices of the Night* (1839), the source of many of Ida's favorite poems. Twenty-three of the forty poems in that volume Longfellow had translated himself from other languages such as Spanish, Italian, French, Anglo-Saxon, Danish, German, and Swedish. Writers of the American Renaissance dabbled in translation, but no one came close to assembling a portfolio as extensive as Longfellow's, who would go on to complete the first full translation, by an American, of Dante's *Divine Comedy*. For him, translation was more than an impulse or a poetic idea; it had become a way of life. One of the most compelling manifestations of that drive toward reinvention is the self-translation he attempted a few years after his last travel to Florence in 1868, when he had enjoyed walking across the river Arno on the famous Ponte Vecchio. Longfellow wrote "The Old Bridge at Florence" in English first, imagining what that Florentine monument, allegedly rebuilt by the painter and architect Taddeo Gaddi after a devastating flood in 1333, would say if it were able to speak.

> Taddeo Gaddi built me. I am old,
>> Five centuries old. I plant my foot of stone
>> Upon the Arno, as St. Michael's own
>> Was planted on the dragon. Fold by fold
> Beneath me as it struggles, I behold
>> Its glistening scales. Twice hath it overthrown
>> My kindred and companions. Me alone
>> It moveth not, but is by me controlled.
> I can remember when the Medici
>> Were driven from Florence; longer still ago
>> The final wars of Ghibelline and Guelf.
> Florence adorns me with her jewelry;
>> And when I think that Michael Angelo
>> Hath leaned on me, I glory in myself.   (*Works*, 318)

---

[28] Emily Dickinson, "The Soul selects her own Society – " (1862), *The Poems of Emily Dickinson*, ed. R. W. Franklin (Cambridge, MA: Belknap, 1999), 189.

The poem, an Italian sonnet, starts with an assertion of power by the iconic bridge. Proud, independent, older than old, it likens itself to Saint Michael the dragon-slayer. Simply by continuing to be there, it exacts revenge on the river for the damage it has caused. The Italian version, "Il Ponte Vecchio di Firenze," has a slightly different beginning. Notably, Longfellow leaves out the architect's first name, a gesture to a hypothetical Italian reader, who would not have needed that information. As if we had run into it in a social setting, the bridge, instead of merely declaring itself "old," formally introduces itself:

> Gaddi mi fece; il Ponte Vecchio sono;
>> Cinquecent' anni già sull' Arno pianto
>> Il piede, come il suo Michele Santo
>> Piantò sul draco. Mentre ch' io ragiono
> Lo vedo torcere con flebil suono
>> Le rilucenti scaglie. Ha questi affranto
>> Due volte I miei maggior. Me solo intanto
>> Neppure muove, ed io non l' abbandono.
> Io mi rammento quando fur cacciati
>> I Medici; pur quando Ghibellino
>> E Guelfo fecer pace mi rammento.
> Fiorenza I suoi giojelli m' ha prestati;
>> E quando penso ch' Agnolo il divino
>> Su me posava, insuperbir mi sento.   (*Works*, 318)

In the Italian poem, the statement appended to "I am old" in the English original ("five centuries old") becomes part of a longer sentence, a recognition on Longfellow's part that each language has its own distinct rhythms and that Italian demands a fluency his own native language denies. By line four, Longfellow has caught up with his original: "pianto sul draco" reflects, even phonetically, Longfellow's English text. But just as we feel comfortably at home again, Longfellow's text liberates itself from any loyalty it might owe to its source: "While I reason, / I see it twist, with weak sound, / Its glistening scales," would be a literal retranslation of the Italian. The sentence extends Longfellow's simile, making the river Arno seem even more animal-like by adding sound to the purely visual impression evoked in the English text. A particularly effective rewriting of Longfellow's original poem takes place in the first three lines of the sestet (ll. 9–11), which, retranslated, would read like this: "I remember when were overthrown / The Medici; also, when the Ghibelline / And Guelph made peace I remember." The circular, static structure created by the repetition of the verb "rammento"

("I remember") captures the mindset of the bridge, to which the vicissitudes of change mean nothing.

In both the English and the Italian poem, the bridge remembers fondly the sanctifying touch of the artist Michelangelo, who must have used the Ponte Vecchio numerous times as he crossed the Arno. But the Italian reworking, by referring to Michelangelo as "Agnolo il divino," draws on knowledge that again would make sense only to an Italian reader – or at least a reader who is aware of the way Michelangelo signed his *Pietà*, with an interpunct between "Michel" and "Angelus" or "Agnolo," allowing us to read the signature as "Michael the Angel."[29] The Italian translation therefore makes clear what the English version only hints at – namely that the bridge dominates its environment not only physically but also spiritually. But it does so with an important qualification: the blessing it receives comes not from God but from a divine artist's touch. Normally impermeable to outside influences, the bridge shows almost human emotion when remembering how once the body of the great Michelangelo had leaned upon it.

Longfellow's "Ponte Vecchio" is a literal as well as a metaphorical bridge, spanning not only the two halves of an old Italian city, but different cultures, languages, ages, religion, and art. A bridge does not privilege one side of the river over the other; it connects them both. The fact that Longfellow's self-translation muddles the relationship between origin and target – for who's to say which of the two is the original Longfellow poem? – confirms once again the central concept behind Longfellow's mental travel: your home is where your mind resides. In its two incarnations, one meant for English readers, the other written to appeal to an imaginary Italian audience, "The Old Bridge at Florence" / "Il Ponte Vecchio di Firenze" shows Longfellow's ability to think about different cultures as both universally connected and nationally specific, a view inspired by his reading of the German philosopher Johann Gottfried Herder, whom he regarded not as a prophet of nationalism but as the facilitator of a truly cosmopolitan approach to world culture.[30]

Ida von Pechmann was in the habit of dating the poems in her anthology, noting the day, month, and year she had copied them. One of the latest entries

---

[29] Aileen June Wang, "Michelangelo's Signature," *Sixteenth Century Journal* 35.2 (2004): 447–73.

[30] Herder's concept of the "nation" involved love of one's native culture as well as the desire to open oneself to other cultures; see Hans Dietrich Irmscher, "Nationalität und Humanität im Denken Herders," Irmscher, *"Weitstrahlsinniges" Denken: Studien zu Johann Gottfried Herder* (Würzburg: Königshausen & Neumann, 2009), 85–106. For Longfellow's knowledge of Herder, see Irmscher, *Longfellow Redux*, 97–8.

in her book was Longfellow's "Nachtglocken" ("Curfew"), in the translation of Claire von Gleimer, which Ida added in September 1882. The poem
is ostensibly about the coming of the night, and the end to strife and labor
it brings. "Toil comes with the morning, / And rest with the night" (*Works*,
69–70). But it is hard not to read the curfew bells in that poem as the ringing
out of a life, which is precisely what the bells of Cambridge had done a few
months earlier, on March 24, 1882, the day of Longfellow's death.

Weariness pervades "Curfew" from start to finish. It is a surprise to find
that Longfellow was in his late thirties when he wrote it. Significantly, his
last poem, or at least the last poem we know he wrote before he died of
stomach cancer at age seventy-five, was very different in tone. "The Bells of
San Blas" became Longfellow's final addition to the catalog of poems about
bells he had written.[31] Longfellow, although he doesn't get credit for it, was
the supreme poet of inanimate things. If Whitman celebrated the soul and
the gloriously different bodies it inhabits, Longfellow celebrated *stuff*: in his
poems, bridges speak, books remember, clocks beckon and salute, a windmill crosses its arms, and logs in the fireplace sing tunes that bring back
forgotten memories.[32] Bells, however, held a special place in his imagination,
and for good reason: they comfort and console, reminding us of the rhythms
of a shared, larger life that transcends the routines of our daily occupations.
In short, they were the perfect metaphors for his poems, which Longfellow
always wanted to be understood as more than the outpourings of his individual sensibility.

Given this long-standing preoccupation, Longfellow was primed to
pay attention when, weeks before his death, he came across an article in
Harper's Monthly that described a peculiar set of old bronze bells in the old
port settlement of San Blas on the Mexican coast. Salvaged from a church
long gone, the locals had mounted them in rude frames a few feet high to
serve as a kind of makeshift belfry for their current church, the "Tower of
San Blas," as residents called the structure with a mixture of affection and
irony.[33] Longfellow was captivated.

Remarkably, he was still alert and interested enough to engage in the
kind of mind travel he had enjoyed so many times before. His poem begins
with the observation that, to the sailors on the ships that pass by San Blas,

[31] See, for example, "The Belfry of Bruges" (*Works*, 54–5); "Christmas Bells" (*Works*, 289–
90); "The Bells of Lynn' (*Works*, 290–1).
[32] See "The Bridge" (*Works*, 63–4); "To an Old Danish Song Book" (*Works*, 65–6); "The
Old Clock on the Stairs" (*Works*, 67–8); "Chimes" (*Works*, 354); "The Windmill"
(*Works*, 347); "The Fire of Drift-wood" (*Works*, 106–7).
[33] William Henry Bishop, "Typical Journeys and Country Life in Mexico," *Harper's
Monthly* 385 (March 1882): 537–53, 552–3.

those bells mean nothing – a distant noise, not different from the sound of the waves lapping the shore. But to the poet, they are full of significance, rich with history, wild with remembered sound. Even in their stripped-down state, they evoke the Catholic church and its once universal reach: "One sound to all, yet each / Lends a meaning to their speech, / And the meaning is manifold." Before the speaker's inner eye, the Spanish empire, "austere and grand," rises again. But it is a power, he quickly reminds himself, that has faded.

Unlike the bells of Lynn that summon up the spectral moon at night or the Christmas bells that proclaim peace on earth, the bells of San Blas no longer have any work to do. Like Longfellow himself, they are diminished, "green with mould and rust," an echo of what they once were (*Works*, 360). They long for a return of the past, when the "the world with faith was filled," priests ruled the land, and people built churches to honor their saints. But the poem's final stanza – likely the last words Longfellow ever wrote – makes it abundantly clear that a return to those days is neither possible nor desirable. The world belongs to the living, not the dead, exclaims the dying Longfellow, contradicting those who have belittled him as a devotee of the backward look, a purveyor of helpless nostalgia. In a final poem set abroad but written at home, he embarks on one last journey – one that doesn't end, however, and instead leads to a new beginning. Poetry has replaced religion, and Longfellow has a lifetime of work to show for it. Fittingly for this polyglot global poet, his last lines invoke not a specific place but the world, not a somewhere but an *everywhere*:

> O Bells of San Blas, in vain
> Ye call back the Past again!
> > The Past is deaf to your prayer;
> Out of the shadows of night
> The world rolls into light;
> > It is daybreak everywhere.   (*Works*, 360)

PART II

Rethinking the Renaissance

6

ZACHARY MCLEOD HUTCHINS

Sins of the Rising Generation: Religion and the American Renaissance

A century before F. O. Matthiessen made the phrase *American Renaissance* a staple of literary study, Joseph Tracy coined another term that has come to shape our thinking about American religion. The title of his 1842 history gave a name to the transatlantic revivals led by Jonathan Edwards and George Whitefield in the 1730s and 1740s: *The Great Awakening*. Tracy told a familiar story of religious declension in New England; the true piety of seventeenth-century Puritan colonists gave way, in Tracy's telling, to hypocrisy and an insincere embrace of religious duty during the early eighteenth century. As evidence, he offered the testimony of eighteenth-century ministers such as Henry Messinger and Nathanael Leonard. Leonard complained "of an awful degeneracy, and kept days of fasting and prayer, year after year, that God would pour out his Spirit upon us; especially on the rising generation." And although "the generations that have risen up from time to time, have generally been instructed, from their very early youth, in the first principles of our holy religion," Messinger lamented that "the power of godliness has been evident but in comparatively few instances."[1] This complaint that youth and posterity had abandoned religion, and a hope that evangelical revivals would inspire the rising generation with newfound piety, are central to Tracy's understanding of the Great Awakening and its import for his nineteenth-century readers.

Tracy's history, written in the midst of what religious historians have come to call the Second Great Awakening, was meant to provide a model for preachers and revivalists of the 1840s, when William Miller's prediction of an imminent millennium was rousing the nation to a frenzy.[2] Like their

---

[1] Joseph Tracy, *The Great Awakening: A History of the Revival of Religion in the Time of Edwards and Whitefield* (Boston, 1842), 159, 122.

[2] See Nathan O. Hatch, *The Democratization of American Christianity* (New Haven: Yale University Press, 1989), 220–6.

colonial counterparts, nineteenth-century preachers bemoaned the degeneracy of a rising generation straying ever further from the faith of their fathers; as scholars have long argued, the story of American culture is filled with calls to repent and reclaim a lost religious heritage.[3] The Book of Mormon, a volume of American scripture translated by Joseph Smith in 1830, frequently denounces "the wickedness of the rising generation" and youth who "did not believe the tradition of their fathers."[4] And Protestant writers of the American Renaissance read accounts of Edwards, Leonard, and Messinger as a call to reclaim their own wayward youth, penning jeremiads that warn of the consequences of religious declension. "It is impossible," the revivalist Charles Grandison Finney warned in 1836, "that a voluntary state of mind should be hereditary, or transmitted from one generation to another," so parents and teachers must constantly strive to inculcate a love of God in children who "universally adopt the principle of selfishness." Persuading youth to repent was a matter of patriotic duty for preachers because the fate of the nation was at stake. Thus Lyman Beecher wrote to his daughter Catharine in 1830, "The moral destiny of our nation, and all our institutions and hopes, and the world's hopes, turns on the character of the West, and the competition now is for that of preoccupancy in the education of the rising generation, in which Catholics and infidels have got the start of us."[5] The fight to turn children from sin to the God of their parents was at the heart of religious discourse during the Second Great Awakening and the American Renaissance.

This belief in a need to "turn the heart of the fathers to the children, and the heart of the children to their fathers" surfaced not only in sermons and ministerial correspondence but also in antebellum poetry and fiction. In "The Half-Century Sermon," Lydia Sigourney imagines a preacher delivering a valedictory address to his congregation fifty years after it was established. The minister's aim, in Sigourney's poem, is to stimulate youth and children to the devotion of their grandparents:

> His scatter'd locks are white
> With the hoar-frost of time, but in his soul
> There is no Winter. He the uncounted gold

---

3 See Sacvan Bercovitch, *The American Jeremiad* (Madison: The University of Wisconsin Press, 1978).

4 *The Book of Mormon*, trans. Joseph Smith, Jr., ed. Laurie F. Maffly-Kipp (New York: Penguin, 2008), 463, 212.

5 C. G. Finney, *Sermons on Important Subjects* (New York, 1836), 145, 157; Lyman Beecher, *Autobiography, Correspondence, Etc.*, ed. Charles Beecher (New York, 1866), vol. II, 224.

Of many a year's experience richly spreads
To a new generation.[6]

(51–55)

Sigourney, like so many of her contemporaries, reverenced maturity because of its association with personal piety. Her poem celebrates the transmission of holiness by the elderly to the young and expects the young to reverence their elders. Looking to the past as a golden age, she suggests that only a reverence for the lessons of godly forebears will guarantee a similarly prosperous future.

Like Tracy, novelists of the American Renaissance turned to the nation's ecclesiastical history in their examination of the moral imperatives confronting nineteenth-century Americans. Nathaniel Hawthorne revisited the Puritan censure of Anne Hutchinson in *The Scarlet Letter* (1850); John William De Forest dramatized the Salem witch trials in *Witching Times* (1856); and Harriet Beecher Stowe examined the abolitionism of Samuel Hopkins, one of Edwards's eighteenth-century heirs, in *The Minister's Wooing* (1858). But novels reading the nation's sacred past challenged the authority and, often, the conclusions of preachers past and present. Dawn Coleman argues that these novelists and other writers "saw their work as morally independent, capable of offering moral visions at odds with those of church authorities and society's majorities."[7] For Hawthorne, in particular, the ministerial narrative of piety's intergenerational decay rang false. Unlike Tracy and the clergymen whose words he preserved in *The Great Awakening*, Hawthorne privileges youth – the rising generation, in his novel, is not a morally bankrupt cohort divorced from the devotion of ages past and desperate for instruction but a group whose integrity and innocence is an implicit rebuke to their parents and grandparents.

Hawthorne flips the dominant theological narrative of colonial and antebellum North America, rejecting the Calvinist reverence for age and suspicion of youth.[8] In upending this hierarchy Hawthorne reflects a broader cultural shift away from the Calvinist belief that children are born totally depraved, in need of moral discipline administered by their elders. Hawthorne places

---

[6] Malachi 4:6; Lydia Howard Sigourney, *Zinzendorff, and Other Poems* (New York, 1836), 68–9.

[7] Dawn Coleman, *Preaching and the Rise of the American Novel* (Columbus: The Ohio State University Press, 2013), 15; see also Martin Kevorkian, *Writing Beyond Prophecy: Emerson, Hawthorne, and Melville after the American Renaissance* (Baton Rouge: Louisiana State University, 2013).

[8] This valorization of youth is, in part, a product of the revolt against patriarchal authority discussed in Jay Fliegelman, *Prodigals and Pilgrims: The American Revolution Against Patriarchal Authority* (New York: Cambridge University Press, 1982).

intergenerational conflict at the center of his novels, rewriting the dominant narrative of declension with a hope of moral ascension and collective purification as the rising generation rejects the failings of their forebears. Scholars such as Karen Sánchez-Eppler, Patricia Crain, and Courtney Weikle-Mills have drawn attention, in recent years, to the ways in which Hawthorne, Stowe, and other authors of the American Renaissance empowered children in novels such as *The Scarlet Letter* and *Uncle Tom's Cabin*; these authors both wrote for child readers and presented the adolescents in their work as constitutive of an idealized public.[9]

This valorization of youth was a literary expression of the theological liberalism championed by William Ellery Channing and Horace Bushnell, who characterized children as holy and pure – neither the blank slates of John Locke nor the degenerates of John Calvin. The first edition of Bushnell's *Christian Nurture* was published three years before *The Scarlet Letter* and, as E. Brooks Holifield attests, "helped redefine the meaning of a Christian education within American Protestantism."[10] Hawthorne's novel both reflects and promotes that shift, championing a forward-looking religion that turns not to fathers but to children as the best hope for purity and progress. Sacvan Bercovitch writes that of the authors canonized by Matthiessen, "Hawthorne was the most resistant" to jeremiad narratives of declension, and that resistance is manifest in his celebration of youthful innocence and potential.[11]

Reading History, Writing Scripture

Hawthorne's reading and writing of the past is itself established as the product of a generational divide in his sketch of "The Custom-House" that precedes the narrative of *The Scarlet Letter*. Reflecting on his career as a writer, Hawthorne imagines the disdain with which his ancestors might regard his professional accomplishments:

---

[9] See Karen Sánchez-Eppler, "Hawthorne and the Writing of Childhood," in *The Cambridge Companion to Nathaniel Hawthorne*, ed. Richard H. Millington (New York: Cambridge University Press, 2004), 143–61; Karen Sánchez-Eppler, *Dependent States: The Child's Part in Nineteenth-Century American Culture* (Chicago: University of Chicago Press, 2005); Courtney Weikle-Mills, *Imaginary Citizens: Child Readers and the Limits of American Independence, 1640–1868* (Baltimore: Johns Hopkins University Press, 2013); and Patricia Crain, *Reading Children: Literacy, Property, and the Dilemmas of Childhood in Nineteenth-Century America* (Philadelphia: University of Pennsylvania Press, 2016).

[10] E. Brooks Holifield, *Theology in America: Christian Thought from the Age of the Puritans to the Civil War* (New Haven: Yale University Press, 2003), 466.

[11] Bercovitch, *American Jeremiad*, 205.

"What is he?" murmurs one gray shadow of my forefathers to the other. "A writer of story-books! What kind of a business in life, – what mode of glorifying God, or being serviceable to mankind in his day and generation, – may that be? Why, the degenerate fellow might as well have been a fiddler!" Such are the compliments bandied between my great-grandsires and myself, across the gulf of time!

Hawthorne's embrace of the declension narrative is playful, ironic. Even as he vocalizes the censure of his Puritan progenitors, Hawthorne lays claim to the moral high ground; he is the "topmost bough" of his family tree.[12] Hawthorne condemns the violence visited upon Quaker missionaries and Salem witches by his ancestors, William and John Hathorne, whose declarations of degeneracy are subsumed in the fiction of his story-books. Unspoken is the larger truth implicit in this ventriloquized performance: a story of moral decline can only be perpetuated if it is internalized by the rising generation. The piety – and disapproval – of his ancestors survives only in Hawthorne's reading of the past.

In "The Custom-House," Hawthorne claims he first read the story of a forbidden love between Arthur Dimmesdale and Hester Prynne during his time as the Surveyor at Salem. Although Hawthorne was not a young man when he was appointed to that post by the administration of Franklin Pierce, he emphasizes the generational divide separating him from the customs inspectors who work under him. They are "old gentlemen – seated, like Matthew, at the receipt of custom, but not very liable to be summoned thence, like him, for apostolic errands" (SL, 76). These venerable tax collectors may remind Hawthorne of the career Matthew abandoned to follow Jesus Christ, but they possess none of the biblical publican's piety and cannot speak credibly on moral issues. Hawthorne characterizes them as "a set of wearisome old souls, who had ... flung away all the golden grain of practical wisdom, which they had enjoyed so many opportunities of harvesting, and most carefully to have stored their memories with the husks" (SL, 88–9). The mere passage of time, Hawthorne insists, does not automatically bestow insight, authority, or piety upon the old.

Instead of these aged inspectors, Hawthorne invests himself with apostolic authority.[13] The Book of Revelation, with its story of a woman and her child who flee together from the devil into the wilderness, was given to the apostle John when "the voice which I heard from heaven spake unto me again, and

---

[12] Nathaniel Hawthorne, *The Scarlet Letter, a Romance*, ed. John Stephen Martin (Peterborough, ON: Broadview, 2004), 83; hereafter cited parenthetically as (SL).

[13] Contemporaries like Herman Melville and Walt Whitman similarly assumed a prophetic voice; see Lawrence Buell, *New England Literary Culture: From Revolution Through Renaissance* (New York: Cambridge University Press, 1986), 166–90.

said, Go and take the little book which is open in the hand of the angel." [14] Hawthorne explains that he received his own story – of how Prynne and her child Pearl escape the machinations of a devilish Roger Chillingworth in the wilderness of seventeenth-century Massachusetts – through a similarly supernatural exchange. In a vision or flight of fancy, Hawthorne had seen Jonathan Pue, the deceased former Surveyor of Salem, "illuminated by a ray of the splendor that shone so dazzlingly about the throne," and as Pue extended "his own ghostly hand, the obscurely seen, but majestic, figure had imparted to me the scarlet symbol, and the little roll of explanatory manuscript" (*SL* 105). The story book that would have been derided by his deceased ancestors is, Hawthorne suggests, scripture; he, and not his Puritan forebears or the decrepit inspectors, is the recipient of revelation. Hawthorne thus positions himself as a prism through which the sins of the fathers are refracted into new moral imperatives. Shedding divine light on the dark deeds of his ancestors, Hawthorne's narrative provides a blueprint for wringing moral progress from the troubled past.

Against the history of Hutchinson's banishment for her deviance from theological and social norms, Hawthorne offers an imaginative alternative in which Prynne's deviance leads not to retrenchment but to a re-evaluation of community standards and the emergence of new scripture. [15] The immediate consequence of Prynne's adultery is estrangement. "If she entered a church," Hawthorne writes, "it was often her mishap to find herself the text of the discourse. She grew to have a dread of children; for they had imbibed from their parents a vague idea of something horrible in this dreary woman" (*SL*, 148). Prynne becomes a substitute for scripture in Hawthorne's New England, as local ministers analyze her person and deportment rather than the Bible verse or "text" typically located at the head of their sermons. These ministerial reading practices, Hawthorne notes, are adopted by parents who pass on their hypocritical prejudices to the next generation. Weikle-Mills argues that "Hawthorne's idealized portraits of children are often accompanied by skepticism about the natural child's ability to produce a moral society without the force of textual or legal discipline," but Hester's persecution suggests, in turn, his skepticism of the disciplinary readings inherited by children from their parents. [16] Hawthorne makes the reading of Prynne's history and the

---

[14] Revelation 12:1–6, 10:8.
[15] On the relationship between Hutchinson, Puritan history, and *The Scarlet Letter* see Thomas Loebel, "'A' Confession: How to Avoid Speaking the Name of the Father," *Arizona Quarterly: A Journal of American Literature, Culture, and Theory* 59.1 (2003): 1–29; and Michael J. Colacurcio, *Doctrine and Difference: Essays in the Literature of New England* (New York: Routledge, 1997), 177–228.
[16] Weikle-Mills, *Imaginary Citizens*, 199.

moral instruction of Massachusetts youth into mutually reinforcing processes, as ministers and parents convert their reading of the past into scripture for a new generation. Instead of a narrative of declension, in which children fall away from the purity of their predecessors, Hawthorne reads New England's ecclesiastical history as a narrative of hereditary disease in which parents pass their prejudices to their offspring.

And yet: notwithstanding the best efforts of these parents and ministers, Prynne becomes a symbol of charity rather than sin. Seeing her benevolence to the poor, the sick, and the afflicted, many inhabitants of Boston come to see her scarlet letter as a symbol of holiness and strength and "said that it meant Able" (SL, 210). This enlightened forgiveness leads more seasoned members of the community to revise their views, and Hawthorne writes that with the passage of time "their sour and rigid wrinkles were relaxing into something which, in the due course of years, might grow to be an expression of almost benevolence" (SL, 211). In the race to forgive Prynne and acknowledge her piety, age is a handicap – not a boon. Hawthorne locates true religion in the sympathy of youth rather than in the wisdom of experience.

The moral advantages of youth are evident from the narrative's opening pages. When Prynne emerges from the jail, she meets the scorn of Boston's residents, but more particularly a group of spiteful older women – "a hard featured dame of fifty" and an "autumnal matron" who whip their aged companions into a lather (SL, 120). When "the most iron-visaged of the old dames" urges the other crones to strip Prynne naked, it is "their youngest companion" who objects: "O, peace, neighbours, peace!" (SL, 123). This division between old and young similarly undergirds the disagreement between Arthur Dimmesdale and "John Wilson, the eldest clergyman of Boston," who "looked like the darkly engraved portraits which we see prefixed to old volumes of sermons; and had no more right than one of those portraits would have, to step forth, as he now did, and meddle with a question of human guilt, passion, and anguish" (SL, 132). Dimmesdale's moral authority, by contrast, is both unquestioned and a function of his youth. Hawthorne uses the words *young* or *youth* seven times in his opening description of Dimmesdale, who "kept himself simple and childlike; coming forth, when occasion was, with a freshness, and fragrance, and dewy purity of thought, which, as many people said, affected them like the speech of an angel" (SL, 133). Notwithstanding Dimmesdale's secret life of sin, Hawthorne characterizes the young minister as wiser and more holy than Wilson, just as the young woman is a more fit and merciful judge of Prynne's transgression than her aged companions.

Not only are the youngest characters in *The Scarlet Letter* more holy and loving than their elders, but Hawthorne traces from this generational divide a process of moral and cultural refinement leading each successive generation to new heights. Speaking of the aged women who curse Prynne, Hawthorne observes:

> Morally, as well as materially, there was a coarser fibre in those fair wives and maidens of old English birth and breeding, than in their fair descendants, separated from them by a series of six or seven generations; for, throughout that chain of ancestry, every successive mother has transmitted to her child a fainter bloom, a more delicate and briefer beauty, and a slighter physical frame, if not a character of less force and solidity, than her own.
>
> (SL, 119–20)

Reversing the narrative of religious declension promulgated by colonial ministers like Messinger or Leonard and nineteenth-century historians such as Tracy, Hawthorne posits the collective moral advancement of American women and, thus, the nation.[17] In her bestselling novel *The Wide, Wide World* (1850) Hawthorne's contemporary, Susan Warner, similarly asked readers to "Recollect how intellect, refinement, peace, and love write their characters on the countenance and in the course of generations change the very conformation of men" for the better.[18] Each successive generation produces moral progress, as children adopt more refined manners and opinions than those of their parents.

Hawthorne's novel concludes with a prophecy that this progress will continue. "In Heaven's own time," he predicts, "a new truth would be revealed, in order to establish the whole relation between man and woman on a surer ground of mutual happiness." Hawthorne seizes an apostolic mantle in "The Custom-House" and casts *The Scarlet Letter* as scripture, but he stipulates at novel's end that the "angel and apostle of the coming revelation must be a woman" (*SL*, 292). As Claudia Stokes and others have noted, this prophecy was fulfilled in the nineteenth century both by the rise of "women in official positions of religious authority" and by white women writers whose novels, hymns, and poems "conveyed religious lessons in a more discreet and conventionally feminine manner."[19] In his prediction of continued moral improvement, Hawthorne forecast the extension of a religious shift already evident during the Second Great Awakening – the transference of moral authority to a rising generation reared and catechized by hallowed white matrons.

---

[17] On the conflation of women's bodies and the early American nation, see Shirley Samuels, *Romance of the Republic: Women, the Family, and Violence in the Literature of the Early American Nation* (New York: Oxford University Press, 1996).

[18] Susan Warner, *The Wide, Wide World* (New York: The Feminist Press at the City University of New York, 1987), 579.

[19] Claudia Stokes, *The Altar at Home: Sentimental Literature and Nineteenth-Century American Religion* (Philadelphia: University of Pennsylvania Press, 2014), 8, 31.

Pearl and the Problem of Original Sin

The prejudice and hypocrisy of the Puritan society that Hawthorne sketches in unflattering terms are functions, he insists, of the community's reliance on the maturity and experience of adulthood. In *The Scarlet Letter*, colonial Boston is "a community, which owed its origin and progress, and its present state of development, not to the impulses of youth, but to the stern and tempered energies of manhood, and the sombre sagacity of age; accomplishing so much, precisely because it imagined and hoped so little" (*SL*, 131). Hawthorne characterizes hope and imagination and the progress that they make possible as products of youth. But, as he notes, New England Puritans did their best to eliminate childhood and adolescence, believing that youth needed to be taught early in life to recognize their own sinfulness and to overcome their own depravity through a mature and reasoned recognition of God's grace in their lives.[20] Thus, the children of Hawthorne's Boston play "at going to church, perchance; or at scourging Quakers; or taking scalps in a sham-fight with the Indians; or scaring one another with freaks of imitative witchcraft" (*SL*, 155). These are not children but adults-in-training, a rising generation destined to repeat the mistakes – the providential readings of Old Testament violence – made by their parents. Only Pearl seems capable of imagining a genuinely new and hopeful future; only Pearl learns to read Hester's scarlet letter without inheriting the diseased perspective of a prior generation. "Rather than finding her mirror in the mother's face," Crain observes, "Pearl finds it in the A... Pearl reads before she speaks; she literally rather than figuratively takes in the alphabet with mother's milk."[21] This tension between Pearl and the other children of Boston, between the Puritan emphasis on age and Hawthorne's valorization of youth as the engine of progress, places Prynne's daughter at the novel's center.

When Prynne and Pearl enter Boston for the first time, a mob of miniature Puritan adults-in-training greet the pair with jeers and fistfuls of mud, ready to drive the scarlet letter and its likeness from their presence. In the face of this persecution

> Pearl, who was a dauntless child, after frowning, stamping her foot, and shaking her little hand with a variety of threatening gestures, suddenly made a rush at the knot of her enemies, and put them all to flight. She resembled, in her fierce pursuit of them, an infant pestilence, – the scarlet fever, or some such

---

[20] On the Puritan view of children, see Judith S. Graham, *Puritan Family Life: The Diary of Samuel Sewall* (Boston: Northeastern University Press, 2000), 78–98.

[21] Patricia Crain, *The Story of A: The Alphabetization of America from The New England Primer to The Scarlet Letter* (Palo Alto: Stanford University Press, 2000), 197–8.

half-fledged angel of judgment, – whose mission was to punish the sins of the
rising generation. (*SL*, 161–2)

Hawthorne borrows the language of declension to describe Pearl's attack, as
though the Puritan children she chastises had abandoned the faith of their
fathers, but their mud-slinging is only a physical manifestation of the verbal
abuse hurled by their parents at Prynne and her daughter. Pearl's chastise-
ment is aimed, in truth, not at the children she charges but at the adults who
have trained their progeny to persecute Quakers and Indians, witches and
adulterers. Pearl, far more than her adversaries, is clearly the representative
of a new and rising generation; less clear is whether her departure from
Puritan norms will lead to a life of depravity and sin or to a life of piety and
a more enlightened and sympathetic engagement with her neighbors.

Throughout *The Scarlet Letter*, Hawthorne raises the question of whether
Pearl has been tainted by the adulterous circumstances of her conception.
She is, on the one hand, an "innocent … worthy to have been brought forth
in Eden; worthy to have been left there, to be the plaything of the angels,
after the world's first parents were driven out" (*SL*, 151). Yet Hawthorne
also describes Pearl as "a born outcast of the infantile world. An imp of
evil, emblem and product of sin, she had no right among christened infants"
(*SL*, 154). Like the speaker in Walt Whitman's *Song of Myself* (1855), Pearl
might boast, "I contradict myself; / I am large … I contain multitudes."[22]
This multiplicity makes Prynne's daughter into a representative of childhood as an institution: "in this one child there were many children" (*SL*,
152). The matter of Pearl's salvation and whether the circumstances of her
conception have irrevocably damned her is, thus, a referendum on the larger
question of original sin and, more generally, the spiritual status of each new
generation.

Dimmesdale's public confession in the marketplace clarifies the state of
Pearl's soul; in foregrounding the sins of a father, Hawthorne absolves the
child of whatever taint she may have seemed to carry. After declaring his
guilt, Dimmesdale begs his illegitimate daughter for a kiss:

> Pearl kissed his lips. A spell was broken. The great scene of grief, in which the
> wild infant bore a part, had developed all her sympathies; and as her tears fell
> upon her father's cheek, they were the pledge that she would grow up amid
> human joy and sorrow, nor for ever do battle with the world, but be a woman
> in it. Towards her mother, too, Pearl's errand as a messenger of anguish was all
> fulfilled. (*SL*, 287)

---

[22] Walt Whitman, *Song of Myself, and Other Poems by Walt Whitman*, ed. Robert Hass
(Berkeley: Counterpoint, 2010), 69. See Barbara Garlitz, "Pearl: 1850–1955," *PMLA*
72.4 (1957): 689–99.

Hawthorne intimates that the enmity characterizing Pearl's earliest relations with the inhabitants of Boston will cease. Dimmesdale's confession frees her of responsibility for sins committed before her birth and breaks the spell of the Calvinist doctrines of original sin and total depravity that had identified Pearl as a dangerously fallen human being.

In emancipating Pearl from the burden of original sin and rejecting the tenets of Calvinist thought, Hawthorne embraces the liberal theology espoused by earlier novelists, including Catherine Sedgwick, Lydia Child, and Henry Ware Jr.[23] Ann Douglas pejoratively styled this liberal turn *The Feminization of American Culture*, at least in part because women played such a central role in shaping the literary and religious climate of the antebellum United States.[24] But Hawthorne was hardly the only prominent male author to condemn Calvinist doctrines. Oliver Wendell Holmes explained that he wrote *Elsie Venner* (1861) "to test the doctrine of 'original sin' and human responsibility for the disordered volition coming under that technical denomination."[25] His novel traces the life of a young woman whose mother was bitten by a snake before giving birth; this daughter suffers unjustly all her life because of an event that took place before she could exercise her agency. Holmes and Hawthorne wrote to undermine the moral foundations of Calvinism, providing a literary foundation for the more liberal theology of Bushnell and Channing.

Virtues of the Rising Generation

In *An Essay Concerning Human Understanding* (1689) John Locke presented a theory of cognitive development that would call Calvin's emphasis on original sin and the depravity of humankind into question.[26] Locke asked his readers to "suppose the mind to be, as we say, white paper, void of all characters, without any ideas."[27] Representing the human mind as a white paper or blank slate, Locke resists the Calvinist claim that all infants enter the world inclined to wickedness; instead of this predisposition to sin, Locke posits moral and intellectual neutrality. His influence on American literature

---

[23] For an overview of liberal, anti-Calvinist fiction in the American Renaissance, see David S. Reynolds, *Faith in Fiction: The Emergence of Religious Literature in America* (Cambridge, MA: Harvard University Press, 1981), 96–122.

[24] Ann Douglas, *The Feminization of American Culture* (New York: Alfred A. Knopf, 1977).

[25] Oliver Wendell Holmes, *Elsie Venner: A Romance of Destiny* (Boston, 1891), ix–x.

[26] For Locke's views on original sin, see John Marshall, *John Locke: Resistance, Religion and Responsibility* (New York: Cambridge University Press, 1994), 145–6.

[27] John Locke, *An Essay Concerning Human Understanding* (New York: Penguin, 1997), 109.

and culture is perhaps most evident in the bestselling *Autobiography* of Benjamin Franklin as the statesman keeps, on an ivory slate which can be wiped clean each day, a tally of setbacks in his quest for moral perfection. With the guidance of Franklin and others, Americans came to think of children as neutral and independent agents.[28]

When Bushnell published his *Views of Christian Nurture* in 1847, Locke's conception of infants and children as blank slates was still a relatively progressive view of human development whose implications occupied Hawthorne and his contemporaries.[29] But Bushnell would push past Locke's view of children as morally neutral agents to suggest that infants and children might exert a positive influence of righteousness in the home. The views of Calvin, Locke, and Bushnell coexisted in North America throughout the nineteenth century, but the pendulum of public opinion swung steadily away from the negative outlook of Calvin to the neutral and positive positions of Locke and Bushnell. Ministers, educators, and parents increasingly idealized infants and children, projecting their hopes for moral progress onto the rising generation.

Ordained a Congregational minister, Bushnell was, ostensibly, committed to Calvinism. But *Views of Christian Nurture* drew censure from Bennet Tyler and other Congregational clergymen who accused Bushnell of doing away with the doctrine of native depravity.[30] Bushnell insists that "it is not sin which [the child] derives from his parents; at least, not sin in any sense which imports blame, but only some prejudice to the perfect harmony of this mold, some kind of pravity or obliquity which inclines him to evil."[31] To readers like Tyler, Bushnell's words too closely resembled the Unitarian thinking of William Ellery Channing, who proclaimed that sin "is not some mysterious thing wrought into our souls at birth" and that sin brings "a consciousness that we have sunk beneath our proper good."[32] Channing characterizes goodness as the proper or natural state of humanity, and Bushnell's affirmations of Calvinist theology are so weak

[28] See Gillian Brown, *The Consent of the Governed: The Lockean Legacy in Early American Culture* (Cambridge, MA: Harvard University Press, 2001), 22–4.

[29] See Sánchez-Eppler, *Dependent States*, 63–4. The second half of Herman Melville's 1855 diptych, "The Paradise of Bachelors and the Tartarus of Maids," is set in a paper factory, where the narrator witnesses the production of those blank sheets of paper imagined by Locke.

[30] Holifield, *Theology in America*, 455.

[31] Horace Bushnell, *Christian Nurture* (New York, 1861), 23.

[32] William Ellery Channing, "The Evil of Sin," in *The Complete Works of William Ellery Channing* (New York, 1884), 266–7.

that he also seems to suggest infants come into the world as good and holy influences.

While exhorting parents to instill Christian principles into their progeny at a young age, Bushnell describes children in terms of their capacity for righteousness. He exhorts his readers that "the aim, effort, and expectation should be, not, as is commonly assumed, that the child is to grow up in sin, to be converted after he comes to a mature age; but that he is to open on the world as one that is spiritually renewed, not remembering the time when he went through a technical experience, but seeming rather to have loved what is good from his earliest years." Bushnell's aim is compatible with Calvinist doctrine, but his description of conversion – justification, or the putting off of original sin – as a mere "technical experience" and his description of a child walking in holiness "from his earliest years" invite misreading. Indeed, Bushnell anticipates such a misreading:

> There are many who assume the radical goodness of human nature, and the work of Christian education is, in their view, only to educate or educe the good that is in us. Let no one be disturbed by the suspicion of a coincidence between what I have here said and such a theory. The natural pravity of man is plainly asserted in the Scriptures, and, if it were not, the familiar laws of physiology would require us to believe, what amounts to the same thing ... so that, view the matter as we will, there is no so unreasonable assumption, none so wide of all just philosophy, as that which proposes to form a child to virtue, by simply educing or drawing out what is in him.

Notwithstanding Bushnell's fervid denial that children are predisposed to virtue, that is precisely the message that readers drew from his insistence that every "child must not only be touched with some gentle emotions toward what is right, but he must love it with a fixed love, love it for the sake of its principle, receive it it [sic] as a vital and formative power."[33] Bushnell's sermons helped turn the public gaze away from the sins of the rising generation and toward their virtues.

Like Bushnell, members of the Transcendentalist circle with which Hawthorne associated became advocates for the spiritual capacity of children. Bronson Alcott urged clergy to "[l]et the children have a larger share in the religious services than hitherto" and reminded his readers that "true worship is childlike."[34] Real wisdom, Ralph Waldo Emerson insisted, was more often displayed in the curiosity of children than in the solemn self-assurance of ministers: "The first questions are always to be asked, and the

[33] Bushnell, *Christian Nurture*, 10, 22–4.
[34] Amos Bronson Alcott, *Concord Days* (Boston, 1888), 268.

wisest doctor is gravelled by the inquisitiveness of a child."[35] Hawthorne's associates praised children as exemplars capable of contributing far more to the spiritual and social communities that had so often marginalized them than they had hitherto demonstrated.

Appropriately, then, the attention of Hawthorne's Puritans shifts at novel's end from Pearl's moral shortcomings to the development of her assets and character. News that she had inherited Chillingworth's fortune "wrought a very material change in the public estimation" of her worth, and Hawthorne assures the reader that Pearl grew to "the flush and bloom of early woman-hood ... her wild, rich nature had been softened and subdued, and made capable of a woman's gentle happiness" (*SL*, 290–1). Indeed, Pearl resembles nothing so much as the "angel and apostle" whose coming Prynne predicts "at some brighter period, when the world should have grown ripe for it," a woman "lofty, pure, and beautiful; and wise, moreover, not through dusky grief, but the ethereal medium of joy" (*SL*, 292). Hawthorne focuses his hopes for American democracy and social progress on young women. Disregarding the popular narratives of declension authored by Puritan ministers and reiterated during the Second Great Awakening by revivalists like Tracy, Hawthorne highlights the virtues of children and articulates a hope that the youth of the rising generation will abandon the sins of their fathers.

Hawthorne's expression of faith in youth and the women who rear them, as agents of apocalyptic social change, anticipated the success of a novel written just months after *The Scarlet Letter* was published. In *Uncle Tom's Cabin*, Stowe presents a child – the idealized Evangeline St. Clare – as a moral exemplar whose life of purity and goodness prompts the reformation of all who meet her. Stowe's portrayal of Eva inspired readers to take action against the evils of slavery and helped turn the tide of public opinion against that peculiar institution. Sánchez-Eppler notes that Stowe was hardly alone in placing Eva at the moral center of her novel: "The record-setting bestsellers of the 1850s contained an unprecedented and diverse crop of child heroines."[36] Hawthorne, Stowe, and other authors of the American Renaissance eager to bring about social change labored, in their reading and rewriting of history and scripture, to bring into being the day foretold by the biblical prophet Isaiah, the day when "a little child shall lead them."[37]

---

[35] Ralph Waldo Emerson, *Emerson: Essays and Lectures* (New York: The Library of America, 1983), 407.
[36] Sánchez-Eppler, *Dependent States*, 13.
[37] Isaiah 11:6.

7

BARBARA HOCHMAN

Uncle Tom's Cabin and the Struggle Over Meaning: From Slavery to Race

> He hath made of one blood the nations of men for to dwell on the face of the earth.
>> *A Key to Uncle Tom's Cabin* (1853)

> I'se dark Topsy, as you see;
> None of you half and half for me
> Black or white it's best to be.
>> "Oh! I'se So Wicked," George Howard (1854)[1]

When *Uncle Tom's Cabin* (*UTC*) first appeared in 1851, fiction was an increasingly popular but controversial form of leisure activity, rarely considered art. Like television in the 1950s, antebellum novels often drew disapproval from educators, ministers, and parents who charged them with fostering passivity and fantasy, especially in the young. *UTC* helped legitimize the genre; its religious intensity in particular gained it entry into many homes which had previously scorned fiction.[2] But despite its moral and religious seriousness, *UTC* had an exceptional capacity to absorb and entertain. Although Stowe's text sometimes sounds like a sermon, it incorporates motifs and rhetorical strategies from a wide range of secular texts – newspaper articles and runaway ads, slave narratives, sensationalism, sentimental fiction, and minstrelsy. *UTC* outsold all other fiction of the period – its closest competitors were Susanna Rowson's *Charlotte Temple*, Maria Susanna Cummins' *The Lamplighter*, and George Lippard's notorious crime novel *Quaker City*.[3]

---

[1] George Howard wrote the song. His wife Cornelia often performed it. *Uncle Tom's Cabin & American Culture*, ed. Stephen Railton. http://utc.iath.virginia.edu/songs/sowickedf.html/.

[2] Barbara Hochman, *Uncle Tom's Cabin and the Reading Revolution: Race, Literacy, Childhood and Fiction 1851–1911* (Amherst: University of Massachusetts Press, 2011), 81–2.

[3] Claims vary as to the most popular nineteenth-century novel before *UTC*. See Ann Douglas, "Introduction," in *Charlotte Temple and Lucy Temple*, ed. Ann Douglas

97

In 1941, when Matthiessen's *American Renaissance* appeared, the novel was a well-established literary genre. Yet American fiction was still marginalized in scholarship and in the classroom. Matthiessen helped establish an academic canon of American fiction that retained its shape for over two generations. His examples embody the philosophical content and subtly ironic texture that he saw as the hallmark of serious literature. He was instrumental in consolidating the influential imperatives of the burgeoning "new criticism." But by these standards, *UTC* was left out: its direct engagement with politics, its messianic Christianity, its sentimental strategies, its very popularity, and Stowe's gender all militated against it. *American Renaissance* mentions *UTC* just twice, in passing. Only in the 1970s with the work of feminist scholars such as Ann Douglas and Elizabeth Ammons did *UTC* gain serious consideration. A decade later, when the work of Jane Tompkins and others made a text's "cultural work" its claim to significance, *UTC* entered the canon.[4]

Stowe's novel accomplished several kinds of cultural work in the antebellum period: it helped raise the status of fiction in literary culture; it gave political content to the idea of women's moral influence in society; it had an impact on public sentiment about slavery that helped trigger emancipation. Lincoln's alleged comment "so you're the little lady who started this great war" began to be cited in the 1890s and still circulates widely.[5] *UTC* made the case against slavery so forcefully that it drew vitriolic condemnation from supporters of the "peculiar institution." But neither Stowe's text nor its impact can be confined to the antislavery frame.

Stowe is often critiqued for her use of racist stereotypes – the antics of Sam and Andy, Aunt Chloe (a cook "in the very bone and center of her soul") and the loyal, self-sacrificing Tom himself.[6] The novel still draws fire for Stowe's failure to affirm the social equality of African-Americans, as reflected in the removal of Eliza, George, and Topsy to Africa at the end of the tale.

(New York: Penguin, 1991), vii–viii; Susan Williams, "'Promoting an Extensive Sale': The Production and Reception of The Lamplighter," *The New England Quarterly* 69 (June 1996): 179–200; Paul Erickson, "New Books, New Men: City-mysteries Fiction, Authorship, and the Literary Market," *Early American Studies* 1.1 (2003): 283.

[4] See especially Ellen Moers, *Literary Women: The Great Writers* (New York: Oxford University Press, 1985); Elizabeth Ammons, "Heroines in *Uncle Tom's Cabin*," *American Literature* (May 1977): 161–79; Ann Douglas, *The Feminization of American Culture* (New York: Knopf, 1977); and Jane Tompkins' *Sensational Designs. Sensational Designs: The Cultural Work of American Fiction, 1790–1860* (New York: Oxford University Press, 1985).

[5] It is cited on the back cover of the Oxford edition, among others. For the history of Lincoln's alleged comment see Daniel R. Vollaro, "Lincoln, Stowe, and the 'Little Woman/Great War' Story: The Making and Breaking of a Great American Anecdote," *Journal of the Abraham Lincoln Association* 30.1 (Winter 2009): 18–34.

[6] Harriet Beecher Stowe, *Uncle Tom's Cabin* (New York: Oxford University Press, 1998), 26.

But despite the racial essentialism implicit in many of the book's events and images, Stowe's representation of racial merger – sexual intimacy across the color line – pervades the text, inscribed in the body of every light-skinned character. I argue that this aspect of the book unsettles the binary of racial difference and exposes the sexual exploitation of slave women. However, Stowe tempered her critique with a tactic she called "prudence," creating a delicate balance.

The publication history and reception of *UTC* destabilized that balance. As isolated aspects of the book became prominent in illustrations, children's editions, material artifacts, and stage performances, Stowe's tale became increasingly racist. Attempting to take the book back, Stowe wrote several follow-up texts. Prefaces for two children's editions, verses for one of them,[7] and *The Key to UTC* appeared in 1853; *The Christian Slave* appeared in 1855. None of these rivaled the impact of the novel, but the quid pro quo reflects the beginning of an ongoing struggle over the meaning of *UTC*. In what follows, I examine some of the forms in which Stowe's narrative circulated in antebellum America, paying special attention to the representation of color and race. But first I want to say more about the rhetorical equilibrium Stowe initially achieved, and repeatedly sought to re-establish, especially with regard to the representation of racial merger.

Stowe's Poetics of Daring and Prudence: Neither Black or White Yet Both

UTC was a direct response to the Fugitive Slave Act of 1850 which made slavery the immediate business of the North as well as the South by urging all citizens to thwart runaways. Capturing an escaped slave could bring a reward; fugitives were returned to the South without a hearing. Helping a slave escape risked a fine and a jail sentence. As a resident of Cincinnati in the 1840s Stowe had witnessed both the plight of fugitive slaves and violence against abolitionists. By 1850 her anguish over slavery had made her impatient with critiques that left the peculiar institution intact. Writing *UTC* Stowe drew on Theodore Weld's detailed compilation, *American Slavery as It Is: Testimony of a Thousand Witnesses*; she frequently cites this book in the *Key*. But she also critiqued Weld's raw presentation of outrages. "With all due credit to my good brother Theodore," Stowe writes, "I must say that

---

[7] The title page of *Pictures and Stories from Uncle Tom's Cabin* (Boston: Jewett, 1853) notes that the verses "have been written by the Authoress." This seems to refer to Stowe, but uncertainty remains. See Hochman, *Uncle Tom's Cabin and the Reading Revolution*, 105.

prudence is not his forte … It is not necessary always to present a disagreeable subject in the most disagreeable way possible and needlessly to shock prejudices."[8] *American Slavery as It Is* did not transform public opinion; Stowe sought greater influence for her book.

In *UTC* Stowe met two rhetorical challenges that were difficult to combine. She tried to engage, even "shock" readers into attention, but she knew that first she would need to breach the defenses of readers inured to abolitionist claims and indifferent to press reports of inhumanity to slaves.[9] "We can become accustomed to very awful things," Stowe comments in the *Key* (209). Many white people who were disturbed about slavery feared the consequences of abolition – especially violence (would ex-slaves take revenge?) and amalgamation (would African-Americans seek legal and social equality, even intimacy?). To neutralize such questions, some tried to ignore the slave controversy, while others accepted proslavery arguments. By proceeding with care, Stowe gave well-worn images and ideas new significance, disarming many resisting readers.

Stowe's caution took several forms in *UTC*. The narrator's emphasis on truth and religious faith helped deflect attacks on the novel as incendiary, prurient, and fantastical. The routine exploitation of slave women is a central motif, but details of abuse are scarce. When Haley the slave-trader expresses eagerness to buy Eliza the text clearly indicates his desire for her as a sexual object, but such desire was "unsayable" by antebellum norms, as Kyla Wazana Tompkins points out; a combination of vernacular speech patterns and imagery positions the opening scene on the border of the "unutterable."[10] Haley's desires are neither specified nor fulfilled. Thus Stowe hints at some of the gravest outrages of slavery while maintaining rhetorical decorum. The words "amalgamation" and "miscegenation" do not appear in the novel. Like her emphasis on Christian perfectionism, this strategy made the book seem less shocking than either slave narratives or the work of abolitionists such as Weld or Lydia Maria Child.[11] The combination of drama, piety, and prudence gave *UTC* greater hearing and made Stowe an international celebrity.

[8] Cited in David S. Reynolds, *Mightier than the Sword: Uncle Tom's Cabin and the Battle for America* (New York: Norton, 2011), 93.
[9] The *Key* cites numerous advertisements offering "negroes" for sale along with mules, corn, and household items. Stowe argues that such ads helped naturalize the equation of slaves with livestock and inanimate objects. Harriet Beecher Stowe, *The Key to Uncle Tom's Cabin* (1852; Bedford, MA: Applewood Books, n.d.) 133–4, 144ff.
[10] Kyla Wazana Tompkins, *Racial Indigestion: Eating Bodies in the Nineteenth Century* (New York: New York University Press 2012), 106.
[11] Child's "A Letter on behalf of that Class of African Americans" and her short story about rape ("Slavery's Pleasant Homes") compromised her career and thus her capacity to persuade others.

Toward the end of *UTC* Cassy, Simon Legree's erstwhile mulatta mistress, tells Tom the story of her life. Within the discursive norms of *UTC*, Cassy's narrative of sexual abuse and its consequences is exceptionally degraded and detailed. But her story reflects a history of amalgamation that is shared by Eliza, George, Emmeline, Adolf, Rosa, and other characters. The exploitation of slave women was common knowledge, especially in the South, but the topic was shrouded in silence. In 1861 Mary Boykin Chesnut describes the Southern plantation as a place where a white man "runs a hideous black harem, with its consequences, under the same roof with his lovely white wife and his beautiful and accomplished daughters." Chesnut concludes: "Mrs. Stowe did not hit the sorest spot. She makes Legree a bachelor."[12]

Knowing her audience, Stowe not only made Legree a bachelor but also delayed her account of Cassy's life (which itself elides many of the "sorest spot[s]") until late in the narrative – when readers who had come so far were unlikely to put the tale down. But characters whose very appearance testifies to miscegenation are central from the start of *UTC*, and imply a world made up of inextricably intertwined, interracial histories. The narrator repeatedly notes the range of color that characterizes the slave population. Describing the slave "warehouse" where Tom, Emmeline, and Lucy await auction, Stowe depicts "numberless sleeping forms of every shade of complexion, from the purest ebony to white" (337). Stowe's attention to the panoply of color does not neutralize her racist stereotypes (the tragic mulatto is a familiar racist trope), but her abolitionism was fueled by her conviction that abuse of slave women was inevitable where masters had unlimited power over slaves. Yael Ben-zvi argues that Stowe was committed to racial purity and therefore believed African-Americans would have to be removed from US soil after emancipation. Molly Farrell makes a related point: Topsy was to be loved and converted but kept out of the family.[13] Yet the preponderance of mixed race characters in *UTC* has contradictory implications. These tensions gave the book additional edge, increasing its circulation and its service to abolition.

Stowe is often criticized for making her most "civilized" characters markedly "white." As Elizabeth Ammons and Susan Belasco suggest, "the farther

---

[12] Mary Boykin Chesnut, *A Diary from Dixie: Electronic Edition*, Documenting the American South. Consulted July 11, 2016. http://docsouth.unc.edu/southlit/chesnut/maryches.html/.

[13] Yael Ben-zvi, "The Racial Geopolitics of Harriet Beecher Stowe's Geography Textbooks," *Legacy* 29.1 (2012); Molly Farrell, "Dying Instruction: Puritan Pedagogy in *Uncle Tom's Cabin*," *American Literature* 82.2 (June 2010): 264–5. See also Arthur Riss, "Racial Essentialism and Family Values in Uncle Tom's Cabin," *American Quarterly* 46.4 (December 1994): 513.

away a black character moves from [racist] stereotypes, the whiter he or she is in ancestry."[14] If, as Elizabeth Barnes argues, Stowe makes sympathy "contingent upon similarity," the whiteness of Eliza and George made them that much easier for white readers to care about.[15] Their "white ancestry" validates their capacity to embody antebellum social norms – domesticity, Christian faith, and motherhood; autonomous individualism, self-culture, and self-restraint. Yet that ancestry – the history that brings Eliza or George into being – is presented only in retrospect, from a distance, if at all. As Brigitte Fielder notes, anxieties about interracial sex were common in the nineteenth-century United States.[16] While the results of miscegenation pervade *UTC*, this crucial aspect of slavery, both underscored and elided throughout, creates unresolved tensions in Stowe's representation of slavery and race.

From Newspaper Serial to Illustrated Book: Racial Binaries and Ambiguities

The wild success of *UTC* when it first appeared in the *National Era* took the editor who had commissioned it by surprise. The novel soon elicited a torrent of public responses not only in the form of literary and political commentary but also in illustrated editions, anti-Tom novels, material artifacts, and theater.[17] These spin-offs reflect disparate interpretations of the text that often depart significantly from the original, although they tend to reproduce the same narrow range of pivotal moments in Stowe's plot – Eliza's escape over the ice, Topsy's comic intransigence, Eva's ecstatic death, and Uncle Tom's violent one.

The first edition of *UTC*, published in two volumes by J. P. Jewett, was soon followed by a lavishly illustrated holiday edition. The book's first

[14] Elizabeth Ammons and Susan Belasco, eds., *Approaches to Teaching Stowe's Uncle Tom's Cabin* (New York: Modern Language Association, 2000), 2.

[15] Elizabeth Barnes, *States of Sympathy: Seduction and Democracy in the American Novel* (New York: Columbia University Press, 1997), 92. See also Hochman, *Uncle Tom's Cabin and the Reading Revolution*, 41–50.

[16] Brigitte Fielder, "Visualizing Racial Mixture and Movement: Music, Notation, Illustration," *Journal of Nineteenth-Century Americanists* 3.1 (Spring 2015): 149–50.

[17] Among many discussions of illustrations, anti-Tom novels, objects, and stage adaptations, see especially Marcus Wood, *Blind Memory: Visual Representations of Slavery in England and America 1780–1865* (New York: Routledge, 2000); Joy Jordan-Lake, *Whitewashing Uncle Tom's Cabin: Nineteenth-Century Women Novelists Respond to Stowe* (Nashville: Vanderbilt University Press, 2005); Robin Bernstein, *Racial Innocence: Performing American Childhood from Slavery to Civil Rights* (New York: New York University Press, 2011); Eric Lott, *Love and Theft Blackface Minstrelsy and the American Working Class* (New York: Oxford University Press, 1995); Sarah Meer, *Uncle Tom Mania: Slavery, Minstrelsy, and Transatlantic Culture in the 1850s* (Athens: University of Georgia Press, 2005).

American illustrator, Hammat Billings, employed sentimental tropes, reinforcing Stowe's emphasis on the spiritual equality of slave and free. Billings's illustrations of *UTC* depict not only white outrage over slavery (Quakers help fugitives, a white man spits on a runaway ad), but also the despair, courage, and initiative of slaves. His six illustrations for the first edition include Eliza delaying her departure from the Shelby plantation to warn Tom that he is sold, George fighting for his freedom, and Cassy risking Legree's fury by comforting Tom. In addition, like Stowe's narrative, Billings's illustrations emphasize slave literacy. Scenes of Bible reading in particular offered reassurance that *UTC* endorsed Christian faith, not slave rebellion; but the image of a slave with a book challenged contemporary norms by implying black cognition, interiority, and humanity, differentiating slaves from livestock, household items, and other property.[18] Thus Billings, like Stowe, attempts to strike a balance – representing racial difference while avoiding reductive stereotypes; yet his illustrations also reproduce contradictions inscribed in Stowe's language.

Eva and Topsy were among the widest circulating images of the period and helped to reify a generally accepted set of contrasts: black and white, Christian and heathen, contained and unruly. A famous description of these two characters makes them "representatives of their races. The Saxon, born of ages of cultivation, command, education, physical and moral eminence; the Afric, born of ages of oppression, submission, ignorance, toil and vice!" (254). This passage emphasizes the impact of history ("ages of oppression …") but is often taken as evidence of Stowe's racial essentialism. Many illustrations intensified the racist potential of such passages. Spin-offs deleted the ambiguities of Stowe's language and Billings's engravings.

A popular doll of the antebellum period encapsulates the opposition of Eva and Topsy. The Topsy-Turvy doll pre-dates *UTC* and may have been Stowe's source for Topsy's name.[19] Held one way, the doll is a white figure with a long skirt; turned upside down the skirt falls over the white face, arms, and torso, revealing a black figure with a long skirt in turn. Like the juxtaposition of Eva and Topsy, the doll seems to reinforce the black/white

---

[18] In most states slave literacy was illegal by 1851. See Jennifer Monaghan, "Reading for the Enslaved, Writing for the Free," *Proceedings of the American Antiquarian Society* 108 (1998): 53–80. On black literacy in *UTC* see Hochman, *Uncle Tom's Cabin and the Reading Revolution*, chapter 2.

[19] Karen Sánchez-Eppler, *Touching Liberty: Abolition, Feminism, and the Politics of the Body* (Berkeley: Berkeley University Press, 1997), 174n2. Shirley Samuels argues that the "reversibility" of the doll discloses the "instability of bodily identity." "The Identity of Slavery," in *Culture of Sentiment*, ed. Shirley Samuels (New York: Oxford University Press, 1992), 158. The doll arguably originated as an object sewn by slave women. See Bernstein, *Racial Innocence*, 81–3.

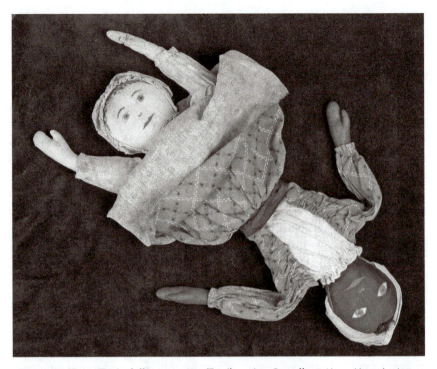

Figure 7.1 Topsy-Turvy doll, 1855–1880; Textile, paint; Overall: 18 ⅛ × 9 ½ × 2 in. (46 × 24.1 × 5.1 cm); object #1961.30; New-York Historical Society.

binary (Figure 7.1). Yet the two figures are indivisible. Each body stops at the waist; each skirt conceals (or reveals) the face and torso of the differently raced doll. In Karen Sanchez-Eppler's words, "the doll's waist simultaneously cordons off her sexual body and marks the boundary between her alternative racial identities" (133–4). The dynamic of sexuality and birth, both deflected and implied as one doll emerges from under the skirt of the other, is inscribed in numerous images of *UTC* that suggest merger and unity while eliding the process, both social and intimate, that brings mulattos and quadroons into being.

Children are key images in *UTC*, but Eva and Topsy seem as far removed from the sexual act that produces children as the Topsy-Turvy doll itself. "Born of ages of cultivation" or "ages of oppression," they are emphatically not framed as the fruit of love or desire. In Topsy's most famous line, she "'Never was born!'" – "'never had no father no mother, nor nothin'" (*UTC*, 249). Stowe's representation of children is the linchpin of her effort to promote abolition while avoiding the most explosive potential of her subject: the role of sexuality and sexual exploitation in producing children – especially mixed-race children.

Color in Question: Addressing White Children

Two children's editions of 1853 approach the representation of sexuality and color with care. *Pictures and Stories of Uncle Tom's Cabin* and *A Peep into Uncle Tom's Cabin* reprint substantial portions of Stowe's text while condensing and editing the novel with a child reader in mind. The first half of *Pictures and Stories* compresses the tale of Eliza, George, and Harry into eleven pages (including two full-page illustrations). These three characters are all light enough to pass for white (as they do in the final phase of their escape), but the book does not allude to racial mixture. It never identifies Harry, Eliza, or George as "negroes" nor does it mention their skin color. In *UTC*, Harry is a "quadroon" whom Haley refers to as "Jim Crow" (9); in *Pictures and Stories* he is a "young child," a "sweet boy," and the "only joy" of his "father and … mother" (5–6). As I have argued elsewhere, this is a narrative strategy that AnaLouise Keating calls "deracialization" – representing characters via context, actions, and language, not racial markers.[20] Underscoring the danger and bravery of Eliza, George, and Harry, the tale invites the white child reader in particular to identify with their situation and feelings. In the second half of the book, by contrast, Tom is "black as jet," with a wife "as black as himself," sons with "very black faces," and a "little black baby" (16). Although Topsy's blackness is also noted, as are Eva's "fair" face and "fair curl[s]" (19, 28), racial ambiguity is omitted from the text.

Directed at children "who live on freedom's ground," *Pictures and Stories* proclaims the value of reading not only the Bible, but also picture books; it thus assumes a privileged reader ("how blessed besides poor Topsy we have been" [24]). It affirms the child reader's capacity for literacy, interpretation and what Patricia Crain calls "self-ownership" – qualities specifically denied to slaves.[21] Yet antebellum children's books, like educational theories of the period, encouraged children's autonomy only up to a point. Children were

[20] See AnaLouise Keating, "Reading 'Whiteness,' Unreading 'Race': (De)Racialized Reading Tactics in the Classroom," in *Reading Sites: Social Difference and Reader Response*, ed. Patrocino P. Schweickart and Elizabeth A. Flynn (New York: Modern Language Association, 2004), 323, 315; Hochman, *Uncle Tom's Cabin and the Reading Revolution*, 112.

[21] See Patricia Crain, *Reading Children: Literacy, Property and the Dilemmas of Childhood in Nineteenth-Century America* (Philadelphia: University of Pennsylvania Press, 2016).

schooled to love and obey their parents, the Bible, and civil law, as Courtney Weikle-Mills argues.[22] Stowe insists, however, that the authority of neither parents nor the law is absolute, a message that *Pictures and Stories* reinforces in multiple ways: Eva's faith, love, and desire to free the slaves is a corrective to her parents, while the representation of George and Eliza legitimizes defiance of masters and civil law. Indeed, despite the massive cuts to Stowe's text, *Pictures and Stories* retains a long prose passage about Senator Bird's defense of the Fugitive Slave Law, and his wife's determination to break it at her first opportunity (10). In the final chapter, as Tom lies dying, the narrator explains that "there was no law to punish the wicked planter, because Tom was black" (30). Thus *Pictures and Stories* not only justifies George and Eliza's actions, but tells children that laws themselves may be "wicked, and abominable" (10).

Stowe's preface to *Pictures and Stories* claims that the book is appropriate for the "youngest readers," though it also addresses their "older brothers or sisters," and indeed their mothers (4, 11). Conceived primarily for young readers, the book elides allusions to sexuality along with racial ambiguity. Stowe's preface to *A Peep into Uncle Tom's Cabin* claims that the "story belongs to children very properly"; yet an "Editor's Introduction," by "Aunt Mary," explains that "in its present form, [*UTC*] cannot be placed in the hands of children."[23] *A Peep* makes Tom the center of the tale, deleting George, Eliza, and Harry entirely. Legree's plantation and Tom's experience gain emphasis, but although *A Peep* includes the sale of the quadroon slave girl Emmeline, it avoids racial mixture as fact, image, or theme; it downplays the intertwining of sexuality, color, and race.

A Peep deletes sexual abuse even from the slave auction episode, while reproducing verbatim much of the scene in which Legree buys Emmeline and Tom. The "horror" that overwhelms Emmeline's mother in *UTC* as she anticipates "her child's being sold to a life of shame" (339) becomes a fear that Emmeline might be "sold to a bad master" (*A Peep*, 356). References to the sale of Emmeline's "body" are edited out of the episode (*UTC*, 339, 344), as is Legree's drawing "the girl towards him," with his "heavy, dirty hand," to examine her "neck and bust" (342–3). Deleting such passages from a children's book is not surprising but, like *Pictures and Stories*, *A Peep* eliminates every suggestion of racial merger (the word "quadroon"

---

[22] Courtney Weikle-Mills, *Imaginary Citizens: Child-Readers and the Limits of American Independence, 1640–1868* (Baltimore: Johns Hopkins University Press, 2012).

[23] "Aunt Mary." *A Peep into Uncle Tom's Cabin* (Boston: Jewett, 1853), iii, v. *Uncle Tom's Cabin & American Culture*, ed. Stephen Railton. http://utc.iath.virginia.edu/childrn/cbcbamart.html. "Aunt Mary" was the daughter of Samson Low, Stowe's British publisher (Hochman, 280, note 89).

never appears, though Emmeline is one). Such changes point to the volatility of scenes and images that might raise uncomfortable questions about the genesis of light-skinned slaves.

Many antebellum children read the full-length *Uncle Tom's Cabin* – or heard it read aloud; in the last installment of the serialized version, Stowe directly addresses the "dear little children who have followed the story."[24] At mid-century the boundary between childhood and adulthood was a matter of debate.[25] Yet an increasing number of books were designed specifically for the young. More than most, *Pictures and Stories* and *A Peep* emphasize the child reader's capacity for judgment and moral responsibility;[26] but the sources and implications of racial mixture were too controversial to touch upon. This issue comes to the forefront in the *Key to Uncle Tom's Cabin*, another follow-up text of 1853. Stowe's *Key* addresses adults only, filling in some of the gaps left by children's editions and *UTC* itself.

Uncle Tom's Cabin Documented: *The Key*

As its title page suggests, the *Key* was to verify "the truth" of *UTC* by presenting "facts and documents." It was designed for adults prepared to read a text without developed characters, sustained drama, or even a continuous storyline. The *Key* was written for readers already familiar with Eliza, Tom, and other figures of *UTC*; it devotes several sections to central characters, substantiating the novel's events and claims. Comprised of news reports, advertisements for runaway slaves, laws, tables, and letters, as well as statements by government officials and clergy on both sides of the slavery question, the *Key* is a fragmented text. It retains the evangelical exhortations of *UTC* but unlike the novel and children's editions, both of which could be "read aloud in the family circle" ("*Farewell*"; *Pictures and Stories,* title page), the *Key* is for adults only. It eschews humor as well as plot, and probes the darkest side of slavery. Yet even the *Key* often insists that there are facts so chilling they cannot be told; Stowe repeatedly "draw[s] a veil" over details "too dreadful to be quoted" (14, 150).

---

[24] Harriet Beecher Stowe, "Farewell to Readers," *National Era* (April 1, 1852). *Uncle Tom's Cabin & American Culture,* ed. Stephen Railton. http://utc.iath.virginia.edu/childrn/cbhp.html. Stowe's "Farewell" was not included when *UTC* appeared in book form.

[25] Weikle-Mills emphasizes the "unstable boundary between childhood and adulthood" in this period (*Imaginary Citizens,* 104).

[26] Abolitionist stories for children – critiquing the law and social norms by definition – often encourage young readers to act on their beliefs (by refusing to eat sugar produced by slave labor, for example) contradicting their parents if necessary. *The Slave's Friend,* an abolitionist periodical for children, includes many such stories.

Unlike many characters of *UTC*, Legree's sex slave Cassy gets no section of her own in the *Key;* but she appears intermittently and Stowe consistently represents her situation as typical of slave women. Citing numerous advertisements for slaves – specifically for "likely girls from 10 to 18 years old" – the *Key* emphasizes that "the existence of this fearful traffic is known to many, the particulars and dreadful extent of it realized by but few" (144). In *UTC* when Cassy tells Tom you "see what I am!" (371), or when Legree asks her "Why can't you be friends with me, as you used to" (378), only a reader who already grasps the basis of Cassy and Legree's relationship will understand the implications of their words. The *Key* is more explicit; it documents "this dreadful commerce" in women, with particular emphasis on the "accursed lot of the woman to whom mixed blood ... has given graces perilous to a slave" (144). Describing women who are "both the child and slave of [their] master," the *Key* employs numerous terms that the novel avoids– licentiousness, amalgamation, concubinage, and more (19, 150, 189, 206).

Throughout the *Key* as elsewhere, Stowe takes the "existing order of society" as a given; yet she attacks not only slavery but also "those irrational barriers and prejudices which separate the human brotherhood into diverse and contending clans" (33). She challenges the separateness of African-Americans in schools and churches, based on the "unchristian prejudice of color" (33, 31). Stowe deplores the fact that Frederick Douglass was not "allowed the common privilege of the omnibus, which conveys every class of white men, from the most refined to the lowest and most disgusting" (32). "Free colored people," she continues, deserve "equal rights and privileges" (32). Then, in a remarkable passage, Stowe backtracks and clarifies: she does not mean to suggest that "all distinctions of society should be broken over, and that people should be obliged to choose their intimate associates from a class unfitted by education and habits to sympathize with them" (32). Nevertheless, since "education and habits" can change, it appears that Stowe's racial essentialism was not always proof against her own doubts. In the final text that I discuss here, these doubts come to the fore.

Stowe's *Christian Slave* Performed by Mrs. Mary Webb

Part of Stowe's "prudence" in composing *UTC* consisted of leaving the worst for last – Legree, Cassy, and Emmeline appear only to readers who have gone along with Stowe's book up to that point. In *The Christian Slave*, Cassy is central. This text was Stowe's response to popular dramatic versions that distorted her novel by intensifying its comic effects, its melodrama, and its racism. George Aiken's stage adaptation of 1852 provided the basis for many others that reproduced portions of *UTC*, adding song and dance, eliminating serious conversations about slavery, highlighting scenes of pursuit, and expanding the role of Topsy: her account of mistreatment becomes a source of broad comedy. Henry J. Conway's version of the play, which appeared almost simultaneously with Aiken's, added dogs to the scene in which Eliza crosses the ice. Internationally popular productions of the 1850s made Stowe's comic effects simpler, cruder, and more racist.[27]

Stowe's *Christian Slave* includes comic effects as well as minstrelized stereotypes, especially in the opening scene of Chloe's kitchen, and in extensive dialogues between Sam and Andy; but it also includes lengthy exchanges about slavery between St. Clare and Ophelia and it focuses with increasing intensity on Tom and Cassy. Indeed, Cassy dominates the last act, and delivers the play's lengthiest monologue. In a volume of the *Christian Slave*, inscribed by Stowe to Mary Webb, Stowe recommends cuts to six scenes while leaving Cassy intact, giving the character additional weight.[28] According to the title page, *The Christian Slave* is "founded on a portion of Uncle Tom's Cabin, dramatized by Harriet Beecher Stowe expressly for the Readings of Mrs. Mary E. Webb." Webb was a free mulatto woman, daughter of a Spanish father and an escaped slave.[29] The sole performer of Stowe's script, she appeared in the United States, Canada, and England, with considerable success. As Sarah Meer has shown, Webb's "race made the spectacle ... British reviewers devoted particular attention to Webb's background, parentage, skin color, and facial features." The attraction of the performance, Laura Korobkin suggests, relied largely on the combination of "Webb's visible blackness with her refinement and vocal cultivation."[30]

Stage productions of *UTC* did not use black performers – they used white performers in blackface. As Meer, Eric Lott, and others have shown, blackface subtly subverts racial difference in ways that range from encouraging

---

[27] Meer, *Uncle Tom Mania*, 106, 123–4.
[28] Susan F. Clark mentions nine cuts; see "Solo Black Performance before the Civil War: Mrs. Stowe, Mrs. Webb, and 'The Christian Slave," *New Theatre Quarterly* 13 (1997): 346, 348n21. However, three of these do not seem to be in Stowe's handwriting. The cuts marked by Stowe remove nothing from Cassy's part. The volume is in the collection of the Harriet Beecher Stowe House.
[29] Clark, "Solo," 342.
[30] Meer, *Uncle Tom Mania*, 188. Laura Korobkin, "Avoiding 'Aunt Tomasina': Charles Dickens Responds to Harriet Beecher Stowe's American Reader, Mary Webb," *ELH* 82.1 (Spring 2015): 123, 124. Taria Nyong'o analyzes the tension between Webb's own experience and the roles that she played; see Tavia Nyong'o, "Hiawatha's Black Atlantic Itineraries," in *Traffic in Poems: Nineteenth-Century Poetry and Transatlantic Exchange*, ed. Meredith McGill (New Brunswick: Rutgers University Press, 2008), 89.

ribald laughter at sexual innuendo and racial fixity to "upsetting the meaning enshrined in polite and educated language."[31] On the surface, however,
minstrelsy reinforces racial binaries. Comic effects dramatize the idea of
difference, restated visually in burnt cork and ragged costumes; white performers can be black on stage as masquerade only. I want to end this chapter
by suggesting that in creating her own version of *UTC* for performance
Stowe not only critiques Aiken and others, but complicates the binary structure of racial difference, by writing this text "expressly" for "Mrs. Webb,"
a "refined" product of miscegenation who, like Cassy herself, is educated,
comely, and well spoken.

The implications of Webb's reading become especially bewildering if one
reflects on this seemingly decorous performance as inverse blackface. Dwight
Conquerwood suggests that Webb's one-woman show was both a "counteperformance to minstrelsy and ... complicit with it."[32] Indeed her reading
must have made chaos out of racial binaries, as she impersonated not only
Cassy (whose racial profile matches her own) but Chloe and Tom, their
children, little George Shelby, Marie and Ophelia, St. Clare – and others.
The figures of Topsy, Sam, and Andy were readily adaptable to the minstrel
stage, but Webb's reading ironizes the very boundaries that most stage versions of *UTC* reified. Her contemporaneous label, "the Black Siddons" – an
allusion to the white British actress, Sarah Siddons – reflects a need among
viewers to stabilize such fluidity.[33]

For most commentators, Webb's "blackness" was central. For some her
virtuosic performance testified to African-American progress, along with
"femininity and good taste."[34] Her training in elocution, deportment, and
"refinement" was evidence of racial achievement, a point emphasized both
in Stowe's letter of introduction to the Duchess of Sutherland and in a biographical sketch of Webb, written by her husband Frank Webb. Although
Mary Webb was not a slave, not a fugitive, and not simply "black," her
blackness was visible enough to provide a central descriptive term both
in contemporaneous reviews and current scholarship. A broadside of the

[31] Meer, *Uncle Tom Mania*, 126.
[32] Dwight Conquerwood, "Rethinking Elocution: The Trope of the Talking Book and
other Figures of Speech," *Text and Performance Quarterly* 20.4 (2000): 333.
[33] On Webb as the "Black Siddons" see Clark, "Solo," 342; Meer, *Uncle Tom Mania*, 188;
Nyong'o, "Hiawatha's," 90. *Home Dramas for Young People*, an anthology for children
(ed. Eliza Lee Follen [Boston: James Munroe and Co., 1859]), includes "Extracts from
the Christian Slave" that give overwhelming prominence to Sam and Andy, Chloe, and
Topsy, educating white children in comic blackface performance and anticipating racist
children's editions of the 1890s. On editions of the 1890s see Hochman, *Uncle Tom's
Cabin and the Reading Revolution*, chapter 7.
[34] Meer, *Uncle Tom Mania*, 188–9.

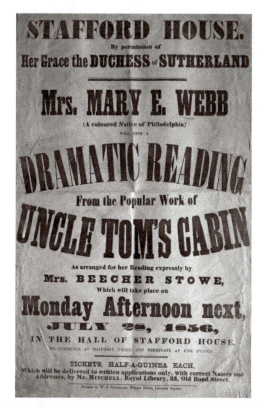

Figure 7.2 Broadside of Mary Webb's Stafford House performance of *The Christian Slave*, 1856. Harriet Beecher Stowe Center, Hartford, CT.

period describes her as a "coloured Native of Philadelphia" (Figure 7.2). The ubiquitous emphasis on Webb as racial other – a "coloured Native ..." – suggests that a mixed race woman performing both blackness and whiteness threatened social legibility and interpretive norms.

Webb enacted male and female figures, children and adults, in multiple registers. Declaiming both proper "white" speech, and vernacular "black" speech, singing "way down upon the Sewanee River" in Uncle Tom's voice, asserting Marie's pro-slavery position, and narrating Cassy's history of abuse, Webb's performance scrambled the very distinctions that slavery and racial essentialism relied on. If antebellum audiences found the performance uncanny, they did not say so: they responded "sympathetic[ally]," applauded "rapturously," and praised her "remarkably effective" rendition of Tom's "peculiar negro intonation" (cited in Clark, "Solo," 347). Stowe's novel itself includes a variety of cross-racial impersonations: Sam mimics a (white) politician, Adolf models himself on St. Clare, and Topsy dresses up in Ophelia's shawl; as noted, Harry, George, and Eliza don disguises when passing for white. Only some of these moments have minstrelized overtones; all challenge racial fixity.[35] *The Christian Slave* had no traceably subversive effect on racial essentialism. But whatever may have impelled Stowe to make Cassy – and Webb – central to this performance, *The Christian Slave* reflects tensions that made *UTC* a popular sensation, as well as an ongoing focus of discussion both inside and outside the academy.

[35] On Adolf, see Michael Borgstom, "Passing Over: Setting the Record Straight in *Uncle Tom's Cabin*," *PMLA* 118. 5 (October 2003): 1290–304; on Topsy see Elizabeth Young, *Disarming the Nation: Women's Writing and the American Civil War* (Chicago: University of Chicago Press, 1999), 42, and Hochman, *Uncle Tom's Cabin and the Reading Revolution*, 120–1. The disguises of the Harris family include gender reversals as well. For a useful account of passing as a challenge to identity boundaries see Elaine Ginsberg, *Passing and the Fictions of Identity* (Durham, NC: Duke University Press, 1996).

8

MARK RIFKIN

The (Im)Possibilities of Indianness: George Copway and the Problem of Representativity

As a rubric for research and pedagogy, the American Renaissance has not been particularly generative in prompting sustained study of Indigenous peoples' articulations of their own identities, histories, and futures. The portrayal of Indians by white writers has served as a meaningful topic of analysis in with this larger category,[1] but discussion of Native self-representation has been rather limited, especially due to the fact that those literary figures treated as central to the American Renaissance wrote in New England and New York – places that often at the time and afterwards inaccurately were cast as no longer having a substantive Native presence.[2] Moreover, scholars who draw on the concept of the American Renaissance tend to focus on the 1840s and 1850s, and while negotiations and conflicts with Native peoples certainly continued throughout this time, covering a much wider swath of territory and in many ways growing more intensive, those decades lie beyond what usually is taken to be the "removal era" in Indian policy, which culminates with the Cherokee Trail of Tears in 1839. Ongoing Native presence, never mind authorship, then, is often implicitly effaced

---

[1] For examples, see Renée L. Bergland, *The National Uncanny: Indian Ghosts and American Subjects* (Hanover: University Press of New England, 2000); Lucy Maddox, *Removals: Nineteenth-Century American Literature and the Politics of Indian Affairs* (New York: Oxford University Press, 1991); Laura L. Mielke, *Moving Encounters: Sympathy and the Indian Question in Antebellum Literature* (Amherst: University of Massachusetts Press, 2008); and Susan Scheckel, *The Insistence of the Indian: Race and Nationalism in Nineteenth-Century American Culture* (Princeton: Princeton University Press, 1998).

[2] See Mark Rifkin, *Settler Common Sense: Queerness and Everyday Colonialism in the American Renaissance* (Minneapolis: University of Minnesota Press, 2014). For discussion of narratives of Indian vanishing in New England, see Amy E. Den Ouden, *Beyond Conquest: Native Peoples and the Struggle for History in New England* (Lincoln: University of Nebraska Press, 2005); Jean O'Brien, *Firsting and Lasting: Writing Indians Out of Existence in New England* (Minneapolis: University of Minnesota Press, 2010).

in mid-nineteenth-century American literary studies.[3] A writer like George Copway, then, can be lost.[4] He was perhaps the most famous Native public writer and speaker in the United States in the mid-nineteenth century, certainly in the East, with the first edition of his autobiography going into seven printings in its first year.[5] Born in 1818 in Rice Lake in what is now Ontario, Copway was raised as part of the Mississauga people of that village, and after his family's conversion to Methodism around 1830, he went on to serve as missionary to a range of Anishinaabe bands before leaving for the United States in 1846 and becoming an important figure in Northeastern literary circles, the very sites from which come the authors conventionally associated with the American Renaissance.[6] How does non-engagement with writers like Copway contribute to the erasure of

[3] For examples of engagement with Native writing across this period, connecting it to earlier and later work, see David Carlson, *Sovereign Selves: American Indian Autobiography and the Law* (Urbana: University of Illinois Press, 2006); Maureen Konkle, *Writing Indian Nations: Native Intellectuals and the Politics of Historiography, 1827–1863* (Chapel Hill: University of North Carolina Press, 2004); Mark Rifkin, *Manifesting America: The Imperial Construction of U.S. National Space* (New York: Oxford University Press, 2009); Phillip H. Round, *Removable Type: Histories of the Book in Indian Country* (Chapel Hill: University of North Carolina Press, 2010).

[4] For discussion of the complex questions raised by efforts to determine what counts as Native "writing," both during this period and before it, see Lisa Brooks, *The Common Pot: The Recovery of Native Space in the Northeast* (Minneapolis: University of Minnesota Press, 2008); Matt Cohen, *The Networked Wilderness: Communicating in Early New England* (Minneapolis: University of Minnesota Press, 2009); Birgit Brander Rasmussen, *Queequeg's Coffin: Indigenous Literacies and Early American Literature* (Durham, NC: Duke University Press, 2012); Round, *Removable*; Hilary E. Wyss, *English Letters and Indian Literacies: Reading, Writing, and New England Missionary Schools, 1750–1830* (Philadelphia: University of Pennsylvania Press, 2012).

[5] A. LaVonne Brown Ruoff, "The Literary and Methodist Contexts of George Copway's *Life, Letters and Speeches*," in George Copway (Kahgegagahbowh), *Life, Letters & Speeches*, ed. A LaVonne Brownn Ruoff and Donald B. Smith (Lincoln: University of Nebraska Press, 1997), 1–23.

[6] His immigration to the United States, though, occurred after he was reported by his uncle to the Indian Department for misappropriation of band funds as well as having been expelled from the Canadian Conference of the Methodist Church. On Copway's background, in addition to his autobiography to which I will turn shortly, see Bernd C. Peyer, *The Tutor'd Mind: Indian Missionary-Writers in Antebellum America* (Amherst: University of Massachusetts Press, 1997), 224–77; Ruoff, "Literary"; Donald B. Smith, "Kahgegahbowh: Canada's First Literary Celebrity in the United States," in Copway, *Life*, 23–60. On Mississauga history and politics in this general period see D. Peter MacLeod, "The Anishinaabe Point of View: The History of the Great Lakes Region to 1800 in Nineteenth-Century Mississauga, Odawa, and Ojibwa Historiography," *Canadian Historical Review* 83.2 (1992): 194–210; Brian Osborne and Michael Ripmeester, "The Missassaugas Between Two Worlds: Strategic Adjustments to Changing Landscapes of Power," *The Canadian Journal of Native Studies* 17.2 (1997): 259–91; Donald B. Smith, *Sacred Feathers: The Reverend Peter Jones (Kahkewaquonaby) and the Mississauga Indians*, 2nd ed. (Toronto: University of Toronto Press, 2013).

Indigenous peoples from American literary studies? How does such erasure further reinforce narratives of Native disappearance and/or irrelevance in ways that treat colonial violence against Indigenous peoples as if it (and they) were a thing of the past rather than a persistent presence influencing US national life, politics, and culture?[7]

Drawing on the American Renaissance as an analytic and historical prism, though, can also prove useful in reframing approaches to nineteenth-century Native writing specifically because of the attention doing so brings to questions of figuration. Native writing often bears the burden of being seen as representative, as speaking for the particular people from which the author comes. While certainly emerging out of complex and ongoing Indigenous histories, and often taking part in public conversations about Native sovereignty and self-determination, texts by Native writers should not be understood as inherently performing a collective act – as necessarily expressing the sentiments of a given Native nation. Yet, such texts often are viewed in just this way, both in the nineteenth century and today. To the extent that the literary – as both a kind of text and a mode of analysis – is taken as depending on the absence of instrumental purpose (unlike, say, government documents), the attribution of a representative function to Native texts (seeing them as seeking to achieve particular policy ends for a given group) implicitly tends to disqualify them as objects of interpretation. Representativity, then, appears as if it were a defining characteristic of the text, instead of a complex rhetorical effect that arises within the text. Whatever one might say about the writers and works often collated under the rubric of "the American Renaissance," they are not read as political surrogates for the population at large. Although their texts are interpreted as participating within existing public discussions and debates, these authors are not treated literally as spokespeople, and that fact allows us to engage with how their acts of writing reflect on and negotiate existing social and political dynamics *as texts*, instead of seeing them as inherently representative of a collective will or perspective.[8]

---

[7] The fact that Copway was from land now claimed by Canada but that he gained fame in the United States, which is where his various books were published, also points toward the need to incorporate transnational geographies into the study of "American" literature in this period. See Anna Brickhouse, *Transamerican Literary Relations and the Nineteenth-Century Public Sphere* (Cambridge: Cambridge University Press, 2004); Kirsten Silva Gruesz, *Ambassadors of Culture: The Transamerican Origins of Latino Writing* (Princeton: Princeton University Press, 2002); Gretchen Murphy, *Hemispheric Imaginings: The Monroe Doctrine and Narratives of U.S. Empire* (Durham, NC: Duke University Press, 2005).

[8] I am not suggesting that "politics" and the "literary" (whatever those terms might reference) do not exist in dynamic relation or that there is some clear, clean dividing

Treating Native textualities in this same way opens up the possibility for attending more to the significance of when and how they portray themselves as representative. In *Life, Letters and Speeches of Kah-ge-ga-gah-bowh or, G. Copway, Chief Ojibway Nation*, for example, Copway repeatedly invokes Ojibwe nationhood and his own supposed status as a "chief."[9] This pattern functions as a rhetorical strategy through which he constructs himself as a representative, a spokesman not simply for the Mississaugas but for Indians more generally. We could seek to judge whether he actually did function as a designated spokesperson for the Mississaugas or other Native people(s), but rather than aiming to assess the accuracy of such claims, evaluating whether the text is in essence telling the truth, we, instead, could read such claims *as figurations*, as performing certain kinds of political and cultural work. How does he employ a rhetoric of representativity in order to validate his own entry into public discourse, to legitimize his role as an *Indian* writer amid prevalent racialized expectations of Native savagery? What is at stake in portraying Native governance, and his relation to it, in the ways Copway does? While creating an authorial identity for Copway by presenting him as speaking for Native people(s), *Life* offers a portrait of Indigenous governance as dependent on a *civilizing* process through which Indians learn how to become proper political subjects. Reading for the ways Copway casts himself as representative draws attention to how Native writers respond to non-native expectations of Indian public speech as well as to

---

line that separates the supposed sphere of one from that of the other. Rather, I'm trying to highlight the ways attributions of political surrogacy to Native texts tend to direct attention away from how such representative status emerges through what might be characterized as the texts' own literary effects (in response to non-native pressures and assumptions). For a collection of studies that explore the relation between politics and the literary in the mid-nineteenth-century United States, see Lauren Berlant, *The Anatomy of National Fantasy: Hawthorne, Utopia, and Everyday Life* (Chicago: University of Chicago Press, 1991); Christopher Castiglia, *Interior States: Institutional Consciousness and the Inner Life of Democracy in the Antebellum United States* (Durham, NC: Duke University Press, 2008); Jay Grossman, *Reconstituting the American Renaissance: Emerson, Whitman, and the Politics of Representation* (Durham, NC: Duke University Press, 2003); Robert S. Levine, *Dislocating Race and Nation: Episodes in Nineteenth-Century American Literary Nationalism* (Chapel Hill: University of North Carolina Press, 2009); Caleb Smith, *The Oracle and the Curse: A Poetics of Justice from the Revolution to the Civil War* (Cambridge, MA: Harvard University Press, 2013); and Priscilla Wald, *Constituting Americans: Cultural Anxiety and Narrative Form* (Durham, NC: Duke University Press, 1994).

9 I'm drawing on the revised 1850 edition printed in Copway, *Life*. Page citations will be parenthetical.

the constrained and constraining vision of Native political identity that results from that way of depicting Native peoplehood.[10]

Copway peppers the text with declarations and intimations of his status as an Anishinaabe political figure.[11] All the editions of his autobiography proclaim him to be a "Chief" of the "Ojibway Nation."[12] Furthermore, he notes, "My father still lives … and is one of the chiefs of Rice Lake Indian Village," after observing of the Crane clan (to which he belongs through patrilineal inheritance) "except in a few instances, the chiefs are of this tribe" (72),[13] and he describes his father as exercising control over one of the two branches of the main river near the village (the other of which belonged to George Poudash, "one of the principal chiefs of our nation" (75)). In his outline of Christian Anishninaabeg villages, he also includes "Copway" among the list of "Chiefs" for those at Rice Lake (157). These moments all contribute to conveying a sense that Copway holds some position of leadership among the Mississauga (specifically at Rice Lake), either directly or by association with his father. In addition, he describes his presence at two regional Anishinaabe councils (held in 1840 and 1845) at which leaders gathered to discuss issues of concern and to draft petitions to the Canadian government, particularly with respect to securing land tenure

[10] Here I implicitly draw on the distinction (and unacknowledged collusion) between representation-as-portrait and representation-as-proxy. See Gayatri Chakravorty Spivak, *A Critique of Postcolonial Reason: Toward a History of the Vanishing Present* (Cambridge, MA: Havard University Press, 1999), 256–64.

[11] In *Dancing on Our Turtle's Back: Stories of Nishnaabeg Re-creation, Resurgence and a New Emergence*, Leanne Simpson notes, "*Nishnaabeg* is translated as 'the people' and refers to Ojibwe, Odawa (Ottawa), Potawatomi, Michi Saagig (Mississauga), Salteaux, Chippewa and Omámíwinini (Algonquin) people. Nishnaabeg people are also known as Nishinaabeg, Anishinaabeg, Anishinaabek, and Anishinabek, reflecting different spelling systems and different dialects" (Winnipeg: ARP Books, 2011), 25. The Mississaugas comprise a number of different bands who share linguistic, cultural, and kinship ties to other *Nishnaabeg* peoples, and in the nineteenth century, "Ojibwe" often was used as the generic, encompassing term for these groups, as in Copway's work. While "Anishinaabeg" is plural and "Anishinaabe" is singular, the latter also is acceptable when used as an adjective, which is what I have done throughout the chapter.

[12] A search in Worldcat for books Copway authored indicates that in all of the extant editions of his autobiography (in its multiple printings at various times and places) he is so identified.

[13] In nineteenth-century ethnological writing, "tribe" often is used to designate what now commonly would be known as a "clan," a kinship-based grouping in which membership is passed intergenerationally and which is part of a larger people or nation. On the importance of clan affiliations (or *doodemag*) in Anishinaabe history, see Michael A. McDonnell, *Masters of Empire: Great Lakes Indians and the Making of America* (New York: Hill & Wang, 2015); Michael Witgen, *An Infinity of Nations: How the Native New World Shaped Early North America* (Philadelphia: University of Pennsylvania Press, 2012).

given increasing white encroachments.[14] He intimates his inclusion among the assembled delegates, at one point noting with respect to the Governor General's failure to respond to the General Council's petition, "we received but little satisfaction" (127), and he indicates his "appoint[ment] by my people at Rice Lake, to transact some business for them at Toronto" (128). For the latter council, Copway actually was elected to serve as vice president for the meeting (146).[15] He characterizes the recent "General Councils of the Christianized Ojebwes" as "hav[ing] been convened and conducted, in the same manner as public and other business meetings are conducted among the whites" (145), and he indicates his appointment by the council to act as their agent in securing subscriptions to build a manual labor school (149). Although one might raise questions about the accuracy of Copway casting himself in this leadership role, especially given the biographical facts of his emigration to the United States and lack of continued sustained contact with Mississauga people, what work does the rhetoric of representativity perform in and for the text? How does enacting this metonymic linkage – Copway standing for and as the "Ojibway Nation" – frame his speech and the text's relation to its readers?

These invocations of political surrogacy implicitly portray the narrative as engaged in something like a diplomatic negotiation. In the preface to the 1850 edition, Copway describes his aim as to "present the *present state* and *prospects* of my poor countrymen" in order to "assist in rescuing them from an untimely and unchristian grave," asserting that his "motto" is "*My poor People*" (65). The act of writing appears to constitute such *assistance* as part of "rescuing" his people from the situation in which they find themselves. Although appealing to white "benevolence," Copway specifically indicates that the need for such compassion and care arises in the context of his "countrymen" having been "once the lords of the land on which the white man lives" (65), and he later notes, "The Ojebwes each claimed, and claim to this day, hunting grounds, river, lakes, and whole districts of country" (71). In these moments, Copway highlights settler displacement of Native peoples as a key part of their currently constrained "prospects" while also insisting on their continued landedness. The text situates its address to readers within an ongoing history of Ojibwe dispossession, presenting the narrative as part of an effort to stanch such losses. In simultaneously claiming a position of political authority and decrying the theft of Indigenous lands, he casts himself as an agent acting for his nation, parlaying with the settler public over access to Native territories.

[14] On Mississauga councils in this period, see Smith, *Sacred*, 173–208.
[15] Smith, "Kahgegagahbowh," 32.

He further suggests the need for learned interlocutors, such as himself, in order to avoid forms of settler exploitation and expropriation. With respect to Mississauga sales of land in 1818, Copway remarks, "Much of the back country still remains unsold, and I hope the scales will be removed from the eyes of my poor countrymen, that they may see the robberies perpetrated upon them, before they surrender another foot of territory" (75), and he later notes, "since that time, some of us have learned to read, and to our utter astonishment ... we find that we have been most grossly abused, deceived, and cheated" (94). Learning to read opens the possibility of removing "the scales" from their eyes. They would become able to see the ways their apparent consent to the surrender of vast stretches of land has depended on a series of false premises and outright lies, such that these transactions amount to little more than "robberies" perpetrated against "unlettered and ignorant Indians" (143). These moments envision a future moment of diplomatic relation in which overtures for land cessions could and should be refused definitively, and in doing so, they implicitly present Copway as a literate ambassador who would not fall for such state-orchestrated schemes. If the text addresses how a lack of knowledge (of English, government intent, white duplicity) vitiates putative Ojibwe assent, it also constructs for and through Copway a kind of political subjectivity that would better enable his "countrymen" to retain what remains of their prior status as "lords of the land."

However, given that the text does not partake directly in such diplomatic negotiation, how might we understand the stakes of Copway's efforts to craft such a subjectivity? Or, put another way, what is made possible by this subject-position, by this particular figuration of representativity in ways separate from Ojibwe (geo)politics per se? Even as scholars raise questions about Copway's motives in writing and his claims about his own status as chief and missionary,[16] they tend take his account of Native landedness and governance as expressive of a project of sovereignty whose horizon is increased Anishinaabe self-determination. Maureen Konkle argues that "throughout his writing" Copway suggests "that were Ojibwe people able to achieve social stability, they would not abandon each other or the Ojibwe Nation but would instead fight to remain together on [their] territory."[17] The text's account of Anishinaabe histories and politics, though, cannot be sundered from Copway's self-presentation as political spokesperson, as the

---

[16] Konkle, *Writing*, 191; Peyer, *Tutor'd*, 236–7; Cathy Rex, "Survivance and Fluidity: George Copway's *The Life, History, and Travels of Kah-ge-ga-gah-bowh*," *Studies in American Indian Literatures* 18.2 (2006): 2; Cheryl Walker, *Indian Nation: Native American Literature and Nineteenth-Century Nationalisms* (Durham, NC: Duke University Press, 1997), 91.

[17] Konkle, *Writing*, 189, 192.

voice of "the Ojibwe Nation." The invocation of Mississauga governance constitutes a speaking position for Copway – as "chief" – within non-native public discourse that he otherwise would lack.

Copway's presentation of himself as a "chief" can be read as creating the potential for a public voice, since otherwise his turn to writing as an Indian would signify his fall from noble savagery and, thus, his status as simply a degraded non-white subject. Bernd Peyer suggests, "Copway seemed to personify the two predominant strands in liberal white attitudes toward Indians romantic primitivism (the vanishing act) and benevolent reformism (the transformation act)."[18] However, these two ways of envisioning Indians were less distinct "strands" than interwoven aspects of a narrative of civilized becoming in which Native people(s) either remained backwardly (if nobly) Indian or transitioned through Christianizing cultivation into being regular civic subjects of the settler state.[19] The text prominently features an example of this discursive and conceptual framing in its account of what it terms the "Ojibwe General Council" meeting in 1840. At the end of that discussion, Copway includes the response of Lord J. Russell to the Council's petition. In arguing against the provision of government aid to the Mississaugas, Russell asserts the following: "All my observation has completely satisfied me, that the direct interference of the Government is only advantageous of the Indians who can still follow their accustomed pursuits, and that if they become settlers, they should be compelled to fall into the ranks of the rest of Her Majesty's subjects, exercising the same independent control over their own property and their own actions, and subject to the same general laws as other citizens." He further notes that when such "accustomed pursuits" are abandoned and Native collectivities continue to exist as such, "the Indian loses all the good qualities of his wild state, and acquires nothing but the vices of civilization," "becom[ing] a drunkard and debauchee" and continuing to "occup[y] valuable land, unprofitably to himself and injuriously to the country," thereby "giv[ing] infinite trouble to the Government" (135–6). This supposed in-between stage, neither in a "wild state" nor simply living "as other citizens," marks the persistence of Indigenous collective landedness and self-governance. The continuing existence of such Native sovereignties means that the settler government must grapple with them in trying to exert jurisdiction and to make more land available for non-native occupation. That fact of Indigenous political endurance appears here as degeneration,

[18] Peyer, *Tutor'd*, 243.
[19] See Steven Conn, *History's Shadow: Native Americans and Historical Consciousness in the Nineteenth Century* (Chicago: University of Chicago Press, 2004); O'Brien, *Firsting*.

as creating "trouble" for the government and simply multiplying popular "vices."

Trading on the fact of ongoing negotiations between settler governments and Native peoples over land cessions and boundaries, Copway asserts his own status as a leader, and that depiction of *Life* as engaged in a quasi-diplomatic negotiation with non-native readers enables him implicitly to present his writing (the actual text and his ability to produce it) as an act of political mediation, rather than as evidence of Copway's fall from a "wild state" into the "vices of civilization." In this way, he positions himself as serving a necessary function in Indian–white relations – as inhabiting the putative middle space between *wildness* and *civilization* – instead of being merely the degraded, semi-civilized bearer of an inherently incapacitating Indianness. Although Copway does critique the ongoing history of settler occupation, his insistence on *Ojibwe* sovereignty, then, can be read as a means of licensing his own literate public speech, presenting his writing as legitimate in its ability to speak for – to represent – Anishinaabe political interests in negotiation with non-Indians.

While creating a space for Copway as an Indian writer by portraying himself as spokesperson, *Life* also endorses the idea that Indians need to become *civilized*, to abandon their supposedly anachronistic ways of being in order to adopt enlightened modern modes of living, and that way of figuring Native prospects for the future also shapes how the text depicts what counts as viable Indigenous governance. When discussing the 1845 council of what the narrative refers to as Christian Ojibwe bands, he notes, "Never was I more delighted than with the appearance of this body. As I sat and looked at them, I contrasted their former (degraded) with their present (elevated) condition. The Gospel, I thought, had done all this," and he adds, "This assembly was not convened for the purpose of devising schemes of murder; plans by which they could kill their enemies; but to adopt measures by which peace, harmony, and love, might be secured" (148). Native self-governance requires a shift from "degraded" ways to "elevated" ones, turning from "devising schemes of murder" to adopting policy to secure social order, such as determining jurisdictional boundaries, promoting conversion to Christianity, incentivizing the turn to agriculture, and creating educational institutions. The "social stability" to which Konkle points as Copway's aim, then, depends not simply on bringing an end to white projects of expansion and expropriation but on transforming Native sociality so as to bring it into alignment with white norms. Copway envisions his own political representativity as predicated on his disowning of a tainted past in which Indianness correlates with barbarism. As he says of conflict among Anishinaabe and Dakota peoples in the western Great Lakes region,

"Christianity and education alone, will check their malevolent and hostile feelings, and thus put an end to their bloody wars," and he characterizes his time living in that region as being "surrounded by savages" (141). Although Copway insists on the presence of a politics of Native territoriality prior to white intervention, the substance of Native collectivity before Christianization (and its general introduction of enlightenment) appears to be little more than scheming as part of "bloody wars." Copway's account presents the right to Indigenous self-governance – including a people exerting authority over their own lands – as dependent on them having embraced dominant settler practices and formulations and having renounced whatever is cast as having preceded white presence (what supposedly comes before and is superseded by "Christianity and education").

Copway's narrative promotes the continued existence of Native peoples, but in doing so, it repeatedly suggests that Indian life must be fundamentally reordered. The persistence of Indigenous polities in *Life* depends on their undergoing this civilizing shift, which the text casts in evolutionary terms. In Copway's account, there is no Native governance absent its being, as quoted earlier, "convened and conducted" as "public and other business meetings are conducted among the whites." *Life*, then, does not so much contest or overturn the framework of Indian law and policy as draw on it in order to illustrate Copway's representativity. Critics often approach prevalent ways of talking about Indianness in the nineteenth century as if there were a static opposition between civilization and savagery and as if presenting Indians as capable of achieving the former inherently challenged forms of settler colonial domination. Scholars have characterized Copway's writing as mediating "the confrontation between tradition and modernity" and as "transcend[ing] and refigur[ing] the nineteenth-century binaristic options available to him."[20] From this perspective, any Native effort to suggest movement between these binaries constitutes a radical act of (political) agency that defies settler notions of inherent, unchanging Native difference. In Cathy Rex's terms, Copway "is performing a fluid self that cannot be swallowed up and contained by the established 'authentic' representation of Native Americans."[21] However, savagery is not so much the opposite of civilization as the logically necessary precursor through which civilization gains meaning: savagery has to exist as that which comes before civilization in order for the trajectory of supposed development/progress to make sense.

---

[20] Konkle, *Writing*, 191; Rex, "Survivance," 25. For similar formulations, see Walker, *Indian Nation*, 84–110; Joshua David Bellin, *Demon of the Continent: Indians and the Shaping of American Literature* (Philadelphia: University of Pennsylvania Press, 2001), 131–53.
[21] Rex, "Survivance," 6.

Life's insistence on the existence of or potential for civilized Indianness does not displace that binary; rather, it takes up the dominant story of Indian transformation/evolution in ways that displace other possibilities for portraying Indigenous collective identities, sovereignties, temporalities, and modes of self-articulation.

Copway's depiction of Anishinaabe governance and diplomacy less resists the terms of US and Canadian Indian policy than inhabits the forms of political subjectivity generated by such policy. Indian policy in the period simultaneously insists that Indians cultivate white social norms (become *civilized*) and that they speak in a tribally unified political voice (for the purposes of both collective accountability for violence against non-native persons and property and collective assent to land cessions in treaties), and given those two imperatives, the status of civilized chief becomes a possibility, one that Copway presents himself as occupying. David Carlson argues that Native autobiographers in the nineteenth-century (like Copway in *Life*) "produced their acts of self-definition in the shadow of a hegemonic legal system designed explicitly to reshape their sense of identity," "reveal[ing] a *process* of self-definition whose engine was engagement with legal models of Indianness."[22] In this way, the kinds of subjectivity at play in such texts can be interpreted as a response to existing discourses of Indian law and policy, including the ways they demand that Native peoples adopt certain forms of representativity (such as the kinds of centralized governance found in ostensibly civilized societies). Carlson suggests that when authors take up such models of Indian identity they are "writing back to power," "push[ing] back against colonial domination," but the employment of these non-native political and conceptual frameworks also can normalize them in ways that disown the existence of other possibilities for how Indigenous peoples organize, express, and govern themselves.[23] In positioning himself as a representative of and for the "Ojibwe" people, Copway presents his own personal story as standing in for the proper trajectory of development for Indigenous peoples more broadly. Cheryl Walker observes, "Copway urges his reader to see him as a text, a personification of Indian progress toward acculturation,"[24] but Copway less positions himself as a subject of interpretive ambiguity (a text open to interpretation), than as a kind of allegory – an embodiment of the only way forward for the "Ojibway Nation." If Copway personifies progress through his demonstration of civilized/civilizing literacy, he also casts himself as a "chief," portraying his own story as metonymic

---

[22] Carlson, *Sovereign*, 6, 14.
[23] *Ibid.*, 12, 179.
[24] Walker, *Indian Nation*, 84.

of Anishinaabe political possibilities writ large. *Life* merges selfhood and sovereignty, the former defining the terms of the latter. In order to signify as a proper leader, one must undergo the process of civilization, performing both an intimate familiarity with Indianness as conventionally conceived by whites and an acquired distance from it.

Rather than understanding non-Christian practices as part of ways of living distinct from dominant Euro-American ideals, Copway casts Natives as either embarking upon a process of civilized becoming or as tending toward extinction. Early in his narrative, he says of his childhood, "I loved the woods, and the chase. I had the nature for it, and gloried in nothing else. The mind for letters was in me, *but was asleep*, till the dawn of Christianity arose, and woke the slumbers of the soul into energy and action" (69). Becoming acquainted with "letters" wakes the newly enlightened Native into accessing what had lain dormant within him. The very act of writing, then, does not so much capture forms of Native sociality otherwise inaccessible to non-natives as transmute them, turning them in a more properly civilized direction. He says of the effects of his own literacy, "I loved to hunt the bear, the beaver, and the deer, but now, the occupation has no charms for me. I will now take the goose quil, for my *bow*, and its point for my *arrow*" (79). He depicts the technologies of writing through those of hunting, potentially intimating a continuity of usage in which the one builds on the other. Instead, though, the quill completely replaces the bow, moving hunting into the past tense and foregrounding writing as the vehicle for future endeavors. After his conversion, "As I looked at the trees, the hills, and the vallies [*sic*], Oh how beautiful they all appeared! I looked upon them as it were, with new eyes and new thoughts" (102). While he does not renounce his prior relation to the landscape, its meaning is refigured through his "new eyes"; his connection to the land (and, by extension, that of other Christianized Natives) becomes oriented around "new thoughts" generated by the process of enlightenment. His discussion of non-Christian Native lifeways does not so much indicate the value of any particular rituals, commitments, or social forms as authenticate his own status as a civilized Indian, one whose knowledge of barbarism evidences his having undergone the process of Christian cultivation.

Emphasizing a decisive break – awakening, renunciation, novelty – these moments cast conversion as an epochal shift in consciousness and behavior, such that old ways of being no longer play any role.[25] They become the past, but not just Copway's personal past. Rather, his own leap forward serves as a metonymic way of figuring the transformation necessary for Indigenous survival. A. LaVonne Brown Ruoff suggests with respect to *Life* that "[t]he

---

[25] This portrayal of an epochal shift effaces the long history of Mississauga engagement with Euro-American political economies. For examples in the text, see Copway, *Life*,

first section is an ethnographic account of Ojibwe culture," adding, "The ethnographic sections are designed to persuade his audience of the value of tribal culture and essential humanity of Indian people."[26] His portrayal of non-Christian social formations, though, might be characterized as *ethnological* rather than ethnographic: ethnography involves the close observation of everyday practices ostensibly in an effort to understand them on their own terms, whereas ethnology refers to the comparative analysis of living populations through which they are situated within an evolutionary scale, from least to most advanced.[27] The narrative less illustrates "the value of tribal culture" than presents it as something that needs to be surpassed and superseded. When he recalls his time among Mississauga hunters, he thinks, "In our days of ignorance we used to dance around the fire. I shudder when I think of those days of our darkness ... I thank God that those days will never return" (80–1). He later suggests of conflicts among western Ojibwe and Sioux peoples, "Christianity and education alone, will check their malevolent and hostile feelings, and thus put an end to their bloody wars" (141), and he empties such engagements of all political and historical meaning by indicating that "[t]he Sioux and the Ojebwas have been at war from time immemorial" (113). In addition, toward the end of the text, he considers the circumstances of the various peoples in the western Great Lakes region, suggesting that they all "must perish as did their brethren in the Eastern States, unless the white man send them the Gospel, and the blessings of education" (160–1). Copway implicitly situates his earlier elaboration of activities and beliefs prior to conversion within a comparative framework in which such practices cannot help but be found wanting, a "darkness" from which Native people must escape lest they "perish" – either in "bloody wars" of their own making or when exposed to the sustained presence and pressures of Euro-Americans. He reiterates Russell's evolutionary narrative about Indian degeneration in the face of white advancement, with the exceptions that settler incursions may serve as a source of political

---

71–2, 80, 84, 91. On this history of engagement, see McDonnell, *Masters*; Witgen, *Infinity*.

[26] Ruoff, "Literary," 7, 9.

[27] On nineteenth-century ethnology, see Bellin, *Demon*, 131–53; Robert E. Bieder, *Science Encounters the Indian, 1820–1880: The Early Years of American Ethnology* (Norman: University of Oklahoma Press, 1986); Conn, *History's*; Robert Lawrence Gunn, *Ethnology and Empire: Languages, Literature, and the Making of the North American Borderlands* (New York: New York University Press, 2016); Scott Michaelson, *The Limits of Multiculturalism: Interrogating the Origins of American Anthropology* (Minneapolis: University of Minnesota Press, 1999). On the ethnological character of Copway's writing and his familiarity with major figures in ethnology, see Bellin, *Demon*, 187–199; Peyer, *Tutor'd*, 263–6; Rex, "Survivance," 20–2.

grievance for Native nations and that Native people may rise to the occasion by becoming civilized in the ways Copway has and following the lead of people such as himself. If, in Joshua David Bellin's terms, Copway "trades in ethnologic currency to complicate ethnologic truisms,"[28] he does not displace the ethnological frame, instead situating himself within it as someone on the other side of the movement away from barbarism who can speak for and help enact the transition from unending "tribal" warfare to modern political structures.

The text portrays Native political identity, and Copway's own supposed role as "chief," in ways that reiterate the developmental narrative at play in Indian policy. Lisa Brooks asks, "What happens when we put Native space at the center of America rather than merely striving for inclusion of minority viewpoints or viewing Native Americans as a *part* of or on the *periphery* of America? What does the historical landscape look like when viewed through the networks of waterways and kinship in the northeast," and the aim of such analysis lies in highlighting the "persistence of indigenous political systems, relationships, and epistemologies."[29] Can we, though, approach Native-authored texts as if they inherently conveyed such perspectives, as if they are expressive of broadly held understandings realized in particular Indigenous geographies and political systems? Or, more pointedly, if we implicitly approach all Native texts in this way, how can we track the work performed by the representativity-effect – the ways given texts employ sets of rhetorical maneuvers that make the authors appear representative regardless of the texts' relations to existing (if shifting and uneven) modes of Indigenous governance and decision making? *Life* can be read as a forthright challenge to non-native frameworks only by overlooking the ways it stages its own supposed representativity, including the ways it reinvests in notions of Native identity at play in settler policy. Accepting the text's account of itself as the voice of Anishinaabe political independence sets aside Copway's reliance on an ethnological narrative that depoliticizes vast swaths of Native life as simply savage residues in need of reformation. Addressing the kinds of figuration at play in texts' claims to be representative allows for us to investigate how Native peoplehood enters and circulates within non-native public discourses. This kind of analysis tracks the forms of textual performance Native writers need to enact when trying to authorize their participation in non-native print publics (given existing white expectations about the possibilities for Native expression, individual and collective), as well as drawing attention to the ways that supposed representativity leads to these

---

[28] Bellin, *Demon*, 190.
[29] Brooks, *Common*, xxxv, xlii.

texts implicitly being characterized by scholars as less "literary" (and, thus, less worthy of literary study) than those of authors conventionally classed in "the American Renaissance." The modes of interpretation developed in this chapter further seek to explore how these forms of supposedly representative authorial subjectivity can come to stand for/as Native political processes – less expressing than substituting for engagement with the complex and continuing dynamics of Indigenous sovereignties.

9

ALEXANDRA SOCARIDES

The Poetess at Work

In the August 1, 1844 issue of *Graham's American Monthly Magazine of Literature and Art*, readers encountered an engraving of a single, anonymous, female figure, dressed all in white (Figure 9.1).[1] Round-faced, with ringlets in her hair and a shawl draped around her lap, this girl-on-the-brink-of-womanhood stares up and off into the space beyond the frame's edge. She could be any young woman of her race and class, except that the portfolio case that she simultaneously holds up with her left hand and presses down on with her right elbow, marks her as "The Young Poetess" of the engraving's title.

While this figure's visual anonymity and generic appearance contribute to the cultural abstraction of the mid-nineteenth-century poetess, the poems that accompanied printings of this image give us the terms of that abstraction. The image in *Graham's* is accompanied by a similarly anonymous poem of the same title. In keeping with the situation of relative leisure depicted in the engraving, this short poem defines this "young poetess" in terms of three attributes: her ability to access the divine, her talent for making metaphor, and her capacity to elicit a strong emotional response from those around her.

> She dwells in her ideal dreams,
> A spirit pure and high;
> And Paradise is caught, in gleams,
> From her uplifted eye!
>
> She sees in every plant a sign
> That points to things above:

---

[1] In the back of the issue it states that that "The Young Poetess" is an "Original Picture by Chapman." Later, under "Embellishments of this Number," it states: "The Young Poetess: A beautiful stipple engraving, executed expressly for this magazine, by Rowdon, Wright & Hatch, from an original picture by Chapman." *Graham's American Monthly Magazine of Literature and Art* (August 1, 1844).

Figure 9.1 "The Young Poetess," *Graham's American Monthly Magazine of Literature and Art* (August 1, 1844), 72.
Courtesy, American Antiquarian Society.

> Of earth, yet more than half divine,
> 'Twere heaven to win her love![2]

Everything this poem claims to know about the pictured figure is derived simply from the angle of her eyes. These verses take their lead from the fact that she looks upwards, a pose elevating her to "a spirit pure and high." She is only ever imagined looking down so as to illustrate that she can "see" how earthly things function as symbols for what is above. Such a talent for explaining worldly things in their heavenly terms – for, we might say, understanding the operations of comparison, substitution, and metaphor – makes her a creature of both earth and heaven, such that she too becomes the plant that might be read as something more than just a plant. This poem ends by

---

[2] "The Young Poetess," *Graham's American Monthly Magazine of Literature and Art* (August 1, 1844): 72.

reveling in the sensation of some unspecified others who might be loved by such a remarkable creature.

Four years after this joint appearance of image and poem in *Graham's*, the same image appeared in the April 1, 1848 issue of the *Wreath*, now accompanied by a different poem of the same title by D. Bates:

> Away, wing'd coursers, that wait on the soul
>   On your pinions free and strong;
> And gather me gems without control,
>   In the beautiful land of song.
> 'Tis a pleasant land where ye oft before
>   Have gathered me flowers bright;
> And in those gardens are many more,
>   As fair to the taste and sight.
>
> How deep is the stream of affection there –
>   Of love, that is brimming o'er!
> And startling oft are the waves of despair,
>   That break on the peaceful shore.
> And the turbid waters of passion rise,
>   Like boiling springs, on the waste
> Upon whose margin affection dies,
>   And beauty is ever defaced.
>
> I love not the sad and mournful themes,
>   That press down the heart with woe;
> But the pure and purling crystal streams,
>   That sing as they gently flow.
> Then away, wing'd coursers, to scenes that are fair;
>   Leave all that is sad and wrong;
> And bring but the gems that are rich and rare,
>   To wreath in a beautiful song.[3]

This poem approaches the subject of "The Young Poetess" from an entirely different angle, as it does not describe the figure from afar but inhabits her subjectivity. The poem speaks as and for this figure, and in so doing attempts to describe the kind of poetry that she seeks to make. But by having her order her "wing'd coursers" to collect the materials by which she will make her "beautiful song," the poem displaces onto them any work that goes into this making. In fact, the poem spends most of its lines not describing this young poetess' poetry directly but, instead, discussing the "beautiful land of song" from which she asks her coursers to do their collecting. In contrast

---

[3] "The Young Poetess," *Wreath* (April 1, 1848): 102. The poem is marked as "Original" for this publication.

to the place where they have, in the past, collected this material – a place of "affection," "despair," "passion," and "beauty" – she now urges them to "leave all that is sad and wrong" and to go only to "scenes that are fair," a request that works to characterize her poetry as simple and uplifting.

I open this chapter with this image and its accompanying poems because, before discussing who or what the nineteenth-century American "poetess" was, I wanted my reader to have a visual and textual encounter with a figure that would have been familiar to nineteenth-century readers of periodicals like *Graham's* and the *Wreath*. This is not to say that such readers would have known who this young woman was (as the engraving's title and the poems make clear, her identity is beside the point) or that this particular image circulated widely (these are the only two places where I have found it), but because it represents many of the ideas about the poetess that circulated in and through the poetry, stories, biographies, sketches, memoirs, reviews, and portraits of the period.

As most recent criticism on the nineteenth-century American poetess has argued, defining who or what the poetess is has not been a simple task.[4] Instigated, we might say, by a portrait like this one that seeks to represent a singular instance of a kind of person, twentieth- and twenty-first-century criticism has vacillated between recovering the identities of individual women poets and arguing that the poetess was never really a person at all, but was, instead, a type, a trope, an idea, a figure, a category, or an occasion. In fact, as Virginia Jackson has argued, "what you think a Poetess is may depend entirely on your investment in the idea – and certainly depended on very different nineteenth-century investments in the idea."[5] It is the great challenge of all investigations into and explorations of the poetess, then, to balance the fact that real women wrote real poems throughout the nineteenth century and that they were, even at the very time of writing, already being abstracted as well as abstracting themselves. Understanding the poetess as an abstraction is crucial to an analysis of nineteenth-century American women's poetry, especially because so much of this poetry is in

---

[4] The three book-length studies of nineteenth-century American women's poetry that have grappled with the identity and cultural position of the "poetess" are Paula Bennett, *Poets in the Public Sphere: The Emancipatory Project of American Women's Poetry, 1800–1900* (Princeton: Princeton University Press, 2003), Mary Loeffelholz, *From School to Salon: Reading Nineteenth-Century American Women's Poetry* (Princeton: Princeton University Press, 2004), and Eliza Richards, *Gender and the Poetics of Reception in Poe's Circle* (Cambridge: Cambridge University Press, 2004).

[5] Virginia Jackson, "The Poet as Poetess," in *The Cambridge Companion to Nineteenth-Century American Poetry*, ed. Kerry Larson (Cambridge: Cambridge University Press, 2011), 54.

dialogue with that abstraction process. As that abstraction process takes place, the issue that gets most explored, warped, and obscured, is that of the woman poet's poetic labor.[6]

This engraving, and the two different poems that accompany it, participate in a shared effort to shore up the identity of this figure as not only anonymous, solitary, imagined, and idealized, but also utterly passive.[7] It is the passivity involved in the woman poet's literary enterprise that I will explore in this chapter, as it exerts a powerful force on her poetics. As both of these poems make clear, this young poetess is a figure who, through her association with other, imagined spaces where poetry lives (be it "Paradise" or the "land of song"), does not lift a finger to make her poems. The portfolio on her lap may contain the papers on which she may have written her verses, but the reader of either poem is led to look not at that material reality, but at the faraway look in her eyes – a look that conjures up the idea that her mind resides elsewhere, apart from the world in which poems get written down, revised, circulated, and published. Simultaneously endowed with elevating, meaning-making powers and stripped of all responsibility for or agency over those powers, then, the poetess had become, by the end of the 1840s, a highly visible and easily circulated figure. One might say that the saturation of periodical culture with the poetess' poems during this period contributed to this formulation of her identity, since understanding her compositional process *as labor* would have been to undermine a necessary gender dichotomy.

Such an image was reinforced in prose descriptions of the poetess, as we can see, for instance, in Caroline May's "Preface" to *The Female Poets of America* – her 1848 anthology of American women's poetry from Anne Bradstreet to Mary Reed. In what presents as a simple description of the poetesses whose writing fills the pages to come, May writes, "It must be borne in mind that not many ladies in this country are permitted sufficient leisure from the cares and duties of home to devote themselves, either

---

[6] My thinking about the woman poet's struggle with this issue echoes, in some ways, Virginia Jackson's treatment of "the nineteenth-century poetics of misery, or lyric sentimentalism" in *Dickinson's Misery: A Theory of Lyric Reading* (Princeton: Princeton University Press, 2005), 209. Jackson's attention to pain as both that which defines "the experience of the sentimental subject" and "the basis on which she becomes a subject of exchange" (210) has informed the way I am reading the figure of labor. In contrast, though, even when figurations of labor become metaphorical, they are not necessarily implicated in the creation of the ahistorical "lyric" with which Jackson is most directly concerned.

[7] Similar poems titled "The Young Poetess" circulated during this period. See, in particular, William H. Burleight, "The Young Poetess," *The North American Magazine* 5.28 (February 1835): 268, where this figure is also "unconscious of employment."

from choice, or as a means of living, to literary pursuits."[8] In acknowledging the work that women do in the home, May pointedly pits that domestic work against the state of "leisure" in which a woman might write poetry, even when it is done "as a means of living." While otium had long been a classical and romantic trope of the precondition for the making of poetry and was embraced by both British and American male poets of the period – see, for instance, John Keats' "Ode on Indolence" or Walt Whitman's many poses of loafing – such descriptions work to reinforce the idea that women's poetry is produced without the kind of sustained attention and rigor to which they devote themselves to other work. And unlike the productive and positive images of women's prose-writing-as-labor depicted in contemporaneous American novels such as *Ruth Hall* and *Little Women*, the image of the woman poet was, at every turn, one of idleness.

But poetry, for many women poets, was not a genre that they associated with passive acts of inspiration; instead, they understood the making of poetry to entail the kind of labor that was directly tied to poetry's forms and media. The most famous woman poet of the antebellum period, Lydia Sigourney, wrote directly about her poetic labor in *Letters of Life*. While her fame makes her an exceptional case, her attention to the issues of time, public demand, and the diversity of poetic genres makes clear the kinds of pressures under which many women poets worked:

> With the establishment of a poetic name came a host of novel requisitions. Fame gathered from abroad cut out work at home. The number and nature of consequent applications were alike remarkable. Churches requested hymns, to be sung at consecrations, ordinations, and installations; charitable societies, for anniversaries; academies and schools, for exhibitions. Odes were desired for the festivities of New Year and the Fourth of July, for silver and golden weddings, for the voyager wherewith to express his leave-taking, and the lover to propitiate his mistress. Epistles from strangers often solicited elegies and epitaphs; and though the voice of bereavement was to me a sacred thing, yet I felt the inefficacy of balm thus offered to a heart that bled. Sometimes I consoled myself that the multitude of these solicitations bespoke an increasing taste for poetry among the people. But to gratify all was an impossibility.[9]

The pressure Sigourney describes here to write in multiple genres (hymns, odes, elegies, and epitaphs), for a variety of different occasions and

---

[8] Caroline May, ed., *The American Female Poets* (Philadelphia: Lindsay and Blakiston, 1848), vi.

[9] L. H. Sigourney, *Letters of Life* (New York: D. Appleton and Company, 1867), 367–8.

individuals, and under time constraints reveals the making of poetry to be a job that she worked hard at but for which she ultimately felt she was always coming up short. The most sustained treatment of this tension within her poetry is, of course, "To a Shred of Linen," where Sigourney stages the very competing labor expectations that May's anthology reinforces. The poem's opening figures of the "neat lady, train'd in ancient times / of pudding-making, and of sampler work, / And speckless sanctity of household care" and the "spruce beau / Essenc'd and lily-handed" are all too aware of the woman poet's literary desires and abilities, and their attention to her non-attention to her housework sets the drama of the poem in motion. It is within the form of poetry – a "merry thought, or quaint conceit" has been called for as a suitable defense of her actions – that the woman poet catalogues the various kinds of labor that produces the paper on which she writes, a move that, by extension, positions her within the lineage of work being performed here.

If we are tempted to say that the magnitude and specifics of the requests made of Sigourney establish her as an outlier on poetry's labor charts, it's worth remembering that many other women poets labored much more straightforwardly under the pressures of income. The public may not have been demanding their verses at the rate of Sigourney's, but these women's lives depended upon the income from their publications. From Elizabeth Oakes Smith to Frances Osgood to Rose Terry Cooke to the Cary sisters, women poets in the period before the Civil War often kept their families economically afloat through the publication of their poems.

And so I would like to ask: What difference would it make to our understanding of the poetess if we were to acknowledge the direct contradiction that exists between the circumstances of many of these women's lives and the image of her that circulated through her culture? Why is her labor the thing that is expunged from the record? How does this tension – between the way her culture represses the story of women's poetic labor and the way many of their poems foreground that labor – help us see more clearly a quality of nineteenth-century American poetics that women poets were particularly attuned to, namely, its obsession with poetry's made-ness?

While some women poets were vocal about the very real work entailed in making poetry, no poet was more upfront about her labor than Alice Cary. Born and raised in Ohio, Alice and her sister Phoebe started writing as teenagers, before moving to New York City, establishing a well-known salon for writers and intellectuals in their home, and becoming two of the best-known poets of the antebellum period. In her 1873 book about their lives, *A Memorial of Alice and Phoebe Cary, with some of their later poems*, Mary

Clemmer Ames stresses just how difficult it was to become a poet under the conditions into which Alice and Phoebe had been born:

> But the country girls, uncultured in mind and rustic in manners, not needing to be told the immense distance which separated them from the world of letters they longed to enter, would not be discouraged. If they must darn and bake, they would also study and write, and at last publish: if candles were denied them, a saucer of lard with a bit of rag for wick could and did serve instead, and so, for ten long years, they studied and wrote and published without pecuniary recompense.[10]

While this description smacks of a sentimental accounting of the Cary sisters' deprivations, in which the desire to join the "world of letters" trumped the material realities of their lives, Ames was not the only one to invoke the disjunction between their means and their desires. Of the recklessness and financial insecurity of this endeavor, Horace Greeley, in "Eminent Women of the Age," wrote, "I do not know at whose suggestion they resolved to migrate to this city, and attempt to live here by literary labor; it surely was not mine." Of the specifics of their arrival, he wrote, "They hired two or three modest rooms, in an unfashionable neighborhood, and set to work resolutely to earn a living by the pen."[11]

The fact that Alice Cary eventually became one of the most celebrated women poets of her time did not keep her from understanding adverse circumstances as a hindrance to the making of poetry. She wrote specifically about this topic in an article entitled "White Crows" that was published in *Packard's Monthly* in March 1869. She takes her title from Greeley, who had written just two months prior for the same publication, declaring: "I know there is a small class of whom the world says 'They see to the heart of things by intuition; they are poets from impulse only; orators, statesmen, critics, sages, because nature would have it so.' I beg leave to doubt that men of this stamp are a whit more abundant than White Crows."[12] Looking back on her experiences as a poet and as one who had closely observed the world of poets around her, Cary was also resistant to this image of the poet that dominated the public imagination:

> I do not believe that man always passes, in the long run, for what he is worth. It seems to me a hard saying. The vision that the poet or the painter transcribes and leaves a joy and a wonder to all time, may, I believe, have come all the same to some poor, unlettered man, who, lacking the external faculty, so to speak,

---

[10] Mary Clemmer Ames, *A Memorial of Alice and Phoebe Cary, with Some of Their Later Poems* (New York: Hurd and Houghton, 1873), 21.

[11] Horace Greeley, in "Eminent Women of the Age." Quoted in Ames, *Memorial*, 31, 32.

[12] Horace Greeley, *Packard's Monthly: The Young Men's Magazine* 1.1 (January 1869): 5.

could not lay it in all its glorious shape and color on the canvas, or catch and hold it in the fastness of immortal verse. No, I cannot give up my comfortable faith, that in other worlds and far-off ages, there will appear a shining multitude who shall, through death, have come to themselves, and have found expression denied them on earth: beautiful souls, whose bodies were their prisons – who stammered or stood dumb among their kind, bearing alone the slights and disgraces of fortune, and all the while conscious, in their dread isolation, of being peers of the poets and the kings, and of all the royal men and women of the world.[13]

Cary's fantasy of a world where everyone, despite personal circumstances, could be the artist he or she was meant to be speaks directly to the extent to which she pushed past her own circumstances through systematic and sustained work. There is no idealization of the act of writing poetry, especially given the reality of her economic situation.[14]

Cary addressed these issues and their specific relation to both the poetic endeavor and the idealization of that endeavor most directly in her poem "To the Spirit of Song: Apology," which was published as the opening poem to her collection, *Ballads, Lyrics, and Hymns*, in 1865:

> O ever true and comfortable mate,
> > For whom my love outwore the fleeting red
> Of my young cheeks, nor did one jot abate,
> > I pray thee now, as by a dying bed,
> Wait yet a little longer! Hear me tell
> > How much my will transcends my feeble powers:
> > As one with blind eyes feeling out in flowers
> Their tender hues, or, with no skill to spell
> > His poor, poor name, but only makes his mark,
> > And guesses at the sunshine in the dark,
> So I have been. A sense of things divine
> > Lying broad above the little things I knew,
> The while I made my poems for a sign
> > Of the great melodies I felt were true.
> Pray thee accept my sad apology,
> > Sweet master, mending, as we go along,
> > My homely fortunes with a thread of song,

---

[13] Alice Cary, *Packard's Monthly: The Young Men's Magazine* 1.3 (March 1869): 82.

[14] Although they are not my topic here, there are many women who labored in other fields – domestic and other – and wrote poems when they could, but did not count on those poems to make a living. In other words, for these women, there was a division between labor and poetry. See, for instance, the poetry of Maria James, of whom May has written: "Maria James is a striking illustration of the fact that true genius, refinement, and real worth, are often found in stations where we least expect them" (May, *Poets*, 147).

> That all my years harmoniously may run;
>> Less by the tasks accomplished judging me,
> Than by the better things I would have done.
>> I would not lose thy gracious company
> Out of my house and heart for all the good
> Besides, that ever comes to womanhood, –
>> And this is much: I know what I resign,
>> But at that great price I would have thee mine.[15]

In this address to the poet's muse (or "spirit of song"), we encounter an older woman poet reflecting on a lifetime of making poems. Despite the intimate and "comfortable" relationship that she has had with this spirit over the years, her depiction of her vocation is filled with descriptions of just how hard she has had to work. Through the poem's central, extended simile, she seeks to show how the making of poems was more a matter of "will" than of "powers." The poet compares herself to a blind person who lacks the natural talents of the poet: he cannot see the colors of flowers, cannot write his name, and cannot decipher the difference between day and night. In making this comparison, the poet strips herself of the qualities often celebrated in poets and draws a clear distinction between the "little things" she knew and the "sense of things divine" that resided elsewhere. She may have "made [her] poems for a sign / Of the great melodies [she] felt were true," but she does not inhabit that other sphere. In fact, Cary uses the very earthly and material language of women's labor when she refers to her work as "mending" her "thread of song."

The poem's final move is to declare that she would not give up her muse's company for all that normally comes "to womanhood," and she admits that hers has been a life of deprivations. This may sound like a romanticized rendering of her own commitment to poetry – remember that the poem opened by calling the spirit her "ever true and comfortable mate" – but what it reveals, ironically, is a longing for all that her commitment to poetry required she sacrifice. Similarly, in the final stanza of "On the Picture of a Departed Poetess," Elizabeth Eames' describes the price paid by the poetess:

> Clear on the expansion of that snow-white forehead
>> Sits intellectual beauty, meekly throned; –
> Yet, O! the expression tells that thou hast sorrow'd,
>> And in thy yearning, human heart atoned
> For thy soul's lofty gifts! – on earth, O, never
>> Was the deep thirsting of thy bosom still'd! –

---

[15] Alice Cary, *Ballads, Lyrics, and Hymns* (New York: Hurd and Houghton, 1865), iii–iv.

> The "aching void" followed thee here forever,
> The Better Land thy Dream of Love fulfilled.[16]

She paid for her laurels not only in the labor of making poems, but also with the "aching void" she carried throughout her life.

Even after death, at the very moment when idealization of the dead woman is most likely to occur, those who remembered Cary in sermons and poetry drew attention to her as a "worker." Dr. Deems, in his funeral sermon for Cary, said: "I see a number of young people who are come out of tenderness to her memory, to the church to-day, and there may be among them literary people just commencing their career, and they say, 'Would I could write so beautifully and so easily as she did!' it was not easily done. She did nothing easily; but in all this that we read she was an earnest worker; she was faithful, painstaking, careful on improving herself, up to the last moment of her life."[17] "The Singer," a tribute to Cary written after her death by John Greenleaf Whittier, paints a portrait of her as a laborer. The poem's middle stanzas celebrate this quality of her most fully:

> Years passed: through all the land her name
> A pleasant household word became:
> All felt behind the singer stood
> A sweet and gracious womanhood.
>
> Her life was earnest work, not play;
> Her tired feet climbed a weary way;
> And even through her lightest strain
> We heard an undertone of pain.[18]

Perhaps because Cary's immediate legacy was as a woman poet who took the writing of poems as her "earnest work," literary history has been unable to fit her into the narrative about passive poetic inspiration that has largely defined the identity of the poetess.

As we have seen through attention to Alice Cary, the disjunction between a passive visual and textual image of the poetess and the very real labor involved in the making of poems by women writers was productive for women poets as a poetic topic. Women were all too familiar with having their work not be considered "work," but within their poems they had a chance to challenge the image of themselves as idle and passive. I want to end by turning to another woman poet of the period, Frances Osgood, in

---

[16] Quoted in May, *Poets*, 259.
[17] Quoted in Ames, *Memorial*, 150, who says it was published in the "Tribune."
[18] John Greenleaf Whittier, *Poems of John Greenleaf Whittier* (London: George Routledge & Sons, 1857), 371–2.

Figure 9.2 Frontispiece, portrait of Frances Osgood, *The American Female Poets*, ed. Caroline May (Philadelphia: Lindsey & Blakiston, 1848).
Courtesy, American Antiquarian Society.

part because, at the end of the 1840s her portrait came to supplant that of the anonymous poetess that had circulated earlier. In her anthology, May chose an engraving of Osgood as the frontispiece to this collection and, in doing so, inherently called attention to Osgood as representative of the poetess (Figure 9.2). While no longer anonymous or generic, this portrait of Osgood still establishes a certain kind of figure as the face of the American woman poet. Looking straight at the reader and without any accompanying writerly paraphernalia, there is nothing to mark her as a poetess other than her image's placement within this particular anthology. The woman poet, this portrait seems to say, is beautiful but plain, direct but deep. She doesn't give much away, but visually invites the reader to want to know more.

More radical, though, than the move from idealized figure to actual human being is the inclusion of Osgood's poem "Labour" – the first poem that appears in her section of this anthology. In this poem, the woman who greeted the reader upon opening the collection becomes the poet who prompts that reader to think about the benefits of natural and human labor. The poem opens with the epigraph "Laborare est orare" ["To labor is to pray"] and then begins its extended celebration of all different kinds of labor:

> Pause not to dream of the future before us,
> Pause not to weep the wild cares that come o'er us;
> Hark, how Creation's deep musical chorus,
> > Unintermitting, goes up unto Heaven!
> Never the ocean-wave falters in flowing,
> Never the little seed stops in its growing;
> More and more richly the rose-heart keeps glowing,
> > Till from its nourishing stem it is riven.
>
> Labour is worship! the robin is singing;
> Labour is worship! the wild bee is ringing;
> Listen, – that eloquent whisper upspringing
> > Speaks to thy soul from out nature's great heart.
> From the dark cloud flows the life-giving shower,
> From the rough sod blows the soft-breathing flower,
> From the small insect, the rich coral bower;
> > Only man in the plan shrinks from his part.
>
> Labour is life! – 'Tis the still water faileth;
> Idleness ever despairesth, bewaileth;
> Keep the watch wound, for the dark rust assaileth;
> > Flowers droop and die in the stillness of noon.
> Labour is glory! the flying cloud lightens;
> Only the roving wind changes and brightens;
> Idle hearts only, the dark future frightens;
> > Play the sweet keys, wouldst thou keep them in tune.
>
> Labour is rest – from the sorrows that greet us,
> Rest from all petty vexations that meet us,
> Rest from sin-promptings that ever entreat us,
> > Rest from world-syrens that lure us to ill.
> Work – and pure slumbers shall wait on thy pillow;
> Work – thou shalt ride over Care's coming billow;
> Lie not down wearied 'neath Wo's weeping willow;
> > Work with a stout heart and resolute will!
>
> Droop not, though shame, sin, and anguish are round thee;
> Bravely fling off the cold chain that hath bound thee;
> Look to you pure heaven smiling beyond thee!
> > Rest not content in thy darkness – a clod!

Work – for some good – be it ever so slowly;
Cherish some flower – be it ever so lowly;
Labour! All labour is noble and holy: –
  Let thy good deeds be thy prayer to thy God![19]

Osgood calls on the reader not to "dream" or "weep," actions that cause one to "Pause," but instead to acknowledge the ongoing process of labor everywhere. While one need not necessarily read this poem as a celebration of literary labor, Osgood's images suggest that the poet is part of this world, for she invokes the "robin" who is "singing" and the "wild bee" who is "ringing." Additionally, when Osgood writes "Idle hearts only, the dark future frightens," suggesting the negative repercussions of idleness, she posits the poet not as an idle heart but as one of the world's laborers who can solve this problem: "Play the sweet keys, wouldst thou keep them in tune." In six stanzas of eight lines of trochaic pentameter (often with a sprung foot), this highly made object foregrounds its own labor too. Osgood writes, "Work – for some good – be it ever so slowly," slowing down her own line, stressing the line's final sound, which we know by now we will hear two more times in deft echoes of the poem's aaab rhyme scheme. In its very craftedness, this poem becomes a product of the labor that it has depicted.

In conclusion, the rise of the poetess to a full-blown abstraction for idealized passive inspiration that took place in the decades just before the Civil War was accompanied by the rise of a female poetics that foregrounded the labor involved in making poetry. Attention to this strain of poetess poetics within the period we call the American Renaissance is important not simply because it reveals that these women poets were in conversation with their male contemporaries or because it makes visible the work of now-long-forgotten poets like Alice Cary and Frances Osgood who were crucial to the literary culture of the time, but because it registers for us the culture's desire to prescribe exactly *how* women poets be read. It allows us to read, for example, the extensive framing of and edits to Emily Dickinson's poems that would happen later in the century as complicit with the antebellum desire to figure women's poetry from this period as effortless and utterly natural productions. Acknowledging women poets' direct and indirect challenges to the image of passive female poetics takes us one step closer toward seeing this period in their terms.

---

[19] Quoted in May, *Poets*, 382–3.

IO

JENNIFER L. BRADY

Fern, Warner, and the Work of Sentimentality

In Fanny Fern's 1854 novel *Ruth Hall*, the titular heroine experiences early happiness: marriage to a man she loves, the birth of a daughter, the possession of a modest but idyllic home. As the novel progresses, those joys are stripped from her: first, her daughter dies, making the once-loved home a painful reminder of what she has lost. Years pass, and two more daughters are born. When her husband then dies, the pain of his loss is compounded by its thrusting Ruth and her daughters into penury. Her husband's family and her own look on her poverty with distaste, providing neither emotional nor material support to the distressed mother. As she is left to support herself, the novel unflinchingly reports Ruth's struggles, but her fortunes start to turn when she begins writing columns for two papers under the pseudonym "Floy." Still, fortune turns slowly, and the early signs of her professional success coexist with lingering privations.

One night, after writing in the gloom of her boarding house, Ruth discovers two fan letters she had forgotten. The first letter comes from a self-described "rough old man" named John Stokes, who writes frankly, "I don't know who you are" but "those pieces have got the real stuff in 'em." He suggests that she collect her articles into a book "so that your readers may keep them," tells her he will take three copies, and advises that she "might make a plum by the operation." Ruth laughs to herself about the letter – "*I* publish a book?" she says, and continues, "[T]hose articles were written for bread and butter, not fame; and tossed to the printer before the ink was dry."[1] Still, she says she will remember the suggestion.

The second letter is of a different character, written by a dying woman signing herself "Mary R.------." She writes that Floy has become "dear as a sister on whose loving breast I have leaned, though I never saw your face," for "every week your printed words come to me, in my sick

[1] Fanny Fern, *Ruth Hall and Other Writings*, ed. Joyce W. Warren (New Brunswick: Rutgers University Press, 1986), 135, 136.

chamber, like the ministrations of some gentle friend." This writer calls Ruth her "unknown sister" while addressing her by her pseudonym, placing Floy in quotation marks to signal her knowledge of its artifice while insisting on their connection on a more substantive level, heart to heart. In response to this letter, "Ruth's head bowed low upon the table, and her lips moved."[2]

Published in 1854, *Ruth Hall* falls into the period first designated by F. O. Matthiessen as the American Renaissance and long represented by authors like Nathaniel Hawthorne, Herman Melville, and Walt Whitman and their original masterpieces. In contrast, Fern and her popular novel were long forgotten and rarely mentioned in the same breath as these canonical authors and works. Instead, Jane Tompkins in 1985 pointed to what she called "the other American Renaissance," constituted by popular women writers like Fern who were summarily dismissed as "sentimental."[3] That term was meant to signal excessive and therefore inauthentic emotionality, a slavish and unthinking adherence to convention, a feminized lack of originality and hence artistry, a non-transcendent focus on the painfully uninteresting ordinary, and astounding but dubious popularity.

Ruth's encounter with her fan mail casts these markers of the sentimental tradition in a different light. To be sure, Mary's letter traffics in the conventional language and situations of sentimentality, as one woman reaches out to another in prose sodden with suffering and sympathy. But it also records the ability of Ruth's articles to produce deep affective connections between otherwise unknown persons, as her printed words move through the public sphere into the domestic and the realm of private, individual feeling. The sympathetic circuit that binds Ruth and Mary together also explicitly expands to include the reader: the narrator describes the letter as written "in a delicate, beautiful, female hand; just such a one as you, dear Reader, might trace, whose sweet, soft eyes, and long, drooping tresses, are now bending over this page."[4] The sentimental postures each woman assumes – bending over a page, leaning on someone else for support, and finally bowing a head in prayer – replicate each other while synchronizing their affect, drawing them together in sympathy. Yet John Stokes's letter is also a part of the sentimental: his forthright focus on the mechanisms of commerce and the financial benefit "Floy" stands to gain from publishing a book point to sentimental literature's astounding sales, while also recording how commerce

---

[2] *Ibid.*, 137, 136.
[3] Jane Tompkins, *Sensational Designs: The Cultural Work of American Fiction, 1790–1860* (New York: Oxford University Press, 1985), 147–85.
[4] Fern, *Ruth Hall*, 136.

could serve the sentimental purpose of both preserving and circulating a loved object – in this case, Ruth's writing.

Stokes was right: sentimental literature sold. In *Ruth Hall*, another letter brings Ruth an offer to publish her articles as a book, and the success that follows allows her to achieve financial independence. *Ruth Hall* itself sold a remarkable 55,000 copies; Fern's first collection of articles, like the one that Stokes advises her fictional counterpart to publish, was titled *Fern Leaves from Fanny's Port-folio* (1853) and was also hugely successful.[5] Fern was the first woman newspaper columnist and also the most highly paid columnist of her time, woman or man.[6] The other subject of this chapter, Susan Warner, wrote a bestseller titled *The Wide, Wide World* (1850). At the time of its publication, its sales were unprecedented (although they would quickly be topped by *Uncle Tom's Cabin* [1852]). Warner's novel was in its fourteenth edition by 1852.[7] Warner and her sister Anna went on to publish many popular books.

This chapter turns to Warner and Fern, two authors who are distinguished by their extraordinary popularity, to demonstrate the range, conventionality, and self-consciousness of the sentimental tradition. Its premise is that the period that has come to be known as the American Renaissance was remarkable in part because it witnessed the rise of women writers like Warner and Fern, who dominated a newly formed mass print culture by writing in the sentimental tradition. Sentimentality's combination of convention and commerce stands in opposition to the perceived originality and artistry of traditional American Renaissance writers; it is a genre that privileges, to adopt Tompkins's phrase, "the power of the copy as opposed to the original."[8] Rather than placing sentimental works "beneath" the American Renaissance and tracing how they inform its traditional masterpieces, as David Reynolds has done, I place these works on a parallel track in order

---

[5] James D. Hart records that *Fern Leaves* sold 70,000 copies in 1853, and Susan Geary places the sales of *Ruth Hall* between 55,000 and 70,000 copies. By comparison, Hart writes that Nathaniel Hawthorne's *The House of the Seven Gables* sold 6,500 copies in its first year of publication, and Frank Luther Mott estimates that Herman Melville's *Moby-Dick* sold about 1,700 copies in its first twelve years of publication. Hart, *The Popular Book: A History of America's Literary Taste* (New York: Oxford University Press, 1950), 92–3; Geary, "The Domestic Novel as a Commercial Commodity: Making a Best Seller in the 1850s," *Papers of the Bibliographical Society of America* 70 (1976): 390; Mott, *Golden Multitudes: The Story of Best Sellers in the United States* (New York: Macmillan, 1947), 132.

[6] For an excellent biography of Fern, see Joyce W. Warren, *Fanny Fern: An Independent Woman* (New Brunswick: Rutgers University Press, 1992).

[7] Hart, *Popular Book*, 95.

[8] Tompkins, *Sensational Designs*, xvi.

to consider them both on their own terms and in the place that they occupied in the world of antebellum publishing and reading.[9] As Warner's and Fern's work demonstrates, the adoption of convention is not without art, nor was it without readers. A wildly popular form, sentimental writing was omnipresent in the 1850s, saturating newspapers and periodicals, novels, giftbooks, religious tracts, plays, and other mass-market literary forms, and sentimentality reached across mid-century culture in even more ways.

The dominance of sentimentality did not go unremarked or unchallenged. Hawthorne famously complained in an 1855 letter to his publisher William Ticknor that "America is now wholly given over to a d – d mob of scribbling women" and lamented "the public taste [that] is occupied with their trash." Making reference to a bestselling sentimental novel by Maria Cummins, he asked, "What is the mystery of these innumerable editions of the Lamplighter, and other books neither better nor worse? – worse they could not be, and better they need not be, when they sell by the 100.000."[10] Hawthorne's complaints are a commonplace in scholarship on the women writers he criticizes, offered as evidence of their domination of the literary marketplace – and his own sour grapes at his comparably lower sales. Sentimental literature has long been understood as a form that is all too superficial, all too transparent; for much of the twentieth century, the only question about it was Hawthorne's, which is why such trash was so forcefully embraced by the mid-century reading public. This chapter raises more questions about sentimentality by considering Warner's and Fern's savvy, deliberate use of convention and articulating the possibilities and pleasures the embrace of convention offered these authors and their readers. In their reliance on narrative formulas, their accessible and familiar style, and their trafficking in a particular kind of excessive, discursive emotion, sentimental books and authors worked to become familiar to their readers, and readers in turn seized the opportunities for connection and recognition that sentimental convention afforded.[11]

In recompense for its long critical neglect, sentimentality now seems to be everywhere in American literary studies. Invoked in discussions of reform movements, material culture, domesticity, the public sphere, and especially

[9] David S. Reynolds, *Beneath the American Renaissance: The Subversive Imagination in the Age of Emerson and Melville* (Cambridge, MA: Harvard University Press, 1988).

[10] Nathaniel Hawthorne, Letter to William D. Ticknor, January 19, 1855, in Hawthorne, *The Letters, 1853–1856, The Centenary Edition of the Works of Nathaniel Hawthorne*, vol. 17, ed. Thomas Woodson, James A. Rubino, L. Neal Smith, and Norman Holmes Pearson (Columbus: Ohio State University Press, 1987), 304.

[11] Joanne Dobson offers an excellent overview of sentimental form in "Reclaiming Sentimental Literature," *American Literature* 69 (1997): 263–88.

white women's writing, sentimentality has become synonymous with identification, sympathy, intimacy, and exploitation. Ann Douglas and Tompkins
set the initial terms of the critical debate over nineteenth-century sentimental literature with their opposing viewpoints on whether crying in response
to sentimental texts was narcissistic, privatizing, and politically suspect
(Douglas), or the font of sympathy, a spur to political action, and a means
of claiming "sentimental power" (Tompkins). What came to be known as
the Douglas–Tompkins debate is, most fundamentally, an argument about
whether sentimental literature compromised or extended women's agency.
In *The Feminization of American Culture* (1977), Douglas argued that sentimental literature and culture extended a compensatory agency to women
and made them complicit in their downward trajectory "from the exercise
of power to the exertion of 'influence.' "[12] In marked contrast, in *Sensational
Designs: The Cultural Work of American Fiction, 1790–1860* (1985),
Tompkins asked her readers to revisit questions of literary value and consider the "cultural work" of sentimental literature – how, in reflecting the
realities of the culture in which it was embedded, it provided strategies of
survival and even the means of pleasure to readers who could not escape
their circumstances. Tompkins sees sentimental literature as making a claim
to power on behalf of its heroines and women readers, not relinquishing it,
by advising them to turn from a corrupt secular world to a transcendent
spiritual reality.

This debate helped to usher sentimental literature back into critical focus,
but scholars have pushed well beyond it and formulated important new
ways to think about the sentimental tradition.[13] In contrast to the early
understanding of sentimentalism as a genre "written by, for, and about
women," as Tompkins wrote, important work by Joycelyn Moody, Glenn
Hendler, Mary Chapman, Laura Mielke, and others has demonstrated its
use by men, African-Americans, and Native Americans.[14] Rather than dis-
cerning a certain progressive or retrograde political content that inevitably
adheres in sentimentality, scholars have studied it instead as a politically

---

[12] Ann Douglas, *The Feminization of American Culture* (New York: Knopf, 1977), 77.

[13] For a more comprehensive survey of recent studies of sentimentality, see Hildegard
Hoeller, "From Agony to Ecstasy: The New Studies of American Sentimentality,"
ESQ: A Journal of the American Renaissance 52 (2006): 339–69.

[14] Tompkins, *Sensational Designs*, 124–5; Joycelyn Moody, *Sentimental
Confessions: Spiritual Narratives of Nineteenth-Century African American
Women* (Athens: University of Georgia Press, 2001); Mary Chapman and Glenn
Hendler, eds., *Sentimental Men: Masculinity and the Politics of Affect in American
Culture* (Berkeley: University of California Press, 1999); Laura L. Mielke,
Moving Encounters: Sympathy and the Indian Question in Antebellum Literature
(Amherst: University of Massachusetts Press, 2008).

flexible discourse that could be turned to multiple and even opposing ends.[15] At the same time, scholars have been attentive to the power dynamics of sentimentality's extension of sympathy, tracing how the slide from "feel[ing] *like*" the objects of sympathy to "feel[ing] *with*" them threatens to replace their subjectivity with that of the reader.[16] Scholars have also considered sentimental literature through not only a historicist but a formalist lens, crediting its cultural work while not neglecting its aesthetics. In this newly expansive scholarship, scholars like Samuel Otter and Claudia Stokes have come to discern and credit the complexity of sentimentality itself.[17]

As scholars reckon with sentimentality, many turn over the question of what sentimentality means and designates, precisely. June Howard offers a particularly lucid and helpful touchstone: "Most broadly – when we call an artifact or gesture sentimental, we are pointing to its use of some established convention to evoke emotion; we mark a moment when the discursive processes that construct emotion become visible."[18] Similarly, Elizabeth Maddock Dillon argues that sentimentality has a dual nature, joining "affective immediacy" to "political and cultural ideals and aims": she therefore calls sentimentalism "a putting to use of emotion."[19] For both scholars, the visibility of the "discursive processes" that construct emotion and its overt instrumentality account for the suspicion that attaches to sentimentality, the perception of it as manipulative and the emotion it produces as insincere. Against this suspicion, Karen Sánchez-Eppler, in her illuminating work on the circulation of images of dead children in sentimental verse and daguerreotypes, demonstrates the potential for sentimental conventions to allow the replication and circulation of feeling – in this case, the grief over a lost child.[20] Sánchez-Eppler's work suggests that even commercial replication need not diffuse the emotional force of the original or individual event. Indeed, the constructed or mediated nature of sentiment – its packaging of emotion in familiar tropes,

[15] See, for example, Sarah Mesle, "Sentimentalism's Nation: Maria J. McIntosh and the Antebellum Contexts of 'Southern' Fiction," *Studies in American Fiction* 40 (2013): 203–30.

[16] Glenn Hendler, *Public Sentiments: Structures of Feeling in Nineteenth-Century American Literature* (Chapel Hill: University of North Carolina Press, 2001), 5.

[17] Samuel Otter, *Melville's Anatomies* (Berkeley: University of California Press, 1999), 208–54; Claudia Stokes, *The Altar at Home: Sentimental Literature and Nineteenth-Century American Religion* (Philadelphia: University of Pennsylvania Press, 2014).

[18] June Howard, "What Is Sentimentality?" *American Literary History* 11 (1999): 76.

[19] Elizabeth Maddock Dillon, "Sentimental Aesthetics," *American Literature* 76 (2004): 515.

[20] Karen Sánchez-Eppler, *Dependent States: The Child's Part in Nineteenth-Century American Culture* (Chicago: University of Chicago Press, 2005), 101–48.

stereotyped characters, and conventional scenes dense with accumulated meaning – advances its ability to be communicated.

Sentimentality's markers are not only visible to scholars in the twentieth and twenty-first centuries, but were recognized by nineteenth-century readers. To register the formulaic and familiar conventions of sentimentality was to discern its invitation to sympathy and connection – and many accepted that invitation, were enfolded by it, and returned again and again for more. Warner's and Fern's uses of convention allow a re-examination of the form of sentimentality, which holds and stabilizes meaning and feeling and thereby makes them shareable.

In Warner's limited departure from a conventional ending for *The Wide, Wide World* and in the responses it engendered lies a particularly illustrative example of the purposes that conventionality served for authors and readers. *The Wide, Wide World* was Warner's first novel, and she wrote it to make money for her family. Her father had been ruined in the Panic of 1837, plunging Susan, her sister Anna, and her aunt Fanny into difficult financial circumstances and forcing them to relocate from New York City to Constitution Island, across the Hudson River from West Point Academy. This is a conventional story of female authorship in the nineteenth century, and the novel itself tells another kind of conventional story.[21] *The Wide, Wide World* follows its young heroine, Ellen Montgomery, through a series of trials that includes Ellen's painful separation from her mother, who later dies; the death of her best friend and adoptive sister, Alice Humphreys; her separation from the rest of her adoptive family and removal to Scotland; and, more mundanely but most importantly, her persistently unruly passions. Ellen withstands her trials, albeit while crying a really astonishing number of tears, and the novel implies that Ellen will be rewarded, as sentimental heroines usually are, with a desirable marriage.

While Warner intimates that Ellen and her adoptive brother John Humphreys will eventually marry, she playfully withholds the satisfaction of certainty. Near the novel's end, John makes two requests of Ellen – "keep up a regular and full correspondence with me" and "[r]ead no novels" – but he leaves a third request unspoken, telling Ellen "you shall know by and by – the time is not yet."[22] At the novel's conclusion, Warner teasingly reminds her readers of this loose end by narrating Ellen's continuing puzzlement over that third thing. Warner clearly recognizes that her readers

[21] Nina Baym, *Woman's Fiction: A Guide to Novels by and about Women in America, 1820–1870* (Ithaca: Cornell University Press, 1978).

[22] Susan Warner, in *The Wide, Wide World*, ed. Jane Tompkins (New York: Feminist Press at the City University of New York, 1987), 563, 564, 565.

would be impatient to learn of Ellen's romantic future, but she plays with convention and the expectations it fosters. She teases into the novel's final paragraph by writing, "For the gratification of those who are never satisfied, one word shall be added."[23] However, the final paragraph offers very little readerly gratification, speaking only generally of Ellen's development into womanhood and her eventual return to the United States. In readers' letters to Warner and to George Putnam, the novel's publisher, and in reviews and notices in the periodical press, readers voiced their desire for a sequel to *The Wide, Wide World*, which Warner never provided. This missing sequel offers a lens on the dynamics of convention and commerce that governed sentimentality, showing what readers hoped to gain through a continuation of Ellen's story and what Warner stood to lose.

The novel's unsatisfactory ending played a role in the expectation that a sequel would be forthcoming, but it is worth asking what accounts for that dissatisfaction. Sentimental convention, as identified by twentieth-century literary scholars and by nineteenth-century readers, dictates that the novel is driving toward marriage. According to a reviewer in *Godey's Lady's Book*, the novel makes clear where it is headed: "Both love and matrimony are insinuated in the concluding pages; and it does not require much knowledge of the mechanism of fiction to detect in John, from the beginning, the embryo husband of Ellen, notwithstanding their dubbing each other brother and sister; this, after all, is but an old and hackneyed trick of the sentimental school."[24] While a reviewer in the *Monthly Religious Magazine* was pleased that Warner did not narrate the marriage, making "a narrow escape" from turning her book into "a love-tale," the wider perception seemed to be, as a review reprinted from the *New York Evening Post* in *Littell's Living Age* stated, "the 'Wide, Wide World' ... seemed to require a continuation to give perfect completeness to the narrative."[25]

Rumors and false reports about that continuation circulated accordingly. The announcement of Warner's second novel, which would be published in the spring of 1852 under the impenetrable title *Queechy*, fed the rumor mill, as speculation abounded that it would prove a sequel to Ellen's story. It was no such thing. On May 15, 1852, the reviewer in *Norton's Literary Gazette* recorded widespread disappointment: "Grave old men, who almost never condescend to story books, but were unconsciously taken captive by little Ellen of the Wide, Wide World, have eagerly awaited its appearance.

---

[23] *Ibid.*, 569.
[24] "Editor's Table," *Godey's Lady's Book* 43.3 (September 1, 1851): 186.
[25] L. J. H., "The Wide, Wide World," *Monthly Religious Magazine* 8.3 (March 1, 1851): 130; "Queechy," *Littell's Living Age* 34.125 (July 10, 1852): 58.

Bright young girls, who have wondered whether Ellen did really marry "Mr. John" ... have been seeking for some word or hint that should settle the point. But here the book comes at last, and every body has found out that it is *no sequel*."[26] Some readers addressed Putnam directly to ask him about a sequel, prompting him to state firmly in published notices "that no sequel to that work has been written or promised by the author, and that it is not and never has been the author's intention to write such a sequel, however gratifying to her must be the desire of so many that the story should be continued."[27]

But why did readers desire that continuation? Readers' letters propose more answers to that question. Sara Bingham, a young girl writing to Putnam from Detroit in May 1852, asked if there was a sequel to *The Wide, Wide World* either already published or forthcoming. She assured him, "I should not have thought myself any thing about a *sequel*, being all the better pleased for a time at least to allow imagination to have full sway, had I not everywhere been asked, Did you know there was a sequel to The Wide Wide World being published in New York?"[28] Bingham indicated her willingness to relinquish her individual imagination of what might happen next in exchange for her continued participation in the community of readers that first cohered around *The Wide, Wide World*.

Bingham's reluctance to let her imagination "have full sway" parallels other readers' requests for a clarification of *The Wide, Wide World*'s ending. Edward Campbell, writing to Warner in 1855, acknowledged that she may have "intended the *final* 'denouement' to take place in the imaginations of your readers," but nonetheless asked her to "condescend to inform me whether you wished the inferred 'finale' to be the *union of Mr John and Miss Ellen*."[29] H. G. Fenimore, not having Warner's address, wrote to Putnam in April 1852 to ask him to "urge her to write more of it." In doing so, Fenimore positioned himself with other readers disappointed in what he described as the novel's "sudden termination." He wrote that readers wanted more Ellen: "[W]e want to see more of little Ellen amongst her Scotch relations. We want to see her once more established in the home of the Humphreys. We want to know when, how & why

[26] "Queechy," *Norton's Literary Gazette* 2.5 (May 15, 1852): 86.
[27] "THE WIDE WIDE WORLD!" *Alexandria Gazette* (June 17, 1852): 2.
[28] Sara T. Bingham, Letter to George Putnam, May 27, 1852, Constitution Island Association Warner Collection, Special Collections, US Military Academy, West Point, New York.
[29] Edward L. Campbell, Letter to Susan Warner, January 10, 1855, Constitution Island Association Warner Collection, Special Collections, US Military Academy, West Point, New York.

she goes back again. We want to see her sweet piety expand into woman-hood, & we want to see more of the noble, generous John Humphreys."[30] Even as he communicated a precise, detailed imagination of what shape a sequel would take, he did not want to rely on his imagination alone to conjure these scenes. He preferred instead to see them stabilized and then disseminated in print.

These letters offer deeper insight into what a sequel to *The Wide, Wide World* would offer its readers – not necessarily closure, but a confirma-tion of convention and continued connections with characters, their creator, and other readers. As they asked for a sequel, these correspondents tellingly positioned themselves in communities of readers united by Warner's novel. Fenimore so expressed not what he wants, but what "we want"; Bingham's request for information about a sequel was prompted by the "many reports" she heard about it; and even an anonymous reader from Philadelphia who wrote to request a sequel tellingly signed him- or herself "One of many."[31] While part of their aim may have been to position the authorial one against the clamoring, reading many and to carry the point on numbers alone – and even to show Warner that a market already existed for a sequel – these read-ers asked for another sustaining fiction. As they gently protest the tempered force of an imperfectly realized convention, these readers urged Warner to perpetuate the fiction of a unified community of readers responding in kind to a conventionally sentimental book.

Writing a sequel was a risk, however, as a brief mention in *Norton's Literary Adviser* in 1851 makes clear. Of the rumors of a sequel, the notice states, "If she is able to carry into the more advanced life of her characters, the same close observation and accurate knowledge of human nature, which she has displayed in her former production, we shall welcome the Sequel heartily. Otherwise, we should scarcely be willing to have the harmony of that excellent Moral Treatise broken in upon or disturbed."[32] Warner never provided a sequel. An unpublished final chapter to *The Wide, Wide World* does exist, in which Ellen returns to the United States as John Humphreys's wife.[33] Why that final chapter was not published with the rest of the novel remains unclear. Putnam was concerned with the novel's length and made

---

[30] H. G. Fenimore, Letter to George Putnam, April 24, 1852, Constitution Island Association Warner Collection, Special Collections, US Military Academy, West Point, New York.

[31] Letter to Susan Warner, May 1851, Constitution Island Association Warner Collection, Special Collections, US Military Academy, West Point, New York.

[32] Untitled, *Norton's Literary Advertiser* 1.7 (November 15, 1851): 73.

[33] The final chapter is reprinted as an appendix to Tompkins's edition of Warner, *Wide, Wide World*, 571–83.

other cuts to her manuscript, so the final chapter may simply have ended up on the cutting-room floor.

Rather than publishing a sequel or even just this final chapter, Warner wrote additional sentimental and religious texts that traded on without endangering *The Wide, Wide World*'s reputation. Subsequent titles written by Warner were identified as being written by the author of *The Wide, Wide World*, explicitly inviting readers to link the book at hand to that first title. With her sister, Anna, Warner also authored a series of books titled "Ellen Montgomery's Bookshelf," which purported to be books that Ellen herself would have read. In her subsequent work, then, Warner provided the pleasures of familiarity, extension, and iteration that her readers sought in their requests for a sequel. Reviewers particularly found those pleasures in *Queechy*. After writing of the old men and young girls alike disappointed to find *Queechy* was not a sequel to *The Wide, Wide World*, the reviewer in *Norton's Literary Gazette* acknowledged "strong points of resemblance in the plan of the story, and in the characters introduced."[34] A reviewer in *To-day*, published in Boston, promised readers they would "find in this book many of their old friends, not bearing the same names, nor in the same positions precisely, but wearing very much the same characteristics, and suffering similar trials."[35] Here, replicable convention and the consequent meeting of "old friends" assuaged the need for a direct continuation of Ellen's story.

Fanny Fern is often perceived as bucking convention, sentimental or otherwise. Although this chapter began with an example from *Ruth Hall*, that novel explicitly departs from sentimental convention in important ways. Rather than ending with a marriage – or a marriage deferred, as is the case in *The Wide, Wide World* – the novel begins with one but proceeds to show that marriage does not guarantee lifelong protection or happiness for sentimental heroines. Its ending is even more unconventional: a printed bank certificate appears in the novel's final pages, representing Ruth's earnings from her writing and her achievement of financial independence. Not only the narrative arc but also the tone of *Ruth Hall* calls its sentimentality into question: Fern's critiques are scathing, her voice acerbic, her pronouncements often terse, and humor and sarcasm mark her writing. Indeed, although Hawthorne complained of scribbling women, he exempted Fern from that mob on the strength of *Ruth Hall*. He wrote in another letter to his publisher

---

[34] "Queechy," *Norton's Literary Gazette* 2.5 (May 15, 1852): 86.
[35] "Queechy," *To-day* [Boston, MA] (May 15, 1852): 318.

Ticknor, "The woman writes as if the devil was in her; and that is the only condition under which a woman ever writes anything worth reading."[36]

Fern's life also departed from convention. Prompted by financial necessity following the death of her first husband and the failure of her second marriage, Fern turned to her pen. Born Sarah Willis Parson, she assumed the pseudonym Fanny Fern shortly after she began publishing in two Boston periodicals in 1851, the *True Flag* and the *Olive Branch*, and became the first woman columnist in the United States when she began writing for the New York *Musical World and Times* in October 1852. Collections of her articles and two novels soon followed; her identity was revealed in 1855 by an editor infuriated by his portrayal in the semi-autobiographical *Ruth Hall*. Her popularity led to more success: she began writing a weekly column for the *New York Ledger* in January 1856 after its editor, Robert Bonner, made her escalating financial offers that she eventually could not refuse. Fern would continue writing for the *Ledger* until her death in 1872.

Fern produced a great volume of writing over her long career, some of which is easily identified as adhering to sentimental convention and some of which seems to eschew convention entirely. Indeed, scholars have puzzled over what they call Fern's schizophrenia, her easy movement between sentiment and satire, her adoption of characters, and her use of seemingly incompatible voices.[37] Fern's signature style is heavy with hyperbole, bombast, outrage, and sarcasm and punctuated with liberal doses of exclamation marks, italics, and dashes. Yet Fern often circles back to conventional subjects through these unconventional stylistics: her wives are long-suffering, her mothers loving, and Fern's sympathies always engaged. Indeed, Fern's persona and the relationship she cultivated with readers were rooted in the sentimental model, premised on the sympathy she extended to readers, the insistent registering of her own emotions, and her lading convention with this affective freight. As Fern spoke on both conventional and unconventional subjects and emphasized common experiences with her distinctive voice, she demonstrated the flexibility of sentimentality.

Sentimentality's power both to communicate and prompt deep feeling is registered when Fern speaks about the most sentimental of subjects, the dead

---

[36] Hawthorne, Letter to William D. Ticknor, February 2, 1855, in Hawthorne, *Letters*, 308.

[37] For surveys of this problem and apt solutions, see Melissa J. Homestead, *American Women Authors and Literary Property, 1822–1869* (New York: Cambridge University Press, 2005), 150–91; Lara Langer Cohen, *The Fabrication of American Literature: Fraudulence and Antebellum Print Culture* (Philadelphia: University of Pennsylvania Press, 2012), 133–61.

child. In *Ruth Hall*, Ruth's grief over the loss of her daughter Daisy does not loose its hold on her, and eight years later the narrative finds Ruth crying over "a little half-worn shoe, with the impress of a tiny foot."[38] Otter argues that the novel does little to individualize Daisy or to acquaint the reader with her in the brief time she appears, instead using her as "a device: the perfect child." Because the reader still weeps over her death, Fern "demonstrates the power of gesture to call forth emotion," "the force of convention to signify even in the absence of a specific signified."[39] Such force is on display in an article Fern published the previous year in the *Musical World and Times* titled "Little Benny." Here, even less is known of the dead child and nothing of his mother, for the article is prompted merely by the narrator's encounter of a headstone with the inscription "Little Benny." She asks, "Why did my eyes fill?" and goes on, in sentimental trope after trope, to list all the reasons they should not: she "never pillowed his little head ... or smoothed his silky locks, or laved his dimpled limbs," nor did she "watch[ ] the look that comes but once, flit over his cherub face." The narrator continues, "And yet, 'little Benny,' my tears are falling; for, *somewhere*, I know there's an empty crib, a vacant chair, useless robes and toys, a desolate hearth-stone and a weeping mother." Here, sentimental convention and sympathetic knowledge replace direct experience, and both find their lodestone in the weeping mother. The article concludes by returning to the simple phrase "Little Benny" and its authorship: "It was all her full heart could utter; and it was enough. It tells the whole story." Here, Fern demonstrates that sentimental convention is replete with shared meaning and deep feeling, positioning it as the expression of a "full heart" "the whole story," "enough."[40]

Fern is regularly, deeply sympathetic, but her sympathy does not always result in tears; instead, excoriating irony also becomes its register. Her related willingness to puncture romantic notions forms part of her project to extend recognition to those who experience mundane trials and griefs as they live decidedly unromantic lives. In "The Tear of a Wife," Fern lambasts an unknown speaker who calls a wife's tear "a drop of poison to her husband" by ironically and manically endorsing that pronouncement. She instructs wives to ignore everything that might prompt tears – all kinds of bodily aches, "and smoky chimneys, and old coats, and young babies!" She continues, "[Y]ou miserable little whimperer, what have you to cry for?

---

[38] Fern, *Ruth Hall*, 49.
[39] Otter, *Melville's Anatomies*, 233.
[40] Fern, "Little Benny," in Fern, *Ruth Hall*, 255.

A-i-n-t y-o-u m-a-r-r-i-e-d? Isn't that the *summum bonum* – the height of feminine ambition?"[41] Clearly, the answer here is no. "The Tear of a Wife" demonstrates how Fern's style serves a sentimental purpose: her bracing language is expended in defense of tears and in sympathy for what prompts them. Fern again and again offers the ready and broad extension of sympathy – to children, seamstresses, and prostitutes; to mothers and wives stranded in the domestic sphere and physically and mentally broken by the unremitting labor that child-rearing and housework demand; but not to obtuse husbands who are often the object of her biting wit. In recording her sympathies and frustrations, her incredulity and outrage, Fern both shares and legitimates that affect.

Scholars have debated what kind of persona Fern constructed in her writings, whether that persona was stable or fluid, and if Fern herself was knowable through the articles she wrote.[42] Lara Langer Cohen has written convincingly of Fern's "positive claim to artifice" and her savvy grasp of its potential.[43] Perhaps the most obvious example of that claim is her adoption of her pseudonym in her private life, as she came to sign private letters as Fanny Fern and was addressed by her third husband as Fanny. Yet that artifice is not without content: Fern repeatedly acknowledges the possibility of coming to know her on a deeper level through her writing, as her recording of the dying Mary's claim to know Ruth Hall heart to heart makes clear. That acknowledgment appears elsewhere, including in Fern's preface introducing *Fern Leaves*: "Some of the articles are sad, some are gay; each is independent of all the others, and the work is consequently disconnected and fragmentary; but, if the reader will imagine me peeping over his shoulder, quite happy should he pay me the impromptu compliment of a smile or a tear, it is possible we may come to a good understanding by the time the book shall have been perused."[44] Here, disconnected fragments are threaded together by imagining the singular author peeping over the reader's shoulder; "impromptu" emotions, really prompted by the steady use of convention, connect a pseudonymous author and a reader who is one of tens of thousands.

Fern's preface drove her readers into the pages that followed, with the promise that she would accompany them as they read. So do Warner's savvy

---

[41] Fern, "The Tear of a Wife," in Fern, *Ruth Hall*, 236–7.

[42] See, for example, Homestead, *American Women Authors*, 150–91, and Cohen, *Fabrication of American Literature*, 133–61.

[43] Cohen, *Fabrication of American Literature*, 153.

[44] Fanny Fern, *Fern Leaves from Fanny's Port-folio* (Auburn, NY: Derby and Miller, 1853), vi.

use of convention and her winking knowledge about it prompt readers to seek Ellen and her elsewhere – through fan letters, in the pages of subsequent sentimental books, in other readers. In its conventionality, sentimentality prompted iteration, invited connection, and always promised more. That promise gained material expression in the proliferation of sentimental texts – innumerable editions and unprecedented sales, fan letters written by eager readers, columns unfolding across decades of writing for the papers. Fern and Warner demonstrate that a signal effect of sentimentality was to perpetuate itself and to drive readers back into sentimental texts to share familiar pleasures.

11

WYN KELLEY

Melville: The Ocean and the City

Where are we in twenty-first-century considerations of Herman Melville? Taking up Melville's jibe in "Hawthorne and His Mosses," one might ask, "Who reads a book by a writer from the American Renaissance?" More than seventy-five years after F. O. Matthiessen's book, Melville's dominance of a narrowly defined canon seems a relic of the past. Budgets are shrinking – not just financial budgets that support the scholarship and teaching that keep Melville studies alive, but also the budgets of patience and tolerance that make space for a canonical white American male author at a time when such status threatens the democratic ideals even Matthiessen espoused.[1] "Canon building," says Toni Morrison succinctly, "is Empire building. Canon defense is national defense."[2] Yet Morrison claims Melville for a critical praxis that is non-exclusionary, that applauds him for the "dangerous, solitary, radical work" of questioning "the very notion of white progress, the very idea of racial superiority, of whiteness as privileged place."[3]

It is not clear that Morrison's view is shared throughout the large popular culture that continues to embrace Melville's works. A steady stream of novelizations, graphic novels, Hollywood films, and reading marathons in the last five years alone demonstrates Melville's staying power, but it also prolifically mixes its messages.[4] Ta-Nehisi Coates judges the opening

---

[1] On Matthiessen's politics, see Leo Marx, "Double Consciousness and the Cultural Politics of F. O. Matthiessen," *Monthly Review* 34 (1983): 34–55.

[2] Toni Morrison, "Unspeakable Things Unspoken: The Afro-American Presence in American Literature," *Michigan Quarterly Review* 28 (1989): 1–34, 8.

[3] *Ibid.*, 18.

[4] Recent novelizations include Michael Shelden, *Melville in Love: The Secret Life of Herman Melville and the Muse of Moby-Dick* (New York: Ecco/Harper Collins, 2016); and Mark Beauregard, *The Whale: A Love Story* (New York: Viking, 2016). China Miéville's *Railsea* (New York: Del Rey/Ballantine, 2013) borrows plot and descriptive details from *Moby-Dick*. For graphic novels see Alan Moore and Kevin O'Neill, *Nemo Trilogy* (Marietta, GA: Top Shelf Productions, 2015), which contains *Hearts of Ice* (2013), *The Roses of Berlin* (2014), and *River of Ghosts* (2015), all drawing on

paragraph of *Moby-Dick* as the greatest in "not just human history, but galactic and extra-terrestrial history too," and Russ Castronovo accepts Bartleby as the hero of Occupy Wall Street.[5] But critics have observed how Captain Ahab serves radically opposed political and racial discourses, a figure, for example, for both Osama Bin Laden *and* George W. Bush.[6] Melvilleculture is mixed up in other ways too. At reading marathons, conferences, and libraries, on board America's last whaling ship, the *Charles W. Morgan*, or in coffee-shops with a famous Nantucket name, I have met Portuguese-speaking descendants of Cape Verdean and Azorean whaling men, female Japanese scholars stirred by Melville's portrayals of Native Americans, old and young salts from Mystic Seaport, San Francisco, or Szczecin, Poland, not to mention schoolteachers and their students, retirees and four-year-olds, scientists and computer programmers, artists, musicians, and actors, of many nations, races, and religious persuasions – most professing to be inspired by Melville, but not a few ashamed to admit to perplexity and boredom.

How to address or even understand this phenomenon? A facile but still intriguing hypothesis might be that Matthiessen's canon and the so-called myth-and-symbol school of American literature have had more lasting influence than scholars care to admit. For surely one thing that animates Melville's diverse and increasingly global readers, like Ishmael's crowds of New Yorkers pouring through Manhattan's streets to the "extremest limit of the land" before diving into the sea, is the power of Melville's symbols.[7] The white whale is vast and terrifying enough on his own. As the above image from "Loomings" further suggests, Melville's *spatial* symbolism, which

characters or plot elements from *Moby-Dick*. The 2015 film *In the Heart of the Sea* (dir. Ron Howard) merges Nathaniel Philbrick's history, *In the Heart of the Sea: The Tragedy of the Whaleship Essex* (New York: Penguin, 2001), with a fictionalized Melville struggling to write *Moby-Dick*. San Francisco held its first *Moby-Dick* Marathon in October 2015, New York City followed with one in November 2015, and in 2017 the New Bedford Whaling Museum celebrated the twenty-first anniversary of its annual *Moby-Dick* Marathon; the Mystic Seaport Museum of America and the Sea held its thirty-first in August, 2016. Note also Jake Heggie's opera, *Moby-Dick*, which premiered in Dallas, 2010.

5 Ta-Nehisi Coates, "And Now for a Much Deserved Moment of Insanity," *The Atlantic* (May 26, 2011), n.p. Web. Accessed October 9, 2016. www.theAtlantic.com/; Russ Castronovo, "Occupy Bartleby," *J19* 2.2 (2014): 253–72.

6 Edward Said, "Islam and the West are Inadequate Banners," *The Observer* (September 16, 2001). Web. Accessed July 15, 2016. www.theguardian.com/world/2001/sep/16/september11.terrorism3; William Spanos, *Herman Melville and the American Calling: The Fiction After Moby-Dick, 1951–1857* (Albany: SUNY Press, 2008).

7 Herman Melville, *Moby-Dick*, ed. J. Bryant and H. Springer (New York: Pearson, 2007), 22. Further references appear in the text in parentheses.

often juxtaposes oceanic vastness with urban complexity in jarringly contemporary ways, produces awesome effects as well. A text like *Moby-Dick*, *Pierre*, *Clarel*, or *Billy Budd* presents a challenging and often unimaginable terrain. Even when Melville carefully maps his spaces – the stacked decks of his "city afloat" in *White-Jacket*, the "great highway" of waters off the Cape of Good Hope in *Moby-Dick* (222), the labyrinthine streets of *Redburn* and *Pierre*, or the oceanic wasteland of *Clarel*'s Judean desert – readers may feel lost in symbolic depths.[8]

While not directly focusing on Melville's spatial imagination, F. O. Matthiessen offered a vocabulary that readers still turn to today, a binary opposition of Ocean and City as deeply significant and knowable. As this chapter will suggest, interest in Melville's spatial symbols has grown and changed with the development of new models for thinking about space – in historical terms, within ideological frameworks, and more recently in the context of the so-called "spatial turn" in American Studies, as part of an emerging field that has been called literary cartography. Innovative digital tools have provided ways to map symbolic terrains systematically and offer new ways to read and visualize the spatial dimensions of literary texts. Yet, remarkably, it appears that Melville was already mapping his texts in the nineteenth century and that he may have sped past or even undermined what we can learn from digital visualization of his symbolic geographies. Indeed, in his construction of spatial domains, he energetically *un*-mapped the symbolic systems that until recently supported assumptions about literary cartography. That mental agility, the ease that permitted Melville to traverse a large expanse of imaginative space without typical maps, may turn out to be his greatest gift to readers constrained by the ideological undercarriages of digital texts.

Melville's Symbolism, Then and Now

Melville's grateful, seemingly baffled letter to Sophia Hawthorne on receipt of her praise of *Moby-Dick* suggests the difficulties critics face when discussing Melville's spatial symbolism in F. O. Matthiessen's wake. Matthiessen quotes only part of a passage in Melville's letter that begins: "[Y]our allusion for example to the 'Spirit Spout [*sic*] first showed to me that there was

---

[8] Herman Melville, "White-Jacket: Or the World in a Man-of-War," in *The Writings of Herman Melville*, ed. Harrison Hayford, Hershel Parker, and G. Thomas Tanselle (Chicago and Evanston: Northwestern University Press/Newberry Library), 74. Further references appear in the text in parentheses.

a subtile significance in that thing – but I did not, in that case, *mean* it."[9]
Matthiessen's quotation below includes some editing of Melville's text:

> I had some vague idea while writing it, that the whole book was susceptible of
> an allegorical construction, and also that parts of it were – but the specialty of
> many of the particular subordinate allegories were first revealed to me, after
> reading Mr. Hawthorne's letter, which, without citing any particular examples,
> yet intimated the part-and-parcel allegoricalness of the whole.[10]

It may be hard to swallow the idea that until the Hawthornes pointed it out
Melville saw no allegorical significance in *Moby-Dick*. But for Matthiessen,
the letter explained "the unconscious working of the creative mind" (250),
a mind that he thought resembled Hawthorne's and those of "many other
writers of the age who, notwithstanding wide divergences, took for granted
the pre-eminence of spirit over matter" (242) and employed symbolic images
accordingly. If to Sophia Hawthorne Melville expressed uncertainty over
the "subtile significance" of *Moby-Dick*, he seemed to Matthiessen a master of symbol-making, especially in imagining cosmic struggles between man
and society, good and evil, or light and dark. More than any previous critic,
Matthiessen established Melville's dominance of the American canon as a matter of writing in a poetic language that carried considerable symbolic freight.

After *American Renaissance*, speculation over Melville's creative process
and production of symbols had to proceed, at first, on the basis of little more
than Matthiessen's inspired rhetoric. Melville left almost no manuscript
evidence: some scraps of *Typee* and *The Confidence-Man*, an unpublished
story and the unfinished *Billy Budd*, a few letters, some travel diaries. The
first generation of scholars depended on studies of Melville's sources and his
marginalia for an understanding of how his "creative mind" worked. In the
second half of the twentieth century, as New Critical interest in symbolism
gave way to theories of the text as historical artifact, social document, or
expression of imagined communities and transnational identities, Melville's
symbolism has flourished in a popular space, where the white whale remains
the nation's most fluid emblem of excessive signification.

With late-twentieth-century digital texts and editions, academic scholarship and popular culture have continued to coalesce around Melville's
works, especially *Moby-Dick*, with a new interest in exploring his influence

---

[9] Herman Melville, *Correspondence*, ed. Lynn Horth, in *The Writings of Herman Melville*, ed. Harrison Hayford, Hershel Parker, and G. Thomas Tanselle (Evanston and Chicago: Northwestern University Press and the Newberry Library, 1993), 219.
[10] F. O. Matthiessen, *American Renaissance: Art and Expression in the Age of Emerson and Whitman* (New York: Oxford University Press, 1941), 250. Further references appear in the text in parentheses.

on popular culture. In just one example, the twenty-first-century Norton Critical Edition of *Moby-Dick* edited by Hershel Parker includes a section of readings on the presence of Melville's novel in popular arts and new media.[11] The *Melville Electronic Library*, besides offering digital editions of Melville's texts with tools for scholarly interactive editing, also includes "rooms" for manuscripts and family papers, works of art (a gallery of images Melville knew), or maps and itineraries.[12] The work that Matthiessen began by first identifying Melville's symbolism now continues in digital editions and archives that map that symbolism onto a wider range of media – and make it accessible to a far wider range of interested readers.

Spatial Symbols: Ocean and City

One of Matthiessen's symbolic patterns that remains relevant, although it did not attract much attention in *American Renaissance,* is the tension between Ocean and City – a dualism that like the many others that Matthiessen introduced has structured thinking about Melville as a writer of conflicting domains. This duality engaged twentieth-century New Historicist scholars interested in establishing Melville as a social writer of the burgeoning American city, in contrast with the maritime Melville, who came to seem a sort of innocent Caspar Hauser wandering dazedly throughout the modern metropolis. By the late twentieth century, studies of Melville's Ocean and City as symbolic, social, or historical sites had shifted in response to new theories of spatiality – ideas that, even if they seem a long way from *American Renaissance,* might have appeared congenial to Matthiessen's way of thinking.

How so? We can credit Matthiessen with deploying the dualisms that helped popularize the idea of Meville's Ocean and City as radically and spatially distinct. But Matthiessen's argument for symbolic polarities is not so simple, and it rests on complicating political as much as aesthetic categories. While proclaiming an "American bias" (242) toward spirit over matter, Matthiessen also criticized an American bias toward allegorical abstraction. By a logic that equated greatness with tragedy, and tragedy with an awareness of social constraints on character, he argued that both Hawthorne and Melville found in tragedy an avenue to social

---

[11] See, for example, Mary K. Bercaw Edwards and Wyn Kelley, "Melville and the Spoken Word," in *Moby-Dick,* Norton Critical Edition, ed. Hershel Parker (New York: Norton, 2018). The edition also includes an essay by Robert K. Wallace on Melville and the visual arts and another by Timothy Marr on Melville and Islam.

[12] *Melville Electronic Library,* John L. Bryant, Director (Hempstead, NY: Hofstra University). Web. Accessed October 9, 2016. http://mel.hofstra.edu/.

art: "The creation of tragedy demands of its author a mature understanding of the relation of the individual to society, and more especially, of the nature of good and evil. He must have a coherent grasp of social forces, or, at least, of man as a social being ... [f]or the hero of a tragedy is never merely an individual, he is a man in action, in conflict with other individuals in a definite social order" (179). In the last paragraph of *American Renaissance*, Matthiessen claims that Melville did not achieve greatness entirely through his use of symbolism: "The search for the meaning of life that could be symbolized through the struggle between Ahab and the White Whale was neither so lucid nor so universal" as in the epics of Western literature, *Paradise Lost* and *Faust* (656). He credits Melville rather with something perhaps more significant: an apprehension of "the tragedy of extreme individualism, the disasters of the selfish will, the agony of a spirit so walled within itself that it seemed cut off from any possibility of salvation" (656). In responding fully to "perpetual suffering in the heart of man," Matthiessen's Melville "fulfilled what Coleridge held to be the major function of the artist: he brought 'the whole soul of man into activity' " (656).

Matthiessen's book thus ends with a Melville who is involved in social "activity," not contemplation – in the "heroic present," not some "hidden past" (656). This is a socially engaged Melville, and it bespeaks a politically motivated Matthiessen, whom Samuel Otter has shown as reading literary language with awareness of the contradictions of history, with a vision of "an alienated fraternity of discontent with capitalism and secularism," and from a position that "testifies to tension and imbalance as much as, or more than, it claims to reconcile opposing forces."[13] Although Matthiessen offers a view of literature as bridging "the gap between two poles of thought, to reconcile fact and abstraction, the many and the One, society and solitude" (3), Otter's essay suggests that Matthiessen's work endures precisely because of its *failure* to resolve the tensions – literary but also social and political – that it proposes.

If so, then we might reconsider the persistence into our time of a certain conception of Matthiessen's legacy: as showing that Melville deploys rigid, binary symbols that create prolonged struggle before tragic resolution. It has been difficult to shake this popular idea. Even before Donald Pease's influential Cold-War Melville, and perhaps even more vigorously since, the whiteness of Melville's whale and the blackness of his Hawthornian moral vision have come to seem fierce combatants in a war of mutually

---

[13] Samuel Otter, "*American Renaissance* and Us," *Journal of Nineteenth-Century Americanists* 3.2 (2015): 228–35, 229, 230, 234.

assured destruction.[14] In relation to geographical symbolism of Ocean and City, however, Matthiessen was not so polemical nor the conflict he suggested so stark. He may have placed Ocean and City in mutual relief by selecting Melville's nautical *Moby-Dick* in contrast with, if not opposition to, urban *Pierre* (vii). But beyond that basic pairing, Matthiessen did not attend as closely to the city–sea binary as we might expect. He speaks of oceanic rhythms in Whitman's verse and notes that Melville too writes out of "the hitherto unplumbed depths of his being, which were sluiced open by the lulling rhythm" (566) of the sea. But Pierre's New York he sees as a backdrop, not a significant alternate space; "Pierre [has not] succeeded in making any contact with the city around him" (469), and neither, seemingly has Matthiessen. In fact, he speaks only briefly of Ocean and City, as of "Bartleby, the Scrivener," in saying: "'Bartleby' is the tragedy of utter negation, of the enduring hopelessness of a young man who is absolutely alone, 'a bit of wreck in the *mid-Atlantic' which is New York*" (493; emphasis mine). Here Matthiessen simply elides any binary relation between the "mid-Atlantic" and New York itself. They are one.

It fell to later critics to develop Melville's identity as an urban writer in distinction to or productive tension with his maritime career.[15] Many had to reckon with a feature of Melville's nautical fiction that Matthiessen seems to have recognized without much concern: in some of his most compelling passages, Melville writes of city and sea as inhabiting the same imaginative, if not geographical, space. This habit suggests that for Melville, at least, Ocean and City worked as symbols mutually constitutive of rather than antagonistic to each other. In that sense, we may see Melville's work as lending itself to multi-layered digital representations of his geographical imagination.

---

[14] Donald E. Pease, "*Moby-Dick* and the Cold War," in *The American Renaissance Reconsidered*, ed. Walter Benn Michaels and Donald E. Pease (Baltimore: Johns Hopkins University Press, 1985), 113–55. Christopher Castiglia, "Cold War Allegories and the Politics of Criticism," in *The New Cambridge Companion to Herman Melville*, ed. Robert S. Levine (Cambridge: Cambridge University Press, 2014), 219–32.

[15] David S. Reynolds, *Beneath the American Renaissance: The Subversive Imagination in the Age of Emerson and Melville* (New York: Alfred A. Knop, 1988); Dana Brand, *The Spectator and the City in Nineteenth Century New York* (Cambridge: Cambridge University Press, 1991); Hans Bergmann, *God in the Street: New York Writing from the Penny Press to Melville* (Philadelphia: Temple University Press, 1995); Wyn Kelley, *Melville's City: Urban and Literary Form in Nineteenth-Century New York* (Cambridge: Cambridge University Press, 1996); Sheila Post-Lauria, *Correspondent Colorings: Melville in the Marketplace* (Amherst: University of Massachusetts Press, 1996); John Evelev, *Tolerable Entertainment: Herman Melville and Professionalism in Antebellum New York* (Amherst and Boston: University of Massachusetts Press, 2006).

Fluid Space in Melville's Writing

A few examples make this pattern evident and suggest the ways Melville's literary cartography may have prefigured the digital visualizations of our time. Although characters like Redburn and Ishmael leave clearly bounded cities – in each case Manhattan – to embark on a clearly defined sea, or like Israel Potter shuttle back and forth between sea and land, the narrative consciousness of many of Melville's early prose works moves fluidly between different domains. In at least three areas – the ship itself, human character, and narrative discourse – city and sea interpenetrate, breaking down the binaries that otherwise structure narrative movement.

The ship is Melville's most noticeable meeting place of city and sea. In *Redburn*, Melville's protagonist faces the same social challenges whether he is sailing on the *Highlander* or wandering around Liverpool. Like New York's Five Points, the vessel contains a range of racial and social types, each one stimulating the inexperienced Redburn to stretch his tolerance and understanding. The perplexing shipboard world of complex rigging, complicated knots, and confusing rituals reminds him of his first exposure to Manhattan's underworld. Yet when he reaches Liverpool, his journey through its extensive system of walled docks – "each Liverpool dock is a walled town" – surrounded by a maze of crowded streets, suggests that he has hardly left the ship's dense and bewildering structure when he steps ashore.[16] On his return voyage, the quarters of the emigrants, kept below-decks like slaves, appear to Redburn a "crowded jail" (287), where men, women, and children suffer the same conditions that in Liverpool's Lancelot's-Hey lead to death by starvation in a cellar.

The blending of ship and city becomes even more obvious in *White-Jacket*, subtitled a "World in Man-of-War," where Melville maps in detail the social and geographical complexities of this city in the sea. The marines' leader, Jack Chase, appears to celebrate the ship's urban character when he declares, "a man-of-war is to whalemen, as a metropolis is to shire-towns" (16). "With its crew of 800 or 1,000 men, a three-decker is a city on the sea" (144), claims White Jacket, describing the decks as a "Broadway in winter" (117), a naval maneuver as exciting "as great a commotion as if a whole city ward were in a blaze" (67), and the gun decks as combustible realms, "any one of which, touched by the smallest spark, was powerful enough to blow up a whole street of warehouses" (129). On the naval ship, "the sins

---

[16] Herman Melville, *Redburn: His First Voyage*, in *The Writings of Herman Melville*, ed. Harrison Hayford, Hershel Parker, G. Thomas Tanselle (Chicago and Evanston: Northwestern University Press/Newberry Library, 1969), 165. Further references appear in the text in parentheses.

for which the cities of the plain were overthrown still linger in some of these wooden-walled Gomorrahs of the deep" (375–6). With its decks resembling the storeys of boarding houses and its secret recesses similar to New York's hidden rookeries, the *Neversink*'s structure contains White Jacket in an urban environment at sea.

Melville extends the urban metaphor to his seagoing characters as well as his ships. Jackson in *Redburn* "dressed a good deal like a Bowery boy" (56) – or in the parlance of Walt Whitman and George C. Foster, a "b'hoy." The steward Lavender is a "handsome, dandy mulatto, that had once been a barber in West-Broadway" (83). In *White-Jacket* the master-at-arms Bland, like Claggart in *Billy Budd*, is a devious chief of police whom Melville compares with the master Parisian detective Vidocq. Perhaps the most surprising urban characters appear in *Moby-Dick*, which begins in Ishmael's Manhattan. Father Mapple retreats to the Ehrenbreitstein of his pulpit (53), and Captain Ahab's isolation is described as "the masoned, walled-town of a Captain's exclusiveness, which admits but small entrance to any sympathy from the green country without" (475). Ahab's soul is also described as an "Hotel de Cluny" wherein a seeker descends to the ruins of an ancient Roman town (177). The whale's body too is an urban artifact, with its "tail like a Lima tower" (388), the forehead a "dead, impregnable, ininjurable wall" (304), and the brain "like the innermost citadel within the amplified fortifications of Quebec" (313). In extending his urban imagery to ocean mammals, as well as men at sea, Melville suggests the fluid geography of narrative space.

That fluidity exhibits itself in narrators as well, who seldom let a reader forget that they imaginatively navigate both City and Ocean. Tommo in *Typee* stops his narration of life in the Marquesas to remind a reader of his Manhattan location: "Even now, amidst all the bustle and stir of the proud and busy city in which I am dwelling, the image of those three trees seems to come as vividly before my eyes as if they were actually present."[17] In just one example among many, Ishmael's "Town-Ho's Story" extends Tommo's cosmopolitanism through a dazzling array of shifting perspectives, as he addresses cavaliers in Lima, and speaks of Parisian revolutionaries, freebooters in Erie Canal groggeries, captains and mates at sea, and the mysterious whale himself, a "wondrous, inverted visitation" from God (222). In *Pierre*, where the protagonist spends the second half of the novel in New York, Melville's narrator reverses the pattern somewhat, presenting *Pierre* as a heroic voyager who experiences the shocks of life in the earth's remotest sites: "One in a city of hundreds and thousands of human beings, Pierre

[17] Herman Melville, *Typee: A Peep at Polynesian Life*, in *The Writings of Herman Melville*, ed. H. Hayford, H. Parker, and G. T. Tanselle (Chicago and Evanston: Northwestern University Press and the Newberry Library, 1968), 244.

was as solitary as at the Pole."[18] The narrator's style, much like Ishmael's, juxtaposes, often disconcertingly, the extremes of Ocean and City within the same expansive view. At a moment, for example, when he considers leaving his protected life for the uncertainties of New York, "there came into the mind of Pierre, thoughts and fancies never imbibed within the gates of towns; but only given forth by the atmosphere of primeval forests, which, with the eternal ocean, are the only unchanged general objects remaining to this day, from those that originally met the gaze of Adam" (139). Even without mapping the movements of Melville's characters, one can note the geographical fluidity of their thoughts, ranging widely over the boundaries that separate humans from landscapes and each other.

Mapping and Un-Mapping

The kind of discursive fluidity and geographical simultaneity that Matthiessen evoked in his sentence about Bartleby and that in many novels Melville deployed as a matter of course has been brilliantly realized in new forms of twenty-first-century cartography. These have shed light on not only technological but also racial, social, and political issues in the use of geographic symbolism. The development that some scholars have called a "spatial turn" in literary studies has stimulated a wide range of responses to new geographical thinking.

Much of that response has been richly generative and expansive. Models of literary mapping in global space – or global mapping in literary space – have proliferated with the growth of not only digital cartography but also distant reading methods inspired by Franco Moretti, Ryan Cordell, and others.[19] The term "geocriticism" bears a family resemblance to "ecocriticism," as a set of practices merging humanities and scientific thinking in fluid configurations.[20] A number of critics have laid the groundwork for the spatial turn

---

[18] H. Melville, *Pierre, or the Ambiguities*, in *The Writings of Herman Melville*, ed. H. Hayford, H. Parker, and G. T. Tanselle (Chicago and Evanston: Northwestern University Press/Newberry Library, 1971), 338. Further references appear in the text in parentheses.

[19] Franco Moretti, *Graphs, Maps, Trees: Abstract Models for a Literary History* (London: Verso, 2005); Ryan Cordell, "Melville in the First Age of Viral Media," keynote address, Melville Electronic Library's Fifth Annual Meeting (MELCamp 5), cosponsored by the NEH and the MIT Literature and Comparative Media Studies Groups, Massachusetts Institute of Technology, April 30, 2015.

[20] Lawrence Buell, *The Environmental Imagination: Thoreau, Nature Writing, and the Formation of American Culture* (Cambridge, MA: Belknap Press.1995); Bertrand Westphal, *Geocriticism: Real and Fictional Spaces*, trans. Robert T. Tally, Jr. (New York: Palgrave Macmillan, 2011); Robert T. Tally, Jr., *Spatiality* (London: Routledge, 2013).

in literary and cultural studies, lending momentum to postmodern, transat-lantic, and post-national theory.[21] And a wave of titles suggests the impact on American literary criticism of new theories of spatiality: from Rebecca Faery's *Cartographies of Desire* to Martin Brückner's and Hsuan L. Hsu's *American Literary Geographies* to Robert T. Tally, Jr.'s *Melville, Mapping, and Globalization: Literary Cartography in the American Baroque Writer*.[22] I do not mean to suggest that these investigations all point in the same direc-tion or constitute a unified field – the retrospective essays and overviews are beginning to appear – but we might note the energy with which American Studies scholars have seized on digital cartography as a hermeneutic model.[23]

The spatial turn nevertheless has its critics, especially in relation to the tendency in geographically informed narratives toward abstraction. Among some adopters of GIS technology and mapping software for uses in the humanities, the question of tools reveals field-related fractures and fric-tions. For example, in their 2013 report "Deep Mapping and the Spatial Humanities," David J. Bodenhamer, John Corrigan, and Trevor M. Harris point out that "unabridged geo-spatial technologies, such as GIS, that are based on positivist epistemologies [are] often ill-suited to the humanities."[24]

---

[21] Gaston Bachelard, *The Poetics of Space*, trans. Maria Jolas (Boston: Beacon Press, 1958, repr. 1994); Michel Foucault, *The Order of Things: An Archaeology of the Human Sciences* (New York: Random House, 1970); Yi-Fu Tuan, *Space and Place: The Perspective of Experience* (Minneapolis: University of Minnesota Press, 1977); Edward W. Soja, *Postmodern Geographies: The Reassertion of Space in Critical Social Theory* (London: Verso, 1989); and Henri Lefebvre, *The Production of Space*, trans. Donald Nicholson-Smith (Oxford: Blackwell, 1991).

[22] Rebecca Blevins Faery, *Cartographies of Desire: Captivity, Race, and Sex in the Shaping of an American Nation* (Norman: University of Oklahoma Press, 1999); Martin Brückner and Hsuan L. Hsu, *American Literary Geographies: Spatial Practice and Cultural Production 1500–1900* (Newark: University of Delaware Press, 2007); Robert T. Tally, Jr., *Melville, Mapping, and Globalization: Literary Cartography in the American Baroque Writer* (New York: Continuum, 2009); also Bruce Harvey, *American Geographics: U.S. National Narratives and the Representation of the Non-European World, 1830–1865* (Palo Alto: Stanford University Press, 2002); Hsuan L. Hsu, *Geography and the Production of Space in Nineteenth-Century American Literature* (Cambridge: Cambridge University Press, 2010); and Paul Giles, *The Global Remapping of American Literature* (Princeton: Princeton University Press, 2011).

[23] Hester Blum, "Melville and Oceanic Studies," in *The New Cambridge Companion to Herman Melville*, ed. Robert S. Levine (Cambridge: Cambridge University Press, 2014), 22–36; Martin Brückner, "The Cartographic Turn and American Literary Studies: Of Maps, Mappings, and the Limits of Metaphor," in *Turns of Event: Nineteenth-Century American Literary Studies in Motion*, ed. Hester Blum (Philadelphia: University of Pennsylvania Press, 2016), 40–60.

[24] David J. Bodenhamer, John Corrigan, and Trevor M. Harris, "Deep Mapping and the Spatial Humanities," *International Journal of Humanities and Arts Computing* 7.1–2 (2013): 170–5, 170. Web. Accessed November 4, 2015. https://doi.org/10.3366/ijhac.2013.0087.

Similarly, in her chapter in *Debates in the Digital Humanities*, Johanna Drucker emphasizes that "the *ideology* of almost all current information visualization is anathema to humanistic thought, antipathetic to its aims and values."[25] Robert T. Tally, Jr., drawing on Bertrand Westphal and Frederic Jameson, asserts that any contemporary system of cartographic visualization has to be contextualized and analyzed carefully: "The recent spatial turn in literary and cultural studies has, for the most part, been a product of, or response to, the postmodern condition."[26] This response to postmodern conditions, as the authors of *Digital_Humanities* suggest, is deeply imbedded in the ways we now must read skeptically even the richly detailed and digitally enhanced maps and spatial narratives that some designers call "thick maps": for "thick maps betray the contingency of looking, the groundedness of any perspective, and the embodied relationality inherent to any locative investigation."[27] In a recent interview in *PC*, Johanna Drucker likewise warns about special problems of digital visualization in relation to sensitive cultural issues: "We need subtler, more complex, more layered, and more lifecycle and culturally-specific visualizations. Those visualizations are still a long way off, I think, since they would require creating non-standard metrics and data models that do not rely on Cartesian principles, but affective, emergent, and co-dependent data models."[28] With this statement, Drucker addresses a problem with many theories of the spatial turn, namely their seeming neglect of social issues at the heart of American Studies – issues of race and gender, class and religion, nation and homelessness that are also central to any consideration of Melville's art.

There is no question that digital technology opens up new vistas in Melville scholarship, making it possible, for example, to map and even virtually experience multiple environmental layers within a single view. In spatial terms, digital renderings of New York can represent areas, like Battery Park, that were once ocean and are now land, and temporal layers can be visualized as well in the new affordances of digital maps. To the extent that Ocean and City can now inhabit the same virtual space, digital mapping might seem to fulfill the promise of Matthiessen's vision of a New York that is at the same time "mid-Atlantic," and a "mid-Atlantic" that is at once New York.

[25] Johanna Drucker, "Humanistic Theory and Digital Scholarship," in *Debates in the Digital Humanities*, ed. Matthew Gold (Minneapolis: University of Minnesota Press, 2012), 85–95, 86.

[26] Tally, *Spatiality*, 38.

[27] Anne Burdick, Johanna Drucker, Peter Lunenfeld, and Jeffrey Schnapp, *Digital_Humanities* (Cambridge, MA: The MIT Press, 2013), 47.

[28] William Fenton, "Humanizing Maps: An Interview with Johanna Drucker," *PC*, October 1, 2015, n.p. Web. www.pcmag.com/article2/0,2817,2492337,00.asp.

But in their focus on contemporary conditions, current debates about the spatial turn seem to have missed a salient point: the possibility of fluid, resistant, even nonhuman maps and mapping in an earlier time. It is this possibility, among others, that Melville may be wrestling with by undoing or un-mapping conventional maps, especially in *Redburn* and *Moby-Dick*. His unsettling of the categories of sea and land, Ocean and City speaks to Matthiessen's implicit contention that Melville, like Bartleby, inhabits different spatial worlds at once. Melville's *un*-mappings, the ways he unsettles his own mapping projects, may lead to a deeper understanding of his geographical imagination than digital tools can.

Maps appear regularly in Melville's texts, starting with his hand-drawn frontispiece to *Typee* and reaching a witty peak in Ishmael's comment that Kokovoko "is not down in any map; true places never are" (67).[29] For an understanding of Melville's geography of Ocean and City, two particular maps are vital. The first is the map of Liverpool that appears in the guidebook Redburn uses and then discards during his visit. Redburn depends on the guidebook because it steered his beloved late father aright in an earlier time. But now he learns that "this world ... is a *moving* world" (157), and the guidebook no longer guides; the map no longer represents the world Redburn sees in front of him. A Rip Van Winkle in Liverpool, Redburn discovers that his "infallible" (151) guidebook is but a work of fiction after all. Although he feels affection for what he calls the "old Morocco!" (152) (an interesting geographical reference), he puts it aside.

Melville's un-mapping here, or his undoing of the map's legitimacy, grows out of an understanding that space changes, that time shapes space: "its sands are forever shifting" (157). Mapping renders the imagining of place in a two-dimensional medium. But Melville derives humor from Redburn's dawning awareness of what is after all a hoary cliché that time marches on, that the sands of time run their course, and that human histories cannot be fixed in a flat spatial representation. For Redburn, as for Matthiessen's Bartleby, the urban setting takes on the fluidity of the sea, and it seems prescient that Melville's Liverpool is enclosed between two Atlantic voyages, is itself, then, "mid-Atlantic" at the same time that it is insistently urban.

A further irony emerges from Ishmael's consideration of Ahab's chart, another well-known example of Melville's treatment of maps and mapping. Ahab's sea-chart imagines space in ways quite different from a land-map,

---

29 On Melville's *Typee* map, see Christopher N. Phillips, "Mapping Imagination and Experience in Melville's Pacific Novels," in *"Whole Oceans Away": Melville and the Pacific*, ed. Jill Barnum, Wyn Kelley, and Christopher Sten (Kent, OH: Kent State University Press, 2007), 124–38.

namely, as oriented to the sea, an alien place for humans, and toward animals of the sea, with their alien intelligence. Melville un-maps the chart even further by undoing the human biases of mapping, thus in effect using it to create a city of whales.

Like most maps, a sea-chart addresses human needs and interests. Both serve conquest and capitalism. Both inspire dreams of success through exploration and exploitation. But the chart Ahab studies particularly focuses on the denizens of the sea, thus expanding the narrative range and power of conventional maps. It is a version of one of Matthew Fontaine Maury's grandest achievements, the 1851 "Whale Chart" based on his research into whaling captains' logs stored at the Naval Observatory in Washington, DC.[30] By compiling accounts of sightings of different species over time and in different oceans of the world, Maury mapped the likely courses of different groups of whales, noting when and where they might appear in popular feeding grounds throughout the year. Any whaling captain would appreciate this early effort of data mining and visualization, designed to collect and represent a whole archive of findings in one legible document.

Read as Redburn reads his father's guidebook and map, however, as a work of fiction or imagining, the chart looks different. The whaling captains who logged the whales were simply noting when and where certain animals had appeared; Maury tried to record as clearly as possible what the captains had seen. But just as Redburn's world is a moving world, the whales' migrations are constantly in motion, determined by mysterious impulses in their environments and in their bodies. We might even begin to understand that the captains and Maury himself did not make this map. The whales' bodies did – and also their intelligence(s). The map is their text, as much as it is a human one. Ahab, hunched over the chart in his cabin, tries to decipher their movements and understand their decisions as much as to annotate and make sense of a geometrical grid of symbols. Moby Dick "tasks me; he heaps me" (159), says Ahab, the whale refusing to submit to human abstractions of his behavior.

In this respect, the Whale that appears in Chapter 134, "The Chase – Second Day" performs much as the whales do in Maury's chart – by providing his own text or map of his movements. In the midst of their final pursuit of Moby Dick, the men follow his wake and time his surfacings in order to determine when and where he will rise again. In an extended epic simile, Melville establishes the importance of the whale's wake as a

[30] Matthew F. Maury, *Whale Chart*, United States Navy (1851), Norman B. Leventhal Map Center at the Boston Public Library. Web. Accessed July 15, 2016. www .digitalcommonwealth.org/search/commonwealth:x633f952x.

message-bearing medium: "So that to this hunter's wondrous skill, the proverbial evanescence of a thing writ in water, a wake, is to all desired purposes well nigh as reliable as the steadfast land" (485). Melville's reference to the "thing writ in water" implicitly connects Moby Dick's markings of the sea to inscriptions on paper, and it helps, of course, that Melville is also quoting from John Keats's gravestone: "Here lies one whose name was writ in water" (see *MD* note, 568). As I have argued elsewhere, this passage suggests that *Moby-Dick* is the whale's story, not solely Ishmael's or Ahab's, and that although the whale's medium is "evanescent," humans can nevertheless read what Moby Dick has left for them to decipher.[31]

In his book *The Moral Lives of Animals*, which uses *Moby-Dick* to frame an argument about the moral logics by which humans maintain their superiority over the animal world, Dale Peterson argues that Melville was rare among nineteenth-century authors (indeed among many before or since) in assuming that whales had intelligence, advanced social systems, and signs of a consciousness that we might call moral.[32] I would go a step further to suggest that Melville implicitly maps the whales' global imaginings as well. That is, Maury's chart, while showing the whales as having bodies and agencies, cannot fully map their stories. Only Melville's novel can begin to do that, indicating that human maps and other kinds of texts leave a gap for literary imagination to fill. By un-mapping the maps at his disposal Melville can imagine and narrate worlds beyond human ones. The tautology of his title, *Moby-Dick: Or, the Whale*, doubles his insistence on the alien perspective of his novel cartography and suggests that the whales are telling the story of *Moby-Dick*, just as they are charting (placing on charts) their global positioning systems.

This sense of mapping as a shared enterprise crossing national, territorial, or even species boundaries is congenial with Melville's authorial cartographies as well as the methods of crowd-sourced digital maps. It captures life on the ground or at sea from the perspective of those who experience City or Ocean bodily and imaginatively as well. For a consideration of American Renaissance in a new century, it also captures the rhythms of constant, daily renewal of relations among all Earth's living inhabitants – of life lived and mapped, in Timothy Marr's moving phrase, according to a "planetary compass."[33]

---

[31] Wyn Kelley, "The Books of *Moby-Dick*," in *A Companion to the American Novel*, ed. Alfred Bendixen (Oxford: Wiley-Blackwell, 2012), 394–407.

[32] Dale Peterson, *The Moral Lives of Animals* (New York: Bloomsbury Press, 2012).

[33] Timothy Marr, "Melville's Planetary Compass," in *The New Cambridge Companion to Herman Melville*, ed. Robert S. Levine (Cambridge: Cambridge University Press, 2014), 187–201.

PART III

Beyond the Renaissance

12

DAVID HAVEN BLAKE

Whitman, In and Out of the American Renaissance

In his valedictory essay "A Backwards Glance O'er Travel'd Roads" (1888), Walt Whitman wrote that *Leaves of Grass* could never have emerged "from any other era than the latter half of the Nineteenth Century, nor any other land than democratic America, and from the absolute triumph of the National Union Arms."[1] As if it were a rock formation jutting out of the earth, he described his book as an "outcropping" of his emotional and personal state, "an attempt, from first to last, to put *a Person*, a human being (myself, in the latter half of the Nineteenth Century, in America,) freely, fully and truly on record" (*WPP*, 671). Nowhere does Whitman suggest that he was part of a literary or intellectual movement, and nowhere does he suggest that the years before the Civil War were more formative or consequential than the decades that succeeded them. "My Book and I – what a period we have presumed to span!" he marveled. "[T]hose thirty years from 1850 to '80 – and America in them!" (*WPP*, 660). Whitman had begun the preface to the first edition of *Leaves of Grass* with the image of a corpse being slowly taken out of a house as a "stalwart and wellshaped heir" waited to take its place (*WPP*, 5). In closing what came to be known as the Deathbed edition, his "definitive *carte visite* to the coming generations of the New World," Whitman insisted that readers see *Leaves of Grass* alongside a half-century of national events rather than the antebellum years (*WPP*, 656).

And yet many readers today would identify Whitman as the primary poet of the American Renaissance, the period from 1850 to 1855 that saw the publication of Ralph Waldo Emerson's *Representative Men* (1850), Nathaniel Hawthorne's *The Scarlet Letter* (1850), Herman Melville's *Moby-Dick* (1851), Henry David Thoreau's *Walden* (1854), and the first edition of *Leaves of Grass* (1855). When F. O. Matthiessen coined the term in his

---

[1] Walt Whitman, *Complete Poetry and Collected Prose*, ed. Justin Kaplan (New York: Library of America, 1982), 661. Unless otherwise noted, all future references to Whitman's poetry and prose will be to this edition and marked in the text as *WPP*.

1941 book, he marveled at how many "past masterpieces were produced in one extraordinarily concentrated moment of expression."[2] "It may not seem precisely accurate to refer to our mid-nineteenth century as a *re-birth*," he explained, "but that was how the writers themselves judged it. Not as a re-birth of values that had existed previously in America, but as America's way of producing a renaissance, by coming to first maturity and affirming its heritage in the whole expanse of art and culture."[3] In the image of Whitman's stalwart heir taking his rightful place, *Leaves of Grass* embodied the spirit that Matthiessen traced throughout these years. Americans did not repel the past, Whitman wrote, but they calmly knew that, among all nationalities, they themselves were the fittest for the new age (*WPP*, 5).

Matthiessen's *American Renaissance* appealed to an era that saw the United States' ascendance on the world stage. Emerson's claim that "We have listened too long to the courtly muses of Europe" was inspiring to the Harvard undergraduates he addressed in 1837.[4] Over a hundred years later, that sense of maturation must have rung true as the nation debated policies like the Marshall Plan to rebuild a war-torn Europe and Great Britain. Despite his own internationalist vision, Matthiessen's book lent itself to the national exceptionalism that dominated mid-century life.[5] While some enlisted Melville, Whitman, and Thoreau in their efforts to critique the Cold War liberal consensus, others viewed the writers' emergence in the antebellum period as a crucial step in the formation of national identity and global power. In Jonathan Arac's memorable phrase, the story of the American Renaissance became "a postwar myth of empire" and helped drive the nascent field of American Studies.[6] Even with the numerous efforts to expand and transform Matthiessen's original canon, the term continues to be extraordinarily durable and resilient. Whether invoked out of convenience or conviction, scholars have had difficulty critiquing the concept of an American Renaissance without also reinforcing it.[7]

---

[2] F. O. Matthiessen, *American Renaissance: Art and Expression in the Age of Emerson and Whitman* (New York: Oxford University Press, 1941, repr. 1968), vii.

[3] *Ibid.*

[4] Ralph Waldo Emerson, *Essays and Lectures*, ed. Joel Porte (New York: Library of America, 1983), 70. On the impact of the American Scholar address on the students who heard it, see Robert Milder, "The American Scholar as Cultural Event," *Prospects* 16 (1989): 119–47.

[5] On Matthiessen's internationalism, see William E. Cain, *F.O. Matthiessen and the Politics of Criticism* (Madison: University of Wisconsin Press, 1988), 116.

[6] Jonathan Arac, "F.O. Matthiessen, Authorizing an American Renaissance," *New Political Science* 7.1 (1996): 28.

[7] Consider two well-known examples that helped shaped literary studies at the end of the twentieth century: David Reynolds, *Beneath the American Renaissance: The Subversive Imagination in the Age of Emerson and Melville* (Cambridge, MA: Harvard University

For all the attention it has received, Matthiessen surprisingly did not come up with the title *American Renaissance* himself. He had written the book as *Man in the Open Air*, but his editor rejected that title, asking for something more "categorically descriptive."[8] The phrase comes from a passage in one of Whitman's notebooks in which the poet comments that literature is filled with stories about man indoors or under the artificial relations of love or battle, but "never before have we had man in the open air, his attitude adjusted by the seasons."[9] Matthiessen eventually shifted the title to the final section of the book where it introduces a discussion of the value of myth in the Emersonian age. "Man in the Open Air," however, provides an especially good headnote to Whitman and other writers of the period. The phrase aptly describes the aesthetic behind Melville's Ishmael, with his preference for unprotected mastheads and the "pure air of the fore-castle deck."[10] It neatly conveys the impulse behind Thoreau's removal to Walden Pond and his complaint in "Economy" that man has been so domesticated he has lost the capacity "to live in the open air."[11] And of course, it sets the tone for the unencumbered, light-hearted poet who, being "done with indoor complaints," invites his comrades to join his procession in the 1856 poem "Song of the Open Road" (*WPP*, 297). In each of these texts, the image of open air had both scenic and symbolic importance, reflecting the writers' interest in liberating individuals from the encumbrances of custom and history. Whitman cast that freedom as an opportunity for personal transformation. "Read these leaves in the open air every season of every year of your life," he promises, "and your very flesh shall be a great poem" (*WPP*, 11).

The movement from inside to outside is one of the central motifs in *Leaves of Grass*. At the beginning of "Song of Myself," the poet leaves the intoxicating, perfumed atmosphere of "houses and rooms" to embrace the natural world:

> The atmosphere is not a perfume, it has no taste of the distillation, it is
>   odorless,
> It is for my mouth forever, I am in love with it,

---

[8] See Harry Levin, *The Power of Blackness: Hawthorne, Poe, Melville* (New York: Knopf, 1958), vii–viii. On Levin's and Matthiessen's relationship, see also Marjorie Garber, *Loaded Words* (New York: Fordham University Press, 2012), 84.

[9] Walt Whitman, *Notes and Unpublished Prose Manuscripts, Vol. 4*, ed. Edward Grier (New York: New York University Press, 1984), 1536.

[10] Herman Melville, *Moby-Dick, or The Whale*, 2nd ed., ed. Hershel Parker and Harrison Hayford (New York: Norton, 2002), 21.

[11] Henry David Thoreau, *Walden*, ed. J. Lyndon Shanley (Princeton: Princeton University Press, 1989), 28.

Press, 1989) and *The American Renaissance Reconsidered*, ed. Walter Benn Michaels and Donald E. Pease (Baltimore: Johns Hopkins University Press, 1989).

I will go to the bank by the wood and become undisguised and naked,
I am mad for it to be in contact with me.   (*WPP*, 189)

The desire to escape indoor artifice, to take things directly and at first hand, appears prominently in Whitman's sprawling, episodic poem. A rich young woman hides behind the curtains in her fine house as she admires twenty-eight young men cavorting and swimming in the water. If only in her imagination, she, too, leaves the confines of the home and heads to the water to join them (*WPP*, 197–8). "Unscrew the locks from the doors!" the poet later commands. "Unscrew the doors from the jambs!" (*WPP*, 210). As if open air were the natural environment for democratic multiplicity, readers encounter Whitman's poet not in the confines of a library and not by a fireside or hearth, but in the barnyard surrounded by animals (*WPP*, 234) and on city streets as he speaks to his fellow citizens (*WPP*, 235). At the poem's end, the poet departs like air, but in keeping with the grass imagery, he bequeaths himself to the soil: "If you want me again," he tells his readers, "look for me under your bootsoles" (*WPP*, 247).

The psychologist William James praised Whitman for practicing a "religion of healthy-mindedness," and part of that religion emerges in the robust vigor he infuses into his activities.[12] His writings are filled with the pleasures of strength and physical exertion. "I am the teacher of athletes," he explains in "Song of Myself." "He that by me spreads a wider breast than my own proves the width of my own" (*WPP*, 242). In a recently discovered newspaper series titled "Manly Health and Training" (1857), Whitman wrote about the heroic, rejuvenating effects of being able to spring up "in the morning with light feelings, and the disposition to raise the voice in some cheerful song – to feel a pleasure in going forth into the open air."[13] Advising readers about exercise, diet, and nutrition, Whitman celebrated the feeling of being "buoyant in all your limbs and movements," of having "perfect command of your arms, legs, &c., able to strike out, if occasion demand, or to walk long distances, or to endure great labor without exhaustion."[14] This paean to vitality could easily have appeared in a notebook or preface associated with *Leaves of Grass*. Indeed, whether they are reading poetry or journalism, Whitman wants to cultivate in his readers a physical and spiritual expansiveness that radiates out of their individual selves and extends

---

[12] William James, *Writings 1902–1910* (New York: Library of America, 1988), 82.
[13] Mose Velsor [Walt Whitman], "Manly Health and Training, with Off-Hand Hints Toward Their Conditions," in *Walt Whitman Quarterly Review*, ed. Zachary Turpin 33.3 (2016): 216.
[14] *Ibid.*

to the universe. In "the morning atmosphere" of the American Renaissance, writers and readers prepared to be the heirs of newly awakened versions of themselves.[15] "Morning brings back the heroic ages," Thoreau proclaimed, urging his neighbors to stop slumbering through their days.[16] "Long enough have you dream'd contemptible dreams," Whitman tells us in "Song of Myself." "Now I wash the gum from your eyes,/ You must habit yourself to the dazzle of the light and of every moment of your life" (*WPP*, 242).

Like many of his contemporaries, Whitman associated this open-aired individualism with the spirit of New World democracy. Painters such as Thomas Cole, Frederick Edwin Church, and Albert Bierstadt focused their work not on portraiture or classical themes but on the apprehension of the sublime through nature. Writers for John L. O'Sullivan's magazine *Democratic Review* promoted a fervent cultural nationalism and aligned themselves with the Young America movement's emphasis on democratic reforms and the common man. (As part of his long career as a newspaper reporter and editor, Whitman published nearly a dozen stories and articles in the *Democratic Review*, including an anonymous self-review in which he praised the poet of the 1855 edition of *Leaves of Grass* for his "perfect naturalness, health, faith, self-reliance, and all primal expressions of the manliest love and friendship.")[17] And of course, Whitman shared much of this vision with Emerson, who not only encouraged readers to develop "an original relation" to the universe, one free of cultural constraints and conventions, but also zealously insisted that creative and intellectual activity were forms of action and power.[18] On this theme, Emerson was, as Matthiessen described him, "the cow from which the rest drew their milk."[19]

Compared to the skepticism of Melville and the loyalty of Thoreau, Whitman had a particularly complicated relationship with Emerson. An essential anecdote in the history of American literature is that, after receiving Emerson's letter congratulating him on the 1855 *Leaves of Grass*,

---

[15] In lectures and conversation Robert Milder has long spoken of the "morning atmosphere" of the American Renaissance. It appears most notably in *Hawthorne's Habitations: A Literary Life* (New York: Oxford University Press, 2013), 60.

[16] Thoreau, *Walden*, 88.

[17] Walt Whitman [unsigned in original], "Walt Whitman and His Poems." *The United States Review* 5 (September 1855), The Walt Whitman Archive. Gen. Eds. Ed Folsom and Kenneth M. Price. Accessed June 12, 2016. www.whitmanarchive.org.

[18] I refer to Emerson's opening question in "Nature," "Why should not we also enjoy an original relation to the universe?" (Emerson, *Essays and Lectures*, 7) and to his comments in "The American Scholar" that "The true scholar grudges every opportunity of action passed by, as a loss of power" (*ibid.*, 60).

[19] Matthiessen, *American Renaissance*, xii. Matthiessen borrows the phrase from Emerson's essay on Goethe.

Whitman published the contents, without permission, in the *New York Tribune*. He subsequently printed an excerpt from that letter – "I Greet You at the Beginning of A Great Career" – on the spine of the 1856 edition. Reinforcing this sense of connection, Whitman appended his own epistolary essay to that edition in which he addressed Emerson as "Dear Master" and compared him to a ship captain who had discovered new lands.

> Those shores you found. I say you have led The States there – have led Me there. I say that none has ever done, or ever can do, a greater deed for The States, than your deed. Others may line out the lines, build cities, work mines, break up farms; it is yours to have been the original true Captain who put to sea, intuitive, positive, rendering the first report, to be told less by any report, and more by the mariners of a thousand bays, in each tack of their arriving and departing, many years after you. (*WPP*, 1336)

Whitman was remarkably savvy about publicity and promotion, and his praise cleverly aligned *Leaves of Grass* with the most influential intellectual of the age. As Whitman presented it, the great emergence of American letters – the churning presses, the proliferating bookshops, the massive numbers of newspapers and periodicals being sold – was ultimately a sign of the cultural independence that Emerson helped create (*WPP*, 1329).

The morning air of Emerson's work contributed little, however, to the highly sexual, working-class persona that differentiated Whitman from many of his canonized peers. The 1855 *Leaves of Grass* introduced this figure with its frontispiece, a portrait of Whitman dressed in working men's clothes, his shirt collar open, and his right hand resting casually on his hip. A haughty, but also inviting expression appears on his face. As "one of the roughs" in the 1855 version of "Song of Myself," Whitman displayed unusual, even shocking, candor about sex and "the procreant urge of the world" (*WPP*, 50, 190).[20] Declaring his body to be as "clear and sweet" as his soul, he challenges a centuries-old binary that had subordinated the physical to the spiritual worlds. "Welcome is every organ and attribute of me, and of any man hearty and clean,/ Not an inch nor a particle of an inch is vile, and none shall be less familiar than the rest" (*WPP*, 190–1). In "I Sing the Body Electric" he catalogues body parts and loses himself in descriptions of sexual sensation: "Ebb stung by the flow and flow stung by the ebb, love-flesh swelling and deliciously aching,/ Limitless limpid jets of love hot and enormous, quivering jelly of love, white-blow and delirious juice" (*WPP*, 253).

---

[20] Whitman would drop the phrase "one of the roughs" from the Deathbed edition of *Leaves of Grass*.

"Whitman's language is more earthy," Matthiessen explained, "because he was aware, in a way that distinguished him not merely from Emerson but from every other writer of the day, of the power of sex."²¹ As Matthiessen saw it, Whitman's sexuality raised what was primarily a language problem: how does one describe carnality while still maintaining a transcendent, spiritual vision? But the poet who vowed to plunge his "semitic muscle" into the United States ("Song of Myself"), who celebrated the labial folds of vaginas ("Unfolded Out of the Folds"), and who wrote poems to prostitutes ("To a Common Prostitute") barely registers in *American Renaissance*. Walking on the Boston Common in 1860, Emerson tried convincing Whitman to revise the more graphically sexual poems in *Leaves of Grass* or consider eliminating them outright.²² Whitman refused. Eighty-one years later, Matthiessen presented his readers with a version of the polite book that Emerson preferred.

Considering the poet's heroic stature in the gay community, contemporary readers will be surprised that Matthiessen steered *American Renaissance* away from the 1860 Calamus poems that address what Whitman called "the manly love of comrades" ("For You O Democracy," *WPP*, 272). In recent decades, scholars have paid increasing attention to this cluster of lyric poems in which Whitman reflects on the adhesive, homosocial bonds that draw men together in the spirit of democracy. "As I walk by your side or sit near, or remain in the same room with you," he writes in "O You Whom I Often and Silently Come," "Little you know the subtle electric fire that for your sake is playing within me" (*WPP*, 286).

The omission is all the more startling, for as Jay Grossman has demonstrated, Matthiessen knew the Calamus poems well: he and his partner, painter Russell Cheney, used the poems to explain and validate their own homosexual relationship. In fact, in a letter to Matthiessen, Cheney quoted from "When I Heard at the Close of Day" about the peace that one man finds in the arms of another:

> I heard the hissing rustle of the liquid and sands as directed to me whispering
>   to congratulate me,
> For the one I love most lay sleeping by me under the same cover in the
>   cool night,
> In the stillness in the autumn moonbeams his face was inclined toward me,
> And his arm lay lightly around my breast – and that night I was happy.
>
> (*WPP*, 277)²³

²¹ Matthiessen, *American Renaissance*, 523.
²² Jerome Loving, *Walt Whitman: The Song of Himself* (Berkeley: University of California Press, 1999), 241.
²³ Jay Grossman, "The Canon in the Closet: Matthiessen's Whitman, Whitman's Matthiessen," *American Literature* 70.4 (December 1998): 807–8. For an equally

The concept of homosexuality did not exist in 1860, and like his contemporaries, Emerson found nothing unusual in the Calamus poems; his objections focused on the poems about men and women. Writing in the 1930s and 1940s, however, when charges of homosexuality could result in arrest or losing one's job, Matthiessen chose to omit Calamus from his analysis, effectively closeting the poems away from the canon he proposed in *American Renaissance*.[24]

That self-protective act seems fitting in the context of the sexual torment that periodically surfaces in Whitman's work. For all of its celebration of sex and the body, *Leaves of Grass* also describes guilt after masturbation, confusion about a lover's intentions, heart-breaking longing and rejection. Sex plays a crucial role in Whitman's religion of healthy-mindedness, but it is also the source of anguish and self-doubt.

The 1856 poem later titled "Crossing Brooklyn Ferry" is at once Whitman's most transcendental poem and his most psychologically attuned to sexuality. Like a painter working in shadow and light, the poet turns a ferryboat ride between Brooklyn and Manhattan into an extended meditation on time, intimacy, and the physical nature of being. "Crossing Brooklyn Ferry" was originally titled "Sun-Down Poem," and as the tides shift and the sun sets, the poet observes his fellow passengers and meditates both on the passage of time and the ability to connect with others across life and death. "I am with you, you men and women of a generation, or ever so many generations hence,/ Just as you feel when you look on the river and sky, so I felt,/ Just as any of you is one of a living crowd, I was one of a crowd" (*WPP*, 308–9). In contrast to the angst of such poems as "Trickle Drops" and "As I Ebb'd with the Ocean of Life," Whitman assures readers that the same dark patches that fall upon them fell upon him also:

> I too knotted the old knot of contrariety,
> Blabb'd, blush'd, resented, lied, stole, grudg'd,
> Had guile, anger, lust, hot wishes I dared not speak,

insightful view of Matthiessen's sexuality, see Randall Fuller, "Aesthetics, Politics, Homosexuality: F. O. Matthiessen and the Tragedy of the American Scholar," *American Literature* 79.2 (June 2007): 363–91.

[24] Grossman, "Canon in the Closet," 813–17. Matthiessen had good reason to be concerned about keeping his sexuality private. The "Lavender Scare" would soon sweep across the nation and result in the expulsion of numerous homosexuals in academia, the military, and the government. See Margaret A. Nash and Jennifer A. R. Silverman, "'An Indelible Mark': Gay Purges in Higher Education in the 1940s," *History of Education Quarterly* 55:4 (November 2015): 441–59. As late as 1960, literary critic Newton Arvin was banned from his Smith College classroom after being arrested for male pornography. See Barry Werth, *The Scarlet Professor: Newton Arvin: A Literary Life Shattered by Scandal* (New York: Anchor, 2002).

Was wayward, vain, greedy, shallow, sly, cowardly, malignant,
The wolf, the snake, the hog, not wanting in me,
The cheating look, the frivolous word, the adulterous wish, not wanting.

(*WPP*, 311)

Whitman's sympathy extends across the ages, leading him to wonder about the force that pours his meaning into readers. That fusion between writer and reader becomes the basis for a moment of visionary union.[25] Looking into the East River, he sees "fine centrifugal spokes of light" around his head, a halo-effect that crowns his readers as well (*WPP*, 309). At the end, he combines his readers with the crowds waiting on shore and the "dumb, beautiful ministers" of the temporal, physical world. "You furnish your parts towards eternity," he assures them. "Great or small, you furnish your parts toward the soul" (*WPP*, 313).

"Crossing Brooklyn Ferry" sits well in the company of transcendental literature, and indeed, Thoreau identified it as one of his favorite poems in *Leaves of Grass*. But as Ross Castronovo explains, labels such as Transcendentalist and American Renaissance can regulate our reading and set unnecessary limits on what we find in literary texts.[26] "Crossing Brooklyn Ferry" provides a good example. If we focus on the poem as part of a national renaissance, if we interpret it as a meditation on the Emersonian oversoul, then we are likely to overlook its rich engagement with world literature. Wai Chee Dimock steps outside Matthiessen's formulation when she reads the poem alongside the Ancient Greek and Egyptian cultures that Whitman was attracted to throughout his life. Dimock shows that Whitman's ferry does not cross only between Brooklyn and Manhattan; it crosses between the Atlantic, the Aegean, and the Mediterranean. A meditation on "prenational time," the poem replicates the funerary boat ritual of Ancient Egypt. The floodtide washes over the shores of Long Island in the same way it washed over the banks of the Nile.[27]

Taken more broadly, the idea of an American Renaissance makes the period between 1855 and 1865 the center of Whitman's life, pushing the next decades of writing to the side. Matthiessen paid considerable attention

[25] As M. Wynn Thomas commented, we are the subject of Whitman's thoughts and the means by which he can continue thinking. Whitman's sympathy extends across the ages, leading him to wonder about the force that fuses him into readers and pours his meaning into them. See Thomas, *The Lunar Light of Whitman's Poetry* (Cambridge, MA: Harvard University Press, 1987), 98.

[26] Ross Castronovo, "Death to the American Renaissance: History, Heidegger, Poe," *ESQ: A Journal of the American Renaissance* 49.1–3 (2003): 184.

[27] Wai Chee Dimock, "Epic and Lyric. The Aegean, the Nile, and Whitman," in *Walt Whitman, Where the Future Becomes Present*, ed. David Haven Blake and Michael Robertson (Iowa City: University of Iowa Press, 2008), 20, 27–31.

to "When Lilacs Last in the Dooryard Bloom'd," the elegy Whitman wrote about the death of Abraham Lincoln. He has comparatively little to say about *Drum Taps*, the cluster of poems about the Civil War. The war made it difficult to maintain the hopeful, morning atmosphere of Whitman's earlier poems, though in its stead came a series of works that emphasized the verisimilitude of his perception. "Cavalry Crossing a Ford," for example, seems almost photographic in its quiet composition and focus on detail:

> A line in long array, where they wind betwixt green islands,
> They take a serpentine course – their arms flash in the sun – hark to the
>   musical clank,
> Behold the silvery river – in it the splashing horses, loitering, stop to drink,
>   Behold the brown-faced men – each group, each person a picture – the
>   negligent rest on the saddles,
> Some emerge on the opposite bank – others are just entering the ford – while,
> Scarlet and blue and snowy white,
> The guidon flags flutter gaily in the wind.   (*WPP*, 435)

The personality that leaped so vibrantly from the early editions of *Leaves of Grass* presents itself in these poems as a guiding, compositional force. If earlier poems had sought to transform his readers' lives, here the poet only urges us to behold the vision he recreates.

The Civil War transformed Whitman into a national patriarch. He initially visited Washington, DC to see his brother George after he was wounded at the Battle of Fredericksburg. The poet would eventually spend ten years in the nation's capitol. Working in the federal government and volunteering in Union Army hospitals, he saw the war's brutality up close. "The Wound-Dresser" projects Whitman into the future where he tells a future generation about his hospital experience, cleaning a side wound, bandaging an amputated limb, and soothing soldiers by holding their hands. Whitman also wrote letters to the families of the wounded and dying, and while the poem does not depict those acts, it does reflect his bedside presence. "I sit by the restless all the dark night, some are so young," he writes. "Some suffer so much, I recall the experience sweet and sad" (*WPP*, 445). In his pamphlet *The Good Gray Poet* (1866), a lengthy defense of *Leaves of Grass* against charges of indecency, William Douglas O'Connor described Whitman's "sublime ministration" on behalf of Union soldiers and railed against prudish critics of his work.[28] The pamphlet, which Whitman helped

---

[28] William Douglas O'Connor, *The Good Gray Poet: A Vindication* (1866), The Walt Whitman Archive. Gen. Eds. Ed Folsom and Kenneth M. Price. Accessed April 12, 2016. www.whitmanarchive.org.

revise, played a major role in turning him into the "Good Gray Poet," a national figure whose long, white beard and magnetic personality enhanced his reputation as democracy's greatest champion.

Whitman would grow into this persona even more after he suffered a debilitating stroke in 1873 and moved to Camden, New Jersey. In "Manly Health and Training," Whitman had contended that men were physically in their prime between the ages of twenty-three and sixty-five, over forty years in which they could lead healthy, vigorous lives.[29] His stroke at fifty-three precipitated a long decline, and the poet who celebrated the vitality of "man in the open air" had to adjust his self-presentation. In his 1882 memoir *Specimen Days*, Whitman described himself sunbathing naked by Timber Creek in southern New Jersey: "Every day, seclusion – every day at least two or three hours of freedom, bathing, no talk, no bonds, no dress, no books, no *manners*" (*WPP*, 806). The scene echoes the poet's ecstatic disrobing in "Song of Myself," though in this case, he hobbles through the woods seeking recovery and rehabilitation.

The postwar editions of *Leaves of Grass* increasingly turn to historical subjects and brief, lyric anecdotes about the poet's life. Partially modeled after Alfred Lord Tennyson's "Ulysses," Whitman's dramatic monologue "Prayer of Columbus" featured the explorer as a "battered, wreck'd old man," venting his "heavy heart" on a distant "savage shore."[30] "Old, poor, and paralyzed," he shares much in common with the poet in his disillusionment (*WPP*, 540). In the course of his angry prayer to God, the seemingly abandoned Columbus comes to understand that he is a prophet of the New World. Looking from his island solitude, he sees "countless ships" on the distant waves and hears "anthems in new tongues" saluting him (*WPP*, 542). The 1874 poem complements Whitman's prophet-like stance in the essay *Democratic Vistas* (1871) in which he calls upon a "divine literatus" to redeem the nation of its fragmented, incomplete democracy. With invective rarely seen in *Leaves of Grass*, he writes, "Society, in these States, is canker'd, crude, superstitious, and rotten" (*WPP*, 937). It is only through the work of future writers that the nation will discover the spiritual bonds that will realize its great promise.

---

[29] Whitman, "Manly Health and Training," 206.

[30] In the marginalia of a newspaper clipping housed in the Charles E. Feinberg Collection at the Library of Congress, Whitman directly mentions the desire to read Tennyson's "Ulysses" in preparation for his writing a poem conveying the thoughts of Columbus adrift on the island of Jamaica. See [Poem – Columbus], Prayer of Columbus Folder, Box 28, Charles E. Feinberg Collection, Library of Congress digitized at The Walt Whitman Archive. Gen. Eds. Ed Folsom and Kenneth M. Price. Accessed June 12, 2016. www.whitmanarchive.org/manuscripts.

Whitman's portrait of the broken down Columbus dramatically updates the numerous explorer images offered in *Leaves of Grass*. The confident and true Emerson of the 1856 "Dear Master" letter, the sage who led the nation to new shores, becomes the disillusioned Columbus waiting for the future to redeem him. The contrast conveys the difficulty of understanding Whitman in limited historical terms. With all its emphasis on youth and vigor, the idea of an American Renaissance can tempt us to neglect Whitman's many poems about old age and infirmity. As if each volume were an act of resolve, he added a series of annexes to *Leaves of Grass* that marked the passage of time: "Sands at Seventy" in 1888 and "Good-Bye my Fancy" in 1891. If Whitman's desire, as he explained in "A Backwards Glance," was to put himself fully on record, then he would also be obligated to record the sorrows and challenges of old age. Whitman outlived all the other writers Matthiessen canonized in *American Renaissance*. Thoreau and Hawthorne died in the 1860s, and while he lived to the age of seventy-nine, Emerson was gone by 1882. Although they were both born in 1819, Whitman died a year after Melville, in 1892, at the age of seventy-three. Contemplating a vanished past, Melville spent his final years writing *Billy Budd*, a novella about a handsome sailor so fresh and innocent that his shipmates lovingly called him "Baby Budd." Whitman did not dwell on his lost vitality. His imagination turned to what he called "Old Age's Lambent Peaks," finding insight in the collapse of his spirits and body (*WPP*, 635). As he explained in the poem "As I Sit Writing Here," he knew that his "glooms, aches, lethargy, constipation, whimpering *ennui*" would filter into the poems he wrote daily (*WPP*, 614). They, too, would be part of the record that he was compiling.

A more complex portrait of Whitman and the American Renaissance comes from "Passage to India," an 1871 poem also grounded in Columbus. Comparing the technological advancements of the late nineteenth century with the explorer's effort to connect the West with the East, the poem opens with a celebration of the industrial wonders that were bringing the world into closer contact: the building of the Suez Canal in the Middle East, the completion of the trans-continental railroad in North America, and the laying of the trans-Atlantic telegraph cable (*WPP*, 531). Representing the cultural achievements of mankind, each of these inventions becomes an image, for Whitman, of the soul's passage toward the perfection of God. "Crossing Brooklyn Ferry" had seen that unity in the poet's ability to address his readers through time. "Passage to India" sees those connections taking place on a larger, historic scale in which the striving of explorers, scientists, and capitalists helped achieve divine transcendence and unity:

A worship new I sing,
You captains, voyagers, explorers, yours,
You engineers, you architects, machinists, yours,
You, not for trade or transportation only,
But in God's name, and for thy sake O soul.   (*WPP*, 532)

The poem, in effect, spiritualizes the principle of Manifest Destiny, viewing technology's capacity to connect the world as a necessary physical step in the creation of a spiritual union. The passage Whitman describes is at once imperial and spiritual, historical and visionary, exploitative and transcendental. He celebrates this material progress because, ultimately, poets will be the acme of the future civilization that industry will create.

"Passage to India" challenges simple understandings of renaissance and rebirth. The poem's optimism rests in the conviction that history is progressive and that one moment in time builds upon the next. Amid his celebration of technological breakthroughs, Whitman sees an even stronger force: "The Past! the Past! the Past ... the infinite greatness of the past!" (*WPP*, 531). Like an arrow or projectile flying through the air, the present is impelled and shaped by what has preceded it. "[W]hat is the present after all," Whitman asks, "but a growth out of the past?" The poem suggests a different sense of history than readers might commonly associate with the American Renaissance. Writers do not regenerate nations; there are no moments of cultural rebirth. In the midst of rapid technological and corporate change, Whitman saw history unfolding sequentially. Indeed, around the time he was writing "Passage to India," the poet was also following the construction of the Brooklyn Bridge, and he knew its completion would bring about the decline of the ferryboats that crossed the East River in his youth. Whatever his personal misgivings, Whitman celebrated the feat in "Song of the Exposition" as one of the "triumphs of our time" (*WPP*, 347).[31] It is hard to imagine such sentiments in the work of Hawthorne, Emerson, and Thoreau.

As a critical concept, the American Renaissance elucidates only part of *Leaves of Grass*. Whitman revised and expanded his work over four tumultuous decades, filling his work with multiple perspectives and experiences. It is worth remembering that Whitman, who had no qualms about

---

[31] Whitman was personally less enthusiastic about the Brooklyn Bridge than "Song of the Exposition" would indicate. As Arthur Geffen points out, he only mentioned the bridge twice and continued in old age to feel nostalgic for the culture of the ferryboat drivers and their passengers. See Arthur Geffen, "Silence and Denial: Walt Whitman and the Brooklyn Bridge," *Walt Whitman Quarterly Review* 1.4 (1984): 1–11. Online. Accessed August 15, 2016. http://ir.uiowa.edu/wwqr.

contradicting himself, fully expected to baffle readers who read his work too narrowly. In fact, in "Whoever You Are Holding Me Now in Hand," he predicts our failures.

> For these leaves and me you will not understand,
> They will elude you at first and still more afterward, I will certainly elude you,
> Even while you should think you had unquestionably caught me, behold!
> Already you see I have escaped from you. (WPP, 271)

Whitman knew that he was too large and multitudinous to be representative of a scholarly thesis, historical time period, or single identity: he boasts that our comprehension of him will be as limited and provisional as our comprehension of the earth itself. We need not feel anxious about this lack of understanding, for each time Whitman eludes us, he draws us deeper into his work.

13

ZOE TRODD

A Renaissance-Self: Frederick Douglass and the Art of Remaking

In January 1846, while lecturing in Glasgow, Scotland, Frederick Douglass wrote to his editor Richard Webb. The two were exchanging letters about the publication of the Irish edition of the *Narrative of the Life of Frederick Douglass*. Douglass disliked the book's newly commissioned frontispiece portrait of himself, engraved by Henry Adlard. "You asked my opinion of the portrait," Douglass noted. "I gave it, and still adhere to it … I am displeased with it … I am cirtain [*sic*] the engraving is not as good, as the original portrait." He went on to request 300 copies of the *Narrative* as soon as possible, "in a strong box," to use on his British lecture tour, and asked Webb to use "better paper than that used in the first edition" for this second edition of his autobiography.[1]

The exchange reveals three interconnected aspects of Douglass's approach to authorship – aspects that should shape our understanding of the American Renaissance and its context, in spite of Douglass's complete exclusion from F. O. Matthiessen's classic text. First, Douglass was deeply engaged with the processes of publication. He cared about Webb's edits to his words, but also the paper on which those words were printed. He was what Graham Thompson calls an "embedded author" – a term that Thompson uses to explore Herman Melville's magazine fiction of the 1850s. Embedded authorship describes the "chain of material creation … to which writers improvised pragmatic responses." To greater or lesser degrees, authors are "embedded in these material relations," Thompson explains. They have a relationship to a "sequence of material creation." Douglass was what Thompson calls (in relation to Melville) a "surrogate reprinter" – a term for authors who engaged in the material creation of texts. Though they were not themselves responsible for physical reprinting, surrogate reprinters reworked texts with an eye on the processes of physical publication. In fact,

[1] Frederick Douglass to Richard Webb, in *The Frederick Douglass Papers*, ed., John W. Blassingame (New Haven: Yale University Press, 1979–), Series Three, 1:79, 80.

soon after this exchange with Webb, Douglass launched his own newspaper, *The North Star*, in 1847, and shifted from surrogate reprinting to become responsible himself for the physical reprinting of texts. More than most American Renaissance authors, he was deeply embedded in the chain of material creation.[2]

Second, Douglass practised what we might call *touche-à-tout* author-ship – a jack-of-all-trades approach. Not limiting himself to the mode of autobiography, he was a polymath author, who tried multiple modes during and after the era of the American Renaissance. Here in 1846 he grapples with at least four modes: the autobiography about to be published, his self-representation via visual portraits (including the various *Narrative* frontispieces), the speeches he was giving around Britain (at which he wanted copies of the *Narrative,* sent in a "strong box," to disseminate), and the letter form. And as well as autobiographies, private and public letters, speeches and his many self-commissioned visual portraits, Douglass produced non-fiction essays, poetry, a novella, and journalism. Again, more than most American Renaissance authors, he was a jack of all trades – a latter-day Renaissance man.

Third, Douglass's embedded and *touche-à-tout* authorship exemplified the very concept of renaissance: rebirth. As he embedded himself in the authorship processes of reworking and republishing, and practised *touche-à-tout* authorship across multiple modes, he repeatedly remade his own public identity. But more than other American Renaissance authors, he also used that process of self-making to envision what the remade nation might look like. His 1846 letter to Webb would not be the last time he objected to a depiction of himself. And as he repeatedly made clear, these objections did not stem from vanity. His careful self-curation was part of his role as an abolitionist remaker of American democracy – one who, as Matthiessen puts it, was trying to "provide a culture commensurate" with America's potential. For example, in 1849 he discovered another engraving of himself, this time in *A Tribute for the Negro* by the British abolitionist Wilson Armistead. The engraver had portrayed Douglass with a slight smile. Douglass was outraged, and in his newspaper he noted that the portrait had "a much more kindly and amiable expression than is generally thought to characterize the face of a fugitive slave." He then attacked the fallibility of engraving and painting: "Negroes can never have impartial portraits at the hands of white artists," he stated. "It seems to us next to impossible for white men to take likenesses of black men,

---

[2] Graham Thompson, *Herman Melville: Among the Magazines* (Amherst: University of Massachusetts Press, 2018).

without most grossly exaggerating their distinctive features. And the reason is obvious. Artists, like all other white persons, have adopted a theory respecting the distinctive features of Negro physiognomy." The vast majority of whites could not create "impartial" likenesses because of their fixed notions of what African-Americans looked like. Douglass, on the other hand, was continually updating his public persona – including via visual self-representation.[3]

Douglass's approach to authorship, including his embedded responses to material circumstances and his *touche-à-tout* experimentations with multiple genres, reveal his embrace of this proto-modernist conception of the self. He imagined the self as continually evolving and he constantly sought new modes of self-representation and new methods of publication that would better express the self in flux. This exploded the very foundations of both slavery and racism: slavery creates a low ceiling above which no one can rise, and racism reflects the belief that some people are permanently superior to other people. Rejecting rigid hierarchies and repudiating the idea of a fixed self, Douglass's fluid conceptions of selfhood and authorship conjoined art and politics. He even went so far as to say in 1861 that "the moral and social influence of pictures" was more important in shaping national culture than "the making of its laws." Pictures and words mattered so much because they could either fix the self – and therefore the nation – within the current racist hierarchy, or remake self and nation around the founding promise of America's birth certificate.[4]

Douglass therefore spent the decades during and after the American Renaissance authoring a reborn self: a Renaissance self perpetually under construction and reworked across multiple authorial modes. Not only creating the first African-American public persona, he offered America its first sustained look at self-made, self-authored black identity. But key to how we understand his position in this literary era – and therefore the political contours of the American Renaissance – is that he sought to use his proffered vision of self-making to effect a *national* transformation, from a land of slavery to one of freedom. Doing battle for the public image of African-Americans, he embraced aesthetic experimentation and self-reinvention on America's behalf. His creation of a Renaissance-self was part of the

[3] F. O. Matthiessen, *American Renaissance: Art and Expression in the Age of Emerson and Whitman* (Oxford: Oxford University Press, 1941), xv; Douglass, "A Tribute for the Negro," *The North Star*, April 7, 1849, in *The Life and Writings of Frederick Douglass*, ed. Philip S. Foner (New York: International Publishers, 1950), 1:380.

[4] Douglass, "Lecture on Pictures," in *Picturing Frederick Douglass: An Illustrated Biography of the Nineteenth Century's Most Photographed American*, ed. John Stauffer, Zoe Trodd and Celeste-Marie Bernier (New York: W. W. Norton, 2015), 129.

abolitionist struggle to achieve a true American renaissance: the rebirth of America itself.

The Renaissance-Self in Photography

As Douglass's protests over engravings suggest, a key part of his Renaissance-self involved visual representation. There are more than 160 photographic portraits of Douglass – a collection that makes him the most photographed American of the nineteenth century. In his "Notes on the Illustrations" in *American Renaissance*, Matthiessen describes Emerson's fascination with "the developing art of photography" and understanding of the camera "as a powerful symbol for his age's scrutiny of character." But far more than Emerson, Hawthorne, and Whitman, and more than any other nineteenth-century American, it was Douglass who understood the implications of his country's new fascination with the camera from the 1840s onward. Believing that photography was a crucial aid to his vision of a free and democratic society, he turned his half-century before the camera into a visual argument for equality. He knew that he was the embodiment of his cause – that his very look in photographs argued against racial oppression. His commissioned and self-directed photographs made him visually famous and immediately recognizable by millions in his own lifetime: Americans circulated his photographs as portrait engravings in the press, published them as lithographs in books, and collected and displayed them in their albums and homes, at a time when most whites understood America as a white man's nation.[5]

These photographs countered the antislavery visual culture of exposure: drawings and photographs of whipped, branded, auctioned, half-naked slave bodies, circulated before and during the Civil War as an argument for abolition. In contrast, Douglass's portraits make him as unavailable as possible. They offer the viewer no clues, symbolic objects, or accessible messages to help 'read' him. He doesn't hold his own books or stand beneath decorative painted backdrops of stormy skies or Southern landscapes. In this way, by refusing to offer accessible smiles, readable props, and expressive backdrops, Douglass countered the visual culture of exposure that made black bodies *available*. His photographs transformed the black body from an emblem of passive suffering to one of stoic, inscrutable manhood. In this sense, then, they offer a counter-point to Matthiessen's own response to nineteenth-century portraiture. Matthiessen called the *American Renaissance* frontispiece, a Southworth and Hawes daguerreotype from

[5] Matthiessen, *American Renaissance*, xxvi.

1854 of shipbuilder Donald McKay, "the finest daguerreotype I have ever seen," which "reveals the type of character with which the writers of the age were concerned, the common man in his heroic stature, or as Whitman called the new type, 'Man in the Open Air.'" The inaccessible Douglass of photographic portraiture – hidden in plain sight – made him the opposite of a "Man in the Open Air." The photographs' stark minimalism creates an enigmatic persona, rather than opening access to what Matthiessen sees as photography's helpful "scrutiny" of character in the nineteenth century.[6]

These carefully staged and individualized portrayals also worked against the ubiquitous dehumanization of African-Americans in visual culture. The photographs of an impeccably dressed, elegant, and self-possessed Douglass countered racist iconography. Douglass is more dignified, represented, recognized, and *seen* – emerging from behind the blackface mask of racist and stereotyped features bestowed upon him by cartoons and lithographs – than any of the ordinary white citizens who embraced photographic portraits as a way to express and establish middle-class identity. His photographs out-citizen white citizens, telling the country that African-Americans are every bit as worthy of citizenship as whites.

Countering the tendencies of antebellum visual culture, the photographs reflect Douglass's practice of experimenting with his own self-representation. This is particularly clear when he was working with fellow activists and reformers on a sitting. For example, he sat for the abolitionist photographers Benjamin F. Reimer in Philadelphia and Thomas Painter Collins in Westfield, Massachusetts. Reimer is responsible for the first ever photograph of Douglass that shows more than his upper body, a carte-de-visite (CdV) from 1861 where a full-bearded Douglass stands holding a chair, his light-colored trousers visible. Collins is responsible for one of the first portraits after Lincoln issued the Emancipation Proclamation, a CdV from early 1863 of a goateed Douglass in the three-quarter statesman pose that would come to dominate his portraiture in the 1870s and 1880s.[7]

Taking this process of self-representation seriously, Douglass developed his own aesthetic. As well as forgoing smiles, props, and backgrounds, he experimented with different angles and poses. In a sitting with Samuel Montague Fassett in Chicago in late February 1864, he tried one shot with a pointing finger and one without. For Augustus Morand in Brooklyn in May 1863, he tried one three-quarter shot and one face-on shot. Benjamin F. Smith took three photographs in Portland, Maine, in early 1864, each

---

[6] *Ibid.*

[7] For the photographs by Reimer and Collins, see Stauffer et al., *Picturing Frederick Douglass*, cat. #16, 17.

with slight changes to the angle of Douglass's head in relationship to the camera. Alfred B. Crosby and Cyrus W. Curtis took one photograph in profile and one face-on in Lewiston, Maine, in April 1864. Douglass adjusted his tie and posture for James Presley Ball's two photographs in Cincinnati in January 1867. From the moment that the faster and more affordable CdV process made multiple shots more feasible, Douglass experimented with angles, adjusted his clothing and tried out varied gestures.[8]

But perhaps most revealing of Douglass's skill and effort in the process of self-representation is his evolution across the photographic half-century – in spite of his consistency during that same fifty-year period in forgoing smiles, props, and decorative backgrounds. In this sense, the photographs are a kind of visual autobiography. As Douglass wrote his three autobiographies across nearly five decades – 1845, 1855, 1881, and 1892 – he also crafted multiple versions of his life and self in pictures. If he wrote himself into public existence with his autobiographies, he photographed himself into public existence as well. The earliest daguerreotypes, in the 1840s, show him exploring the new medium and finding his visual voice. The act of posing himself for the first time was political. It marked an absolute break from his experience as a slave. In 1847 he told a British audience: "dissatisfaction was constantly manifesting itself in the looks of a slave. [I have] been punished and beaten more for [my] looks than for anything else – for looking dissatisfied because [I] felt dissatisfied – for feeling and looking as [I] felt at the wrongs heaped upon [me]." Now Douglass had to turn those facial expressions into a feature of his new abolitionist identity.[9]

He achieved this over the 1850s, evolving in photographs into a freedom fighter and steely visionary – later to become in the 1870s and 1880s a wise prophet and elder statesman. In the mid–late 1850s, perhaps his most radical era, when he advocated violent resistance to slave catchers and worked with John Brown, his fists are clenched, as though in the act of fighting. A stunning 1855 profile daguerreotype shows a clenched fist, as does a copy print from a lost daguerreotype or ambrotype dating to 1858. Then in an ambrotype from 1859, Douglass folded his arms across his chest in an aggressive pose. Confirming such poses as those of an abolitionist, he abandoned them after the Civil War and Emancipation. By 1865, he has unclenched his fist and unfolded his arms. We see the relaxed hands and spread fingers of postwar Douglass.[10]

---

[8] For the photographs, see Stauffer et al., *Picturing Frederick Douglass*, cat. #28–29, #23–24, #25–27, #33–34, #50–51.

[9] Douglass, "American Slavery is America's Disgrace: An Address Delivered in Sheffield England on 25 March 1847," in Douglass, *Papers*, Series 1, II:10.

[10] For the photographs, see Stauffer et al., *Picturing Frederick Douglass*, cat. #10, 13, 14.

Figure 13.1 Unknown photographer, c. 1853. Sixth-plate daguerreotype (3 ⅛ × 2 ¾ in.).
Courtesy Metropolitan Museum of Art, Open Access for Scholarly Content.

He made a second shift with Emancipation, too. Before the war, Douglass often makes direct eye contact in photographs, staring challengingly back at the viewer. Almost half of the photographs taken before the end of the Civil War (seventeen of thirty-eight) show him staring into the camera (Figure 13.1). After the Civil War, he preferred the statesman-like three-quarter pose (Figure 13.2). Of the postwar photographs, only a quarter feature the direct stare (thirty-two of 122). As well, most of these post-war eye-contact photographs are group shots, where Douglass and other committee members or associates have been photographed together. Of Douglass portraits (posed studio photographs of him alone), there are only twelve postwar images where he makes direct eye-contact. Turning a challenging stare into a visionary gaze, Douglass the fighter and fugitive transforms with legal abolition into Douglass the citizen and great American. As Douglass himself phrased it in the title to his second autobiography, this is a transition – in photographic portraiture at least – from bondage to freedom.

Figure 13.2 George Kendall Warren, c. 1879. 289 Washington Street, Boston, MA. Cabinet card (4 ¼ × 6 ½ in.).
Courtesy Metropolitan Museum of Art, Open Access for Scholarly Content.

The battle visibly shifts, from one for emancipation to one for citizenship and equal rights.

Marking his own transitions across the years still further, Douglass even seemed to revise his look with the publication of each new autobiography, knowing that the first page of the book would feature a frontispiece portrait. The Douglass of the *Narrative* era is clean-shaven with a side-parting in photographs. When he published *My Bondage and My Freedom* in 1855, he grew a goatee and replaced the side-parted hair with a larger Afro-like style. In the 1870s, soon before he published his third autobiography, he reinvented himself one last time and grew a full beard and longer hair. This leonine persona lasted until his death. The autobiographies therefore date his different visual eras as the fugitive slave era of the *Narrative* (1840s), the abolitionist firebrand era of *My Bondage* (1850s and 1860s), and the elder statesman era of *Life and Times* (1870s, 1880s, and 1890s). Like the revisions to his autobiography with each new version, these new personas reveal his interest in a fluid selfhood. The photographs show Douglass embracing the self in flux – reinventing himself visually as he sought to reform the country. They argued against the idea that the self can be reduced to the bare bones of scientific enquiry and they critiqued white tendencies to lock represen-tations of black men and women within fixed boundaries. In *this* sense, therefore, he fully embraced and anticipated Matthiessen's understanding of nineteenth-century photography in *American Renaissance*: Douglass spent fifty years perfecting and refining his own version of "heroic stature," and adjusted his symbolism to be a "powerful symbol of his age" across multiple eras, decades, and shifting ideas of heroism.[11]

The Renaissance-Self in Autobiography

Soon after he sat for his first photograph in 1840, Douglass authored him-self in words too, with the *Narrative* (1845). The photographs' process of self-construction was immediately apparent in the frontispiece to this and to his second autobiography as well. His image is unfinished in the *Narrative*. In *My Bondage and My Freedom*, his partially sketched hands grip the jacket as though about to open it wide, suggesting an ongoing process of discovery or display that imitates the opening of the book. Then, in both the *Narrative* and *My Bondage*, Douglass imagines laying his pen in wide gashes made by frost in the soles of his cracked feet, as though writing between the lines of himself while writing and rewriting his life-story. This image echoes his account of "writing in the spaces left in Master Thomas's copy-book" in the *Narrative*: the slave might have to carve a space between the lines, or find page-space and "copy-book ... [on] the board fence, brick wall, and pavement," as Douglass adds, but there is infinite room for text in the gashes and scars of the self-under-construction. In fact, by writing these autobiographies, commissioning 160 photographs, and authoring *The Heroic Slave* in 1853, Douglass acknowledged that the denial of selfhood to slaves created the need for traces of a counter-narrative. There may be a "diploma written on [his] back" by whips, as he describes it the *Narrative*, but he could write in the "spaces left" and craft an indeterminate self. There could be potentiality and possibility in the crevice, and he could dwell there as a witness-participant and a liminal man-in-the-making.[12]

---

[11] Matthiessen, *American Renaissance*, xxvi.
[12] Douglass, *My Bondage and My Freedom. Part I. – Life as a Slave. Part II. – Life as a Freeman* (New York: Miller, Orton & Mulligan, 1855), 132, 359; Douglass, *Narrative of the Life of Frederick Douglass, an American Slave* (Boston: Anti-Slavery Office, 1845), 44, 43.

Even Douglass's decision to rewrite the *Narrative* as *My Bondage* in 1855 – rather than starting *My Bondage* where the *Narrative* left off – reflected his search for a partially erased American counter-history; what he imagines at one point as the traces of slaves' "footprints." For example, in writing *My Bondage*, he added more dialogue than in the *Narrative* sections he was reworking – as though the dialogue had been missing in 1845. He also quoted some of the key novelistic passages from the *Narrative* (a paragraph about his grandmother, the Chesapeake oration, and a passage using the vernacular of white shipyard workers), as though his first autobiography was an external, authoritative source. Gore Vidal argues that *all* autobiographies are palimpsests – that the autobiographer starts "with life; makes a text; then re-vision ... an afterthought, erasing some but not all of the original while writing something new over the first layer of text." But in his revised autobiography of 1855, Douglass literally wrote between the lines of himself – in the "spaces left" – and crafted a layered, autobiographical palimpsest. And, while a palimpsest is the erasure or alteration of a text to provide room for a new imprint, Douglass's version of a palimpsestic narrative in 1855 reveals what Ashraf Rushdy calls "the present ... written against a background where the past is erased but still legible." Douglass wrote a new document over an old one, but let the old one show through. Through his own self-inscriptions, he highlighted the silences and erasures of America's slave past and present.[13]

Douglass's two antebellum autobiographies fully engage this conflict between sub-version and official version. In his *Narrative*, he confronts the problem of exclusion from recorded history, for he has "no accurate knowledge of my age, never having seen any authentic record containing it" and the parallel problem of having no access to the future, expressed in Master Thomas's instruction to "lay out no plans" and instead achieve "thoughtlessness of the future." In *My Bondage*, he experiences the struggle to be "master of my own time" and the denial of "progress" to the slave, whose "destiny" is "fixed." Denied the slave is both "retrospect" and "prospect," past and future. For the slave there is only an endless present, Douglass suggests. At one point he even slips into an unusual present tense when trying to look "both ways" into the past and future.[14]

---

[13] Douglass, *Narrative*, 102; Gore Vidal, *Palimpsest: A Memoir* (New York: Random House, 1995), 6; Ashraf Rushdy, *Remembering Generations: Race and Family in Contemporary African American Fiction* (Chapel Hill: University of North Carolina Press, 2001), 8.

[14] Douglass, *Narrative*, 1, 103; Douglass, *My Bondage*, 328, 175, 273, 271–2.

He translates these time-wars into a struggle for control over *historical* time. Time and history blend. The "order of civilization" is "reversed" by slavery, the plantation is a "full three hundred years behind the age," and Douglass feels the resulting pathology of wanting to remain "little forever." But in response to this denial of personal and historical time – prospect and retrospect – Douglass attempts to seize control. He stays at a camp meeting longer than expected and eventually hires out his own time. Another victory is the slaves' music, which has no "time." Then, through his autobiographical act across three narratives, Douglass finally takes control of historical time by telling and retelling his own story.[15]

The autobiographies' self-creative space challenged overseers' inscriptions upon the physical space of slave bodies (where the whip writes "on the living parchment of ... their backs") with a different story. His act of writing and rewriting the pages of his autobiography also opened a self-creative space denied him by white abolitionists: "'Give us the facts ... We will take care of the philosophy,'" keep "a little of the plantation manner of speech," and don't "seem too learned," they had told him (trying to "pin" him down). His self-creation in text answered these attempts to "pin" him down to a "simple narrative." Finally, the textual self-creation opened a space of historical record that challenged erasure: what Douglass describes as silences around a "delicate subject," the silent presence of "unmarked" slave graves, the absence of "family records" for the slave, the things that are "speedily hushed up." With his autobiographies' Renaissance-self, Douglass reveals these gaps in America's public memory and insists upon the presence of counter-history. For example, he imagines a different narrative altogether. In both the *Narrative* and *My Bondage* he notes that "circumstance" helped to liberate him from slavery, thereby embedding the voice of counterfactual history: "it is quite probable that, but for the mere circumstance of being thus removed ... instead of being, today, a FREEMAN, I might have been wearing the galling chains of slavery." This suggestion of a different story begins to solve the problem of exclusion from history's space: his self-construction opened the boundlessness that he describes at the end of his famous speech, "The Meaning of July Fourth" (1852), where there are no more "walled cities," the Pacific is at his feet, "[s]pace is comparatively annihilated," and there is hope for abolition.[16]

---

[15] Douglass, *My Bondage*, 51, 64, 44; Douglass, *Narrative*, 13.

[16] Douglass, *My Bondage*, 177, 361–2, 155, 60, 35, 127, 138–9; Douglass, "The Meaning of July Fourth for the Negro" (1852), in *Writings*, II:181–204, 203.

The Renaissance-Self in Fiction and Speeches

Douglass continued answering the problem of historical space in "The Meaning of July Fourth." The speech of course protests the long delay in realizing the ideal of equality expressed in the Declaration of Independence. Choosing to give the speech on July 5, Douglass reminded his white audience that slavery was an anachronism, a rupture in America's narrative of endless progress. But he went further still, and engaged in a process of writing in the "spaces left" to offer a counter-narrative to the celebrations of Independence Day. "The Meaning of July Fourth" includes a speech within the speech that turns Douglass's previous work into a partially visible primary source. In his *Narrative*, Douglass had described himself standing on the banks of Chesapeake Bay, watching "the countless number of sails moving off to the mighty ocean." He had given a speech at this point in the *Narrative*, invoking the free-sailing ships: "You are loosed from your moorings ... I am fast in my chains." Now, in his Fourth of July oration, he used a description of "slave ships ... with their cargoes of human flesh, waiting for favorable winds to waft them down the Chesapeake." Echoing his *Narrative* address, Douglass updated the spatial imagery so that even the free ships contain tight slave spaces (cargoes of human flesh). He retrospectively darkens his earlier image of the Chesapeake "sails." Many in the 600-strong antislavery audience at the July 4th event had undoubtedly read the *Narrative*, might have heard the Chesapeake echo, remembered the younger Frederick's impassioned speech, and got two for the price of one with their 12 ½ cent admission. They were encountering a layered representation three levels deep (bank-side speech, quotation of his speech in the *Narrative*, invocation of the quoted speech in "The Meaning of July Fourth") and simultaneously listening to a slave describe free space and a free man describe slave space. Layering space and time in this way, by embedding an already embedded speech within his 1852 address – by using his previous work as an unacknowledged source and weaving together three different voices – Douglass wrote subversive history in the "spaces left." He offered a glimpse of a narrative sub-version and challenged the exclusive space of national memory; July 4th celebrations and all.[17]

The following year, Douglass added fiction to his growing canon of historical reclamations. Like "The Meaning of July Fourth," his novella *The Heroic Slave* shows him experimenting with the layered counter-histories of literary palimpsests. And like his autobiographies, the novella describes the battles for time and space that necessitate these counter-histories. Madison

[17] Douglass, *Narrative*, 64; Douglass, "The Meaning of July Fourth," 194.

Washington explains that slavery and flight has "turned day into night" and describes his punishment for staying "longer at the mill … than it was thought I ought to have done." But Washington seizes control of time by making it speed up and slow down: after a lengthy account of "two long hours," he skims over "five long years" in a mere phrase. And while Washington must make a swampy cave his home, the novella reverses the dynamic of confined space for slaves. Listwell – the white traveler – is trapped in a "hiding-place" and as Washington departs, Listwell remains "in motionless silence … fastened to the spot." Only upon declaring himself an "abolitionist" does Listwell recover his freedom of movement. Then, as in his other works, Douglass fuses time and space into the space of history and memory. The tavern's space is under attack from "time and dissipation," its stables no longer a "comfortable shelter" for the "noblest steeds." But this time-decayed space is also a site of living history, surrounded by gossips who are as "good as the newspaper for the events of the day." The tavern's "history … is folded in their lips" and they are "equal to the guides at Dryburgh Abbey." They practice a form of folk history.[18]

In contrast to this space of living history, Douglass presents the erasures of American historical memory in the form of Washington's absence from the "American annals." Taking up the particular codings of 1776, Douglass explains that "a man who loved liberty as well as did Patrick Henry – who deserved it as much as Thomas Jefferson – and who fought for it with a valor as high, and arm as strong, and against odds as great, as he who led all the armies for freedom and independence, lives now only in the chattel records of his native State." Here he creates a counter-memory, making abolitionism the Revolution's legacy. But he also critiques those "annals," for their erasures mean that "[g]limpses of [Washington] are all that can now be presented … a few transient incidents." Washington is visible by a "quivering flash of angry lightning," before disappearing, "covered with mystery … enveloped in darkness." Douglass continues this theme of partial history – what he terms "marks, traces, possibles, and probabilities" – throughout his novella. From his hiding place Listwell can only see Washington in brief glimpses, raising his head periodically to see "the sorrow-smitten slave." During the slave revolt, Grant can only see "by the quick flashes of lightning that darted occasionally from the angry sky." Visible in the annals only in "glimpses," Washington also seems visible to observers only in flashes.[19]

---

[18] Douglass, "The Heroic Slave," in *Autographs for Freedom* (Boston: John P. Jewett and Company, 1853), 174–239, 195, 188, 178, 181–2, 206–8.

[19] Douglass, "Heroic Slave," 174, 175, 176, 180, 236–7.

Yet although he critiques the fragmentary nature of "American annals" by giving observers these brief glimpses of the novella's heroic slave, Douglass again embraces the fragments as an alternate history. He gathers the "marks" and "traces" of a partially erased story, from the trace of sorrow that lingers on a brow in the novella's first epigraph, to the "ineffaceable marks on the tavern" and the traces of Washington himself that are "daguerreotyped" on Listwell's "memory." As Washington travels through Virginia's "dismal swamps," he moves through a literary landscape that bears the historical traces of another slave rebellion (the Nat Turner revolt of 1831). And the traces of undocumented voices and folk history also emerge as rumors, hints, overheard snippets, and circulating stories in Douglass's historical romance. Washington eavesdrops on one man and finds this private prayer to be "the most fervent, earnest, and solemn" he has ever heard. Listwell eavesdrops on Washington and on the men in the tavern: from a "private room" he hears "important hints." For both Washington and Listwell, the best stories exist beyond the space of public declaration.[20]

The Heroic Slave is a palimpsestic narrative that makes the archive's absences reveal as much as its selective inclusions. With it, Douglass adapted what was known about the *Creole* affair and endowed Madison Washington with a past. He confronted the codings and erasures of American history: the possibility that black people might be expunged from the official historical annals altogether and the denial of personal history to the American slave. Then, within the black canon, his counter-history became a primary source itself. Resonances of Douglass's transfigured text appeared in William Wells Brown's *The Black Man* (1863), Lydia Maria Child's *The Freedman's Book* (1865), and Pauline Hopkins's "A Dash for Liberty" (1901). In the face of historical erasure, Douglass had recorded a different story in the "spaces left."

The novella also confirms the particular focus of Douglass's lifelong challenge to the official American narrative. Revealing the hidden fissures in American notions of progress with his narrative of Madison Washington's partially hidden, partially erased story, Douglass countered perhaps *the* master-narrative of national history by reinterpreting the meaning of July 4. Washington justifies his violence and claims his freedom with the words: "We have done that which you applaud your fathers for doing, and if we are murderers, so were they." Douglass's counter-memory turns abolitionism (in the form of Madison Washington) into the Revolution's legacy.[21]

[20] *Ibid.*, 174, 206, 188, 192, 197, 211.
[21] *Ibid.*, 235.

In fact, of all the American Renaissance writers, Douglass was the most focused on closing the gap between Revolutionary ideals and antebellum realities. As well as his "Meaning of July Fourth" speech and Madison Washington's declaration in *The Heroic Slave*, Douglass explained in an article for *Frederick Douglass's Paper* in 1854 that slaves "acted out the declaration of independence" through resistance and escape. Illustrating this idea the following year in *My Bondage*, Douglass describes himself and Covey standing as "equals before the law" during their fight: the incident is his own Declaration. Krista Walter explains one reason why Douglass summoned 1776, arguing that he set out to "reclaim a genuine republican language and ideology for the purposes of abolition." Robyn Wiegman acknowledges that Douglass claimed republican ideology but adds that he also sought to establish the ongoing failure to translate that ideology into practice: "By setting the mythology of national origin against the transaction of human beings into property, Douglass casts an ironic addendum to the rhetoric of universal suffrage that accompanies America's nativity narrative, revealing the deeply profound ideological breach on which 'liberty' under a slave economy rests." Douglass was making abolitionism a patriotic movement *and* establishing the limitations of 1776.[22]

But more than this, he also was taking control of time and space and fusing both into a new space of protest memory. Part of Douglass's agenda in creating a narrative sub-version within *The Heroic Slave*, embedding a narrative sub-version in "The Meaning of July Fourth," and using both the novella and the speech to denounce America's past *and* the dominant discourse around that past, was to shift the country in a different direction as it moved forward. He saw the abolitionist campaign, and eventually the Civil War, in apocalyptic terms; as a struggle that would start the country anew and replace one history with another. The second covenant of the Fall allows redemption grace alongside creation grace, and Emancipation and the war were supposed to be the redemption of America's history. The creation of the republic had been flawed – with slavery its original sin – and the war might be the Fall that levelled all things, making all men equal in a true national rebirth.

Of course, the apocalypse birthed no new age. Shocked by the bloodshed of war and the failures of Reconstruction, Douglass was soon forced to acknowledge that the abolitionists' work was *far* from over. The South's

---

[22] Douglass, "Another Righteous Judge," *Frederick Douglass's Paper* (September 29, 1854): 2; Douglass, *My Bondage*, 242; Krista Walter, "Trappings of Nationalism in Frederick Douglass's *The Heroic Slave*," *African American Review* 34.2 (2000): 233–47, 237; Robyn Wiegman, *American Anatomies: Theorizing Race and Gender* (Durham, NC: Duke University Press, 1995), 71.

last Republican governments fell in 1877, federal troops withdrew from the region, and redeemer governments had begun to roll back the gains of Reconstruction and re-establish white supremacist rule in the old Confederate states. In June 1879, a week after William Lloyd Garrison's death, Douglass saw a "second battle for liberty" unfolding. A "spirit of evil has been revived which we had fondly hoped was laid forever," he observed. The nation had only "half learned" the "lessons" taught by abolitionists and so the abolitionist "army" would have to "march on." Douglass was soon reinventing himself again as America's first great antilynching activist. Just as slavery cost America "a million graves," so lynching "may yet bring vengeance," he warned. The old anti-slavery societies had declared victory too soon after the Civil War, he noted, and Douglass would have to continue their work. He revived the abolitionist jeremiad to protest lynching, and he returned to his pre-war imagery of divinely sanctioned vengeance. A postwar renaissance of freedom and equality was nowhere in sight: after the antebellum decades of offering his images and words as the outline trace of a different American story, Douglass would have to remake the nation and reconfigure, again, his Renaissance-self.[23]

[23] Douglass, "Speech on the Death of Garrison," June 2, 1879, in the Frederick Douglass Papers, Manuscript Division, Library of Congress, box 23, reel 15; Douglass, *The Lessons of the Hour* (Baltimore: Press of Thomas & Evans, 1894), 32.

14

MELBA JOYCE BOYD

Frances Ellen Watkins Harper "In the Situation of Ishmael"

You white women speak of rights. I speak of wrongs. I, as a colored
woman, have had in this country an education that had made me feel
as if I were in the situation of Ishmael, my hand against every man, and
every man's hand against me.
(Frances Harper, 1866)

Frances Ellen Watkins Harper spoke these words in her deliverance at the
Woman's Rights Convention at the Church of the Puritans in New York City
in 1866, one year after the end of the Civil War. While the purpose of this historic event was to address the inequality of women, Harper's biblical reference
to Ishmael, the first-born son of Abraham, is a fitting description of her life.
Like Ishmael, Harper was a warrior. Similarly, it appears her father abandoned
her mother before Harper was born, but there is no record of him, which
leaves much of this to speculation. But as an adult, she fought against slavery
and for the rights of women. As a black woman in the position of Ishmael, this
fight was against her own countrymen, even when it came to public transportation, which mirrors the protest of Rosa Parks in 1954, almost 80 years later.
Harper relayed:

> Going from Washington to Baltimore this spring, they put me in the smoking
> car. Aye, in the capital of the nation, where the black man consecrated himself
> to the nation's defense, faithful when the white man was faithless, they put
> me in the smoking car! They did it once; but the next time they tried it, they
> failed; for I would not go in. I felt the fight in me; but I don't want to fight all
> the time … One day I took my seat in a car, and the conductor came to me
> and told me to take another seat. I just screamed "murder." The man said if
> I was black I ought to behave myself. I know that if he was white he was not
> behaving himself. Are there not wrongs to be righted?[1]

---

[1] Frances Harper, *The Proceedings of the Eleventh National Woman's Rights Convention*,
New York, May 10, 1866, Frances Harper Collection, the Historical society of
Pennsylvania, Philadelphia, PA.

In 1976, when the United States celebrated the bicentennial of the founding of the nation, a number of historic sites, including the home of Frances
Ellen Watkins Harper at 1006 Bainbridge Avenue in Philadelphia, were
deemed National Historic Monuments. Born a "free person of colour,"
Harper (1825–1911) was known as "the bronze muse" of the Abolitionist
Movement. One of the most prominent and widely known authors and
activists, she authored eleven books of poetry, four novels, and countless
essays during her lifetime. She toured the nation and spoke fervently for the
rights of all Americans, regardless of their race or sex. Her work effectively
changed racial and gender politics and policies in the United States. She
was in the forefront of the Abolitionist and Woman's Rights Movements;
however, despite her political popularity and literary prominence during her
lifetime, she is still largely unknown to the contemporary, American public.
Her historical invisibility can be correlated with the secondary consideration of African-Americans, especially African-American women.

The common perception of black women during the nineteenth century
is limited to slavery, and even when that image is associated with a heroic
figure, such as Harriet Tubman, it is still limited to her work as a runaway slave, who liberated other slaves. However, she was also a spy for the
union army during the Civil War, and a staunch advocate of women's rights.
A close associate of Tubman, Harper, reported her mistreatment on a public
streetcar:

> The last time I saw that woman [Tubman] her hands were swollen. That
> woman who had led one of Montgomery's most successful expeditions, who
> was brave enough and secretive enough to act as a scout for the American
> army, had her hands all swollen from a conflict with a brutal conductor, who
> undertook to eject her from her place. That woman, whose courage and brav-
> ery won recognition from our army and from every black man in the land, is
> excluded from every thoroughfare of travel.
>
> Talk of giving women the ballot-box? Go on. It is a normal school, and the
> white women of this country need it. While there exists this brutal element in
> society which tramples upon the feeble and treads down the weak, I tell you
> that if there is any class of people who need to be lifted out of their airy noth-
> ingness and selfishness, it is the white women of America.[2]

The anger in Harper's words are indicative of her ongoing struggle as a
black woman, and her continued disappointment with white Americans:

> I never saw so clearly the nature and intent of the Constitution before. Oh,
> was it not strangely inconsistent that man fresh, so fresh, from the baptism of

---

[2] *Ibid.*

the Revolution should make such concessions to the foul spirit of Despotism! That, when fresh from gaining their own liberty, they could permit the African slave trade – could let their national flag hang a sign of death on Guinea's cost and Congo's shore![3]

As Harper indicated in her speech, she did not want to fight all the time. However, during her entire life as an activist and a writer, she would have to experience, witness, and continue to fight against injustice. As an activist, she incorporated her poetry into her lectures against slavery, for women's rights, and for universal education. Her mission to advance the development of a true democracy in the United States brought her into interaction and collaboration with Harriet Tubman, Frederick Douglass, William Still, John Brown, Susan B. Anthony, Mary Shadd Cary, and Ida B. Wells, among many other famous historical figures. The obscurity of black women in American history is directly related to their past and contemporary status in society. Harper's legacy was significantly retrieved in the 1990s when a number of women scholars published books by and about her, recollecting her poetry books, essays, and novels and reconstructing her biography and identifying her appropriate historical and literary stature. More recently, her first book of poetry, *Forest Leaves* (1846), recovered by Joanna Ortner, was a remarkable discovery due to serious archival research.[4] But despite the diligence of scholars and our continued interest in Harper, for the most part, popular knowledge of Harper remains largely blank and as indifferent as it is to black women in general. Hopefully, this chapter will serve to introduce Harper to a larger audience that will be encouraged to seek additional readings to learn more about and from her.

Bury Me in a Free Land

In addition to providing insight into historical and political struggles that affected an entire people, a consideration of Harper's personal struggles, of being orphaned at the age of three and losing her husband after four short years of marriage, demonstrate the vulnerability of her life. On September 24, 1825, Frances Ellen Watkins (Harper) was born a "free person of color" in Baltimore, Maryland. Her mother died when she was not quite three years old, and she was raised and educated by her material uncle, William Watkins, Sr., who ran the Watkins School for Colored Youth. She received a rigorous, classical education, which included lessons in Greek, Latin, and the

---

[3] Frances Harper, [Letter to the Editor], *National Anti-Slavery Standard* 9 (April 1859): 3.
[4] See discussion of Harper's first book of poetry, Forest Leaves, in *Common-Place* 16.2, http://common-place.org/.

Romance languages.[5] This education and the religious tenets of the A. M. E. Church provided the foundation for Harper's activist aesthetics. Watkins was an abolitionist, a member of the African Methodist Episcopal Church, and a writer. He published essays and poetry in William Lloyd Garrison's newspaper, *The Liberator*, and Watkins influenced Frederick Douglass when he was a slave in Baltimore.

Harper's education also included dressmaking, a skill which helped her to secure employment as a domestic for a book merchant, who gave her access to his extensive library. It was during this period that she began writing poetry. When the Ohio Conference of the A. M. E. Church established the Union Seminary School in Wilberforce in 1844, Harper left Baltimore to become the first woman on the faculty. It is possible that she met her future husband, Fenton Harper, during her tenure at Union Seminary. However, also trained in elocution and writing, these talents ultimately determined another destiny.

In 1854, Harper began lecturing against slavery, and because of her poetry, she was soon called "the bronze muse of the Abolitionist Movement." During this same time, her poetry and prose was popularized, appearing in many anti-slavery publications such as *Frederick Douglass' Paper, Anti-Slavery Bugle, Anglo-African Magazine, A. M. E. Church Review, The Liberator, The Provincial Freeman*, and others. The following excerpt from "Our Greatest Want" (1859), which appeared in the *Anglo-African Magazine*, is Harper's clarion call for African-Americans to join the fight against slavery and racism, and to not submit to the illusion of wealth as an equalizing force in race relations and citizenship:

> We have money among us, but how much of it is spent to bring deliverance to our captive brethren? Are our wealthiest men the most liberal sustainers of the Anti-slavery enterprise? Or does the bare fact of their having money, really help mold public opinion and reverse its sentiments? We need what money cannot buy and what affluence is too beggarly to purchase. The greatest want of our people is not simply wealth, nor genius, nor more intelligence, but brave men, and earnest women, whose lives shall represent not a stagnant mass, but a living force of self-sacrificing souls that will stamp themselves not only on the present, but also on the future![6]

As indicated in her address at the Eleventh National Woman's Rights Convention, Harper's prose closely resembles the passionate style of her speeches, but it was probably the power of her poetry that distinguished her at the lectern. Harper's first book of poetry, *Forest Leaves*, was published

[5] James H. A. Johnson, "William Watkins," *A.M.E. Church Review* 3 (1886): 11–12.
[6] Harper, "Our Greatest Want," *Anglo African Magazine* 1 (1859): 160.

when she was only twenty-one years of age. However, her literary stature catapulted in 1854 when she became a lecturer for the Maine Anti-Slavery Society, and her second book of poetry, *Poems on Miscellaneous Subjects*, was published with an introduction by the fiery abolitionist, William Lloyd Garrison. Her poetry became so popular that according to William Still's account in his book, *The Underground Rail Road*,[7] of her first four books, 50,000 copies were in print by 1872.

Harper's poetry was in such demand that the dual publication in 1853 of "Eliza Harris," a poetic abstraction derived from Harriet Beecher Stowe's popular novel, *Uncle Tom's Cabin*, in William Lloyd Garrison's *Liberator* and in *Frederick Douglass' Paper* aggravated a pre-existing antagonism between the two abolitionists. When Douglass left Garrison's New England Anti-Slavery Society to commandeer his own newspaper, it created a rift between the two leaders who also ascribed to different political strategies to end slavery. Whereas Garrison was a pacifist, Douglass believed acts of war were necessary. In this case, Garrison argued that Harper's poem was presented as if it had been especially written for the Douglass periodical. The response, the *Douglass'* publication, included an admission of the error, but it also appealed to Harper to continue to submit literature for their publication.

While Harper was one of the most well-known lecturers and poets of the nineteenth century, women lecturing in public was rare; and in "proper circles," it was considered inappropriate for women to speak before a "promiscuous" audience, one that contained men and women. However, William Watkins, Sr. trained her to become a liberating voice, and she accepted the invitation from the Anti-Slavery Society of Maine, which included a rigorous schedule of travel throughout the Northern United States and Ontario, Canada.

Mary Shadd Cary, the black woman editor of *The Provincial Freeman*, an abolitionist newspaper based in Chatham, Ontario wrote about Harper's appearance in Detroit in a letter to her husband (September, 1858):

> Miss Watkins [Frances Ellen Watkins Harper] & Mr. Nell come back to Detroit and she is to go West a ways. Why the whites and colored people here are just crazy with excitement about her. She is the greatest female speaker ever was here, so wisdom obliges me to keep out of the way as with her prepared lectures there is no chance of a favorable comparison.[8]

---

[7] William Still, *The Underground Rail Road*, rev. ed. (Philadelphia, 1872).
[8] Dorothy Sterling, *We Are Your Sisters* (New York: W. W. Norton, 1984), 174–5.

The black abolitionist, William C. Nell, reported to William Lloyd Garrison about Harper's speech in Detroit "to a crowded meeting of Negroes" at Second Baptist Church, "where Miss Watkins, in the course of one of her very best outbursts of eloquent indignation, protested the kidnapping of two fugitive slaves living in Detroit."[9]

The power of Harper's lectures was rooted in her command of the English language and an elocutionary style that infused her poetry into her speeches, conveying the tragic injustices of slavery with visceral imagery that moved and impressed audiences, black and white. These poems illuminated the invisibility of the oppressed, and gave voice to the disenfranchised. "The Slave Auction," one of her most famous and frequently anthologized poems, projects imagery of a slave auction, a scene that many Northerners had never witnessed. Harper was especially concerned with the abuse of enslaved women, and the opening stanzas emphasize the women's humiliation caught in the gaze of naked exhibition while enduring the horror of being separated from their loved ones. "The interplay between low pitch and elongated syllables creates a slow rhythm, which produces a haunting echo"[10]:

> The sale began – young girls were there,
>> Defenseless in their wretchedness,
> Those stifled sob of deep despair
>> Revealed their anguish and distress.
>
> And mother stood with streaming eyes,
>> And saw their dearest daughter sold;
> Unheeded rose their bitter cries,
>> While tyrants bartered them for god.
>
> And woman, with her love and truth –
>> For those in sable forms may dwell –
> Gaze'd on the husband of her youth,
>> With anguish none many paint or tell.

The power of Harper's poetry resides largely in her capacity to tell a story. Entranced by the sound and the emotional impact of the imagery and the sonic properties of the ballad form, she captured the imagination of the audience. The ballad also accommodates the oral tradition of nineteenth-century culture, and this poetic structure works seamlessly with her oratorical style. Harper's poems were both appealing and informative because

[9] Samuel Sillen, *Women Against Slavery* (New York: Masses & Mainstream, 1955), 71.
[10] Melba Joyce Boyd, *Discarded Legacy: Politics and Poetics in the Life of Frances E. W. Harper, 1825–1911* (Detroit: Wayne State University Press, 1994), 64.

they were based in reality. The poem "The Slave Mother: A Tale of Ohio" is derived from a real slave narrative, a famous case which brought attention to the severity of slavery and to what end a mother would go to save her children from that fate.

The unnamed slave mother is actually Margaret Garner, who kills one of her children, but is stopped before she can kill the other three. The poem begins in the voice of the persona, the mother, but an omniscient narrator weaves in and out of the poetic experience and the woman's foreboding thoughts in frantic anticipation of bounty hunters tracking her trail. Resigned to her inevitable capture, as foreshadowed by warnings and flashing visions, the slave mother, persuaded by desperation, decides to free her children by killing them.

> I will save my precious children
> From their darkly threatened doom,
> I will hew their path to freedom
> Through the portals of the tomb.

Using the first-person narrative brings the woman's voice into deliberation with the experience and into the national conversation about this famous case. Racist perceptions of blacks, including a judgment that slaves were incapable of human feelings, attributed to disgust on the part of many whites about the mother's actions. Therefore, Harper infused the slave mother's emotional and psychological condition into the poem to convey her humanity; however, Harper did trust the audience's capacity to comprehend the slave mother's reasoning. Hence, the last lines of the poem define the mother's actions as "*a deed of fearful daring*," and then raises the rhetorical question through the African American oratorical technique of "call and response," challenging the audience to join the fight against the true culprit: "*Do the icy hands of slavery / Every pure emotion chill?*"

While Harper's inclusion of the woman's experience in slavery was paramount in her poetry, she also gave voice to enslaved men. "The Tennessee Hero" is another poem based on an actual occurrence. The epigraph of the poem reads: "He had heard his comrades plotting to obtain their liberty, and rather than betray them, he received 750 lashes and died." Harper's poetry uncovered truths and dispelled lies about enslaved and free blacks – an arduous, lifelong mission.

Harper's popularity was also related to the frequent appearance of her essays in newspapers and journals, which complemented the politics of her poetics. She wrote against laws that supported slavery and white supremacy, and these ideas formulated her lectures. It is important to note her global knowledge on the subject of slavery, and how the United States had failed its democratic principles:

> But a few months since a man escaped from bondage and found a tempo-
> rary shelter almost beneath the shadow of Bunker Hill. Had that man stood
> upon the deck of an Austrian ship, beneath the shadow of the house of the
> Hapsburgs, he would have found protection. Had he been wrecked upon
> an island or colony of Great Britain, the waves of the tempest-lashed ocean
> would have washed him deliverance. Had he landed upon the territory of
> France and a Frenchman had reduced him to a thing and brought him here
> beneath the protection of our institutions and our laws, for such a nefarious
> deed that Frenchman would have lost his citizenship in France.[11]

Her essays also addressed how federal laws supporting slavery also affected the security of free persons of color. Because of the passage of "The Fugitive Slave Act" by Congress, bounty hunters pursued Margaret Garner into Ohio, and the state court was obliged to follow federal law: "The Fugitive Slave Act has made criminals of the champions of freedom, just like the Dred Scott Decision confirmed the negation of our full citizenship; our word carries no value in argument with whites in the courts, and no state has to recognize our right to vote, although we are taxed at the same rate."[12] Harper also indicted the North's complicity in its support of slavery, which made escape from tyranny nearly impossible for the enslaved: "But the ready North is base enough to do their shameful service."[13]

"Bury Me in a Free Land," possibly Harper's most famous poem, was first published in 1858 in the *Anti-Slavery Bugle*. Exhausted from a rigorous touring schedule for the Anti-Slavery Movement, her health declined dramatically, and she had to retire for some weeks to recover. The opening four lines of the poem first appeared in a letter she wrote to William Still, the conductor of the Underground Rail Road in Philadelphia:

> Well, perhaps it is my lot to die from home and be buried among strangers;
> and yet I do not regret that I espoused this cause; perhaps I have been of some
> service to the cause of human rights, and I hope the consciousness that I have
> not died in vain, will be a halo of peace around my dying bed, a heavenly sun-
> shine lighting up the dark valley and shadow of death.[14]

---

[11] Harper, [Letter], 3.
[12] *Ibid.*
[13] *Ibid.*
[14] Still, *Underground Rail Road*, 763.

Her most anthologized poem, these lines illustrate how artistry transcends centuries:

> *Make me a grave where'er you will,*
> *In a lowly plain, or a lofty hill;*
> *Make it among earth's humblest graves,*
> *But not in a land where men are slaves.*
>
> *I could not rest if around my grave*
> *I heard the steps of a trembling slave;*
> *His shadow above my silent tomb*
> *Would make it a place of fearful gloom.*
>
> *I could not rest if I heard the tread*
> *Of a coffle gang to the shambles led,*
> *And the mother's shriek of wild despair*
> *Rise like a curse on the trembling air.*

Harper recovered from her illness; however, the following year John Brown was captured during the failed raid on Harper's Ferry in Virginia. This was a very tense time for abolitionists because Brown was charged with treason, and the federal government pursued those suspected as being complicit with Brown's plans. Frederick Douglass, for instance, fled to Canada, and then to England. Unintimidated by the government, Harper wrote a letter to Brown, in which she conferred her steadfast commitment:

> Dear Friend: Although the hands of Slavery throw a barrier between you and me, and it may not be my privilege to see you in your prison-house, but Virginia has no bolts or bars through which I dread to send you my sympathy.[15]

Subsequently, she published "The Triumph of Freedom – A Dream,"[16] a prose piece about John Brown configured as the spirit of Agitation and Christ-like.[17] Although Harper's writings were often grounded in her Christian faith, it is important to recognize that the religious doctrine of abolitionists differed from mainstream Christianity. In "The Bible Defense of Slavery," Harper attacks a popular book of the same title that distorts biblical text in order to justify the institution of slavery and white supremacy. What is also distinctive about her religious poetry is her inclusion of the woman's perspective, as in "Ruth and Naomi,"

---

[15] Frances Harper to John Brown, "From A Woman of the Race He Died For," November 25, 1859, in James Redpath, *Echoes of Harper's Ferry* (1860; repr., Salem, NH: Ayer Co., 1969), 418.

[16] Frances Harper, "The Triumph of Freedom – A Dream," in *A Brighter Coming Day: A Frances Harper Reader*, ed. Frances Foster (New York: Feminist Press, 1990), 22.

[17] Boyd, *Discarded Legacy*, 86.

"Rizpah, the Daughter of Ai" (*Poems on Miscellaneous Subjects*, 1854), and "*Vashti*" (*Poems*, 1871). These poems defy patriarchal dogma that pervaded American Christianity and brought forward female biblical figures whose perspectives had been ignored, obscured or repressed by the church. Indeed, Harper's most ambitious and revolutionary work, *Moses: A Story of the Nile* (1869), includes a woman's perspective and influence. Harper's radical reconfigurations of women's roles in community, society and church placed her in controversial situations and conversations, in the situation of Ishmael.

In 1863, President Lincoln signed the Emancipation Proclamation, which inspired Harper to write the poems "President Lincoln's Proclamation of Freedom" and "The Freedom Bill." During this time, Frances Ellen Watkins married Fenton Harper (1860) and was living on a small farm outside of Columbus, Ohio. Fenton was a widower with three children; and in 1862, Frances gave birth to their daughter, Mary. Her responsibilities as wife and mother dominated her life, but she returned to the lectern with her poem "Words for the Hour" to recruit black soldiers. Celebrating the nation's change of heart, she wrote in a letter to William Still: "The shadow of the American Army becomes a covert for the slave, and beneath the American eagle we shall reach a higher destiny."[18] Her marriage ended suddenly when Fenton Harper died on May 23, 1864.

She made a new home with her daughter in Philadelphia, but continued her writing and activism in tandem with Reconstructionist efforts in the Southern states after the Civil War. And, 1869 was a very prolific and innovative year for Harper, publishing a new book of poetry, a short story, and her first novel. At this juncture, her writing engaged more challenging literary forms, as in *Moses: A Story of the Nile* (1869), a long poem written in blank verse. As indicated in some of her biblically based poems, the poem conveys the perspective of the women in Moses's life, attributing his political consciousness to the teachings of his mother, who becomes his nurse and rears him to realize his true religious purpose.

Minnie's Sacrifice, a serialized novel published in *The Christian Recorder* (the official publication of the African Methodist Episcopal Church) includes a shocking ending with the lynching of the main character by the Ku Klux Klan. The theme of the story rejects the idea of mulattos passing for white, encourages her audience to join the Reconstructionist efforts in the South, and emphasizes the pervasive killing of blacks, and the burning of schools and churches by the Klan. A postscript appears at the end of

---

[18] Still, *Underground Rail Road*, 766–7.

the story that explains the meaning of the fiction and makes an appeal to African-Americans to join the Reconstructionist efforts in the South, where they need teachers and workers to help the freedmen and women:

> But while I confess (not wishing to misrepresent the most lawless of the Ku-Klux) that Minnie has only lived and died in my imagination, may I not mostly ask that the lesson of Minnie shall have its place among the educational ideas for the advancement of our race?
>
> The greatest want of our people, if I understand our wants aright, is not simply wealth, nor genius, nor mere intelligence, but live men, and earnest, lovely women, whose lives shall represent not a "stagnant mass, but a living force."[19]

The comment echoes Harper's earlier appeal in "Our Greatest Want" (1859), however, the same year that the story appeared in the *Christian Recorder*, Harper was again in "the situation of Ishmael" when she engaged the debate about the Fifteenth Amendment at the 1869 Equal Rights Association meeting in New York.

Susan B. Anthony and Elizabeth Stanton argued that the organization should oppose the constitutional amendment if it only gave black men the right to vote and excluded women. Harper stated that though Anthony and Stanton were enlightened on the issue of race, most white women were not:

> That might be your idea, but when I was in Boston, there were sixty women who left work because one colored woman went to gain a livelihood in their midst. If the nation could only handle one question, I would not have the black woman put a single straw in the way of the black man.[20]

Harper continued to address the confluence of gender and race, but continues the dialogue in the black community and uses the main character in *Minnie's Sacrifice* to echo and extend her comments at the Equal Rights Association convention:

> And while I would not throw a straw in the way of the colored man, even though I know that he would vote against me as soon as he gets his vote; yet I do think that woman should have some power to defend herself from oppression, and equal laws as if she were a man.[21]

Also a supporter of women's rights and suffrage, Minnie discusses sexist repression in the black community with her husband Louis, aspects Harper raised when lecturing throughout the Southern states during the

[19] Frances Harper, "Minnie's Sacrifice," *A.M.E. Christian Recorder* (March 20, 1869–September 25, 1869).
[20] *Ibid.*
[21] Harper, "Minnie's Sacrifice."

Reconstruction Era, advocating education and attempting to influence the politics of her audiences:

> Yesterday I spoke in Darlington, South Carolina, where two years ago a young girl was cruelly scourged and brutally hung for making an indiscreet comment about wanting to marry a Yankee. Her previous master tried to save her to no avail. She was only 17 years of age.
>
> ...Things are a little more hopeful, for some of the colored people are getting better contracts, and there has been less murdering. I don't know how the colored man will vote, but I hope they are not intimidated at the polls.[22]

Harper's essay, "Coloured Women of America," initially published in London, England in 1878, details her admiration of the freedwomen, chronicling their tenacity and strength:

> The women as a class are quite equal to the men in energy and executive ability. In fact, I find by close observation that the mothers are the levers, which move education. The men talk about it, especially during election time, if they want an office for self or their candidate, but the women work most for it ... I know of girls from sixteen to twenty-two who iron till midnight that they may come to school in the day.[23]

In concert with these freedwomen, Harper expanded her poetic voice by inventing a form of dialect that, unlike her literary contemporaries, does not insult the intelligence of her subjects or her audience. "Sketches of Southern Life" (1872) emulates the slave narrative in the voice of the persona, Chloe:

> I REMEMBER, well remember,
>   That dark and dreadful day,
> When they whispered to me, "Chloe,"
>   Your children's sold away!

The poem opens with the slave mother's most dreaded fear – losing her children at the slave auction. Harper's poem was written for the newly freed, and was used during Reconstruction to teach reading and writing. The long poem outlines slavery, the secret codes the community used to communicate the progress of the Civil War, their political perspectives and race, and the building of their new lives in freedom. These themes affirm the integrity of their humanity when they were slaves and during their relentless pursuit for just lives as free people, as they build homes, schools and churches, reunite with their loved ones, and deal with the terror of the Ku Klux

---

[22] Still, *Underground Rail Road*, 768.
[23] Frances Harper, "Coloured Women of America," *Englishwoman's Review* (January 15, 1878): 10–15.

Klan. In African-American vernacular, Chloe describes the political defeat of President Andrew Johnson, a Southerner who did little to advance the Reconstructionist efforts or to stop racial terrorism: "*They let poor Andy slide*"; and then praises his successor, President Grant, "*for breaking up / The wicked Ku-Klux Klan.*"

Speaking from their own consciousness, their language is interesting, multidimensional, and full of insightful observations and abstract expressions. The dialectic Harper implemented in her poetry operates within a cultural and linguistic frameworks that authenticate indigenous speech. Moreover, since she is a poet and an African-American, her sense of sound is more nuanced and attuned to black voices. With its own cultural perspective and syntax, Harper conceptualized a more appropriate representation of the spoken word and its spatial relationship to the page.[24]

Whereas Harper's writing addressed the horrors of slavery during the Abolitionist Movement, works such as *Minnie's Sacrifice* and "Sketches of Southern Life" demonstrate the historical continuum of violence perpetuated against African-Americans in the aftermath:

> If the United States government can protect money, the property of its citizens against destruction at the hands of the counterfeiter, it can protect the owners of the property against loss of life at the hands of the murderer ... It can go to war, spend millions of dollars and sacrifice thousands of lives to avenge the death of naturalized white citizen slain by a foreign government on foreign soil, but cannot spend a cent to protect a loyal, native-born colored American murdered without provocation by native or alien in Alabama ... It can stop lynching and until it does, it has on its hand the innocent blood of its murdered citizens.[25]

The Woman's Era

Juxtaposed with her ongoing struggle against racial injustice was her resistance to the perseverance of gender repression. In 1869, Harper also published the short story, "The Mission of the Flowers" in the book *Moses: A Story of the Nile*. In addition to the theme of diversity and difference, which appears to be a comment to her white feminist sisters, a most interesting feature of the story is Harper's symbolic manipulation of the rose's intoxicating allure – which throughout Western literature has been symbolic of woman's

---

[24] Boyd, *Discarded Legacy*, 152–3.
[25] Frances Harper, "How to Stop Lynching," *Women's Era* 1.2 (1894): 8–9.

sexual power. In the story, the rose entices, seduces, and even rapes some of the flowers until they all agree to become roses:

> A modest lily that grew near the rose tree shrank instinctively from her; but it was in vain, and with tearful eyes and trembling limbs she yielded, while a quiver of agony convulsed her frame.[26]

This provocative flower fable is directly related to the objectification of women's sexuality. Consequently, "the men grew tired of roses, for they were everywhere." When women are valued only for procreation or sexual pleasure, they are, at best, two-dimensional beings. Hence, on a metaphorical level, sexuality and individuality are also related to the essence of complexity and depth in person and in community."[27]

One of Harper's most popular poems during this period, "A Double Standard" (*Poems*, 1870) which appealed to women across the color line, demonstrates Harper's continued critique of gender discrimination in a common social circumstance – a love affair. The woman persona is condemned by society while her male counterpart escapes public ridicule unscathed:

> *Would you blame the world if it should press*
> *On him a civic crown;*
> *And see me struggling in the depth*
> *Then harshly press me down?*
>
> *Crime has no sex and yet to-day*
> *I wear the brand of shame;*
> *Whilst he amid the gay and proud*
> *Still bears an honored name.*

She elicited Christian values to identify the hypocrisy of social practices and ultimate judgement:

> *No golden weights can turn the scale*
> *Of justice in His sight;*
> *And what is wrong in woman's life*
> *In man's cannot be right.*

Likewise, the poem "John and Jacob – A Dialogue on Woman's Rights" (1885) brings men into the conversation about woman's equality to advocate for universal suffrage. As in "A Double Standard," the men are not identified by race, which illustrates the cross-cultural application of the poem to a broader audience. In Philadelphia, Harper continued to teach Sunday

---

[26] Frances Harper, "Mission of the Flowers," in *Moses: A Story of the Nile*, ed. Frances Harper (Philadelphia, 1869), 47.

[27] Boyd, *Discarded Legacy*, 129–30.

school for the A. M. E. Church, but joined the Unitarian Church because it advocated and practiced racial and gender equality.

"The Woman's Era," a term that symbolized the spirit of black feminism in the 1890s, was first referenced by Harper in a quote from Victor Hugo in "The Woman's Christian Temperance Union and the Colored Woman." This essay explicitly deals with the lynching crisis to illustrate the most critical crisis of the historical period. One of her close allies in this work was Ida B. Wells, who stayed with Harper during the 1892 National Conference of the A. M. E Church in Philadelphia. That same year Harper's most famous novel, *Iola Leroy, Or Shadows Uplifted* (1892), appeared. The female protagonist, who aspires to become a writer, is Iola, which is also Ida B. Wells's pen name.

The following year, Frances Harper and Ida B. Wells attend the 1893 World's Columbian Exposition in Chicago, where the World's Congress of Representative Women met. They join Hallie Q. Brown, Anna Julia Cooper, Fannie Jackson Coppin, Sarah J. Early, Fannie Williams, and Frederick Douglass. The organization circulated a pamphlet, "Why the Negro Is Not Represented in the Columbian Exposition," in several languages to protest this exclusion. Harper delivered a speech, "Woman's Political Future," which reiterates her undaunted and relentless drive since 1854:

> O women of America! Into your hands God has pressed one of the sublimest opportunities that ever came into the hands of the women of any race of people. It is yours to create a healthy public sentiment; to demand justice, simple justice, as the right of every race; to brand with everlasting infamy the lawless and brutal cowardice that lynches, burns, and tortures your own countrymen ...
>
> To grapple with the evils which threaten to undermine the strength of the nation and to lay magazines of powder under the crisis of future generations is no child's play ... Let the hearts of the women of the world respond to the song of the herald angles of peace on earth and good will to men.[28]

Subsequently, black women founded their own organizations and established the journal, *The Women's Era*. Harper was elected vice president of the National Association of Colored Women in 1897.

---

[28] Frances Harper, "Women's Political Future," *World's Congress of Representative Women, 1893 Proceedings*, ed. May Wright Sewall (Chicago, 1894), 433–7.

Conclusion

In 1851, Herman Melville's great American novel, *Moby-Dick*, was published. The opening line is one of the most famous in literature: "Call me Ishmael." Ishmael, the narrator, sails with Captain Ahab, and relays a plot based on a tale told to Melville by a sailor, who survived the sinking of a ship, the *Essex*, by a gigantic whale. A literary association could be correlated with Harper's pronouncement, "in the situation of Ismael." No doubt, she read the works of Melville, whose portrayals of Africans and African-Americans were progressive and served an abolitionist purpose. Considering her national profile, Melville probably was aware of Harper, and could have been conversely influenced by her.

However, the politics in her aesthetics demonstrate her identification with Ishmael, which was the perspective of the paradox – being black and female. "In the situation of Ishmael," Frances Ellen Watkins Harper fought many battles, confronted discrimination and survived dangerous times. She died on February 22, 1911 in Philadelphia at the age of eighty-five. And, despite her modesty, there is a marker in front of her house that honors her life and the space where she lived and aspired to advance freedom for all Americans.

> *I ask no monument, proud and high,*
> *To arrest the gaze of the passers-by;*
> *All that my yearning spirit craves,*
> *Is bury me not in a land of slaves.*
> (Frances E. W. Harper, 1858)

15

LAURA DASSOW WALLS

The Corner-stones of Heaven: Science Comes to Concord

On the last day of August, 1856, Henry Thoreau set out "a-cranberrying." His walk took him across the Great Fields to Beck Stow's Swamp, a half-mile west of the farm where he was born, where he stepped around bags of commercial European cranberries raked up and ready for the market, stripped off shoes and stockings, and waded into the swamp's cold water, squeezing the soft sphagnum moss between his toes. This kind of walk was now Thoreau's primary enterprise, an act of literary composition written first on the land, then in his Journal. It was also an act of scientific investigation, which he would add to his growing databank of natural knowledge: two simultaneous acts of composition, literary and scientific. Six years before, Thoreau had been elected a "corresponding member" of the Boston Society of Natural History; in exchange, he had agreed to "advance the interests of the Society by communication or otherwise, as shall seem good."[1] From then on, Thoreau kept his pledge to be the scientist among poets and the poet among scientists, interweaving nature and history, local and global, heaven and earth: transcendence squeezed between his toes, every object a corner-stone of heaven, every least experience indexing an ecology of place and planet.

Even finding such a small thing as a wild native cranberry would, Thoreau wrote, make his walk significant, for his goal was not merely to taste "an insignificant berry ... but the flavor of your life to that extent," a sauce "no wealth can buy." This particular walk proved especially noteworthy: he located not one but two species of wild cranberry – one nestled away in the green sphagnum, the other resting like ruby jewels on its green breast – and filled two pockets, one species per side. He also found a new species of blueberry, its berries small, black, tough, and hairy: *Gaylussacia dumosa* var. *hirtella*, said Asa Gray's botany. Any new species was cause for celebration,

---

[1] Henry David Thoreau, *Correspondence, Volume 2: 1849–1854* (Princeton: Princeton University Press, forthcoming), 89.

but for Thoreau, finding an inedible hairy wild huckleberry was truly thrilling: it meant a half-hour's walk could carry him into a region "as wild and primitive and unfrequented as a square rod in Labrador." The wild is not somewhere far away – indeed, "there is none such" – for "the surface of the globe" is *everywhere* wild, even to our very bodies, "the bog in our brain and bowels." The undiscovered country lies all around us, even within us. Only our blindness hides it from view.[2]

This Journal passage marks a year of recovery for Thoreau. Soon after *Walden*'s 1854 publication he had been leveled by a near-fatal bout with tuberculosis, which attacked his legs and made walking difficult. But by spring of 1856 he was again outside, working as a surveyor, taking long daily walks, and writing brilliantly in his Journal. Its pages track a still largely unknown Thoreau: the accomplished author, anti-slavery activist, and natural scientist, living happily with his family on Main Street, working out the grand vision for which *Walden* was the dawn. His goal was to practice what he'd learned at Walden Pond: to see, wherever you are, "with the unworn sides of your eye, travel totally new paths." As his August jaunt to Beck Stow's Swamp made clear, such paths did not need to be long or far away. To walk the familiar byways of Concord was to walk the surface of a stellar body, gaining acquaintance with "cohabitants with me of this part of the planet," learning that the planet was not all "garden and cultivated field and crops, that there are square rods in Middlesex County as purely primitive and wild as they were a thousand years ago … little oases of wildness in the desert of our civilization, wild as a square rod on the moon." As Thoreau reached from the flavor of the berries to the flavor of his life, his hands touched the circuit of the heavens: "I believe almost in the personality of such planetary matter, feel something akin to reverence for it, can even worship it as terrene, titanic matter extant in my day." Why, the whole globe was "an aerolite," he exclaimed. "How happens it that we reverence the stones which fall from another planet, and not the stones which belong to this, – another globe, not this, – heaven, and not earth? … Is not our broad back-door-stone as good as any corner-stone in heaven?"[3]

From cranberry culture to the corner-stone of heaven? It seems a leap, but as readers of *Walden* know, even Thoreau's most extravagant writing was deeply rooted in agriculture – specifically, in the mixed-husbandry horticulture that had characterized the Concord River valley for two hundred years, but was swiftly giving way to globalized industrial agriculture. This

---

[2] Henry David Thoreau, *Journal of Henry David Thoreau*, 14 vols. (Boston: Houghton Mifflin, 1906), IX: 35–43.

[3] *Ibid.*, IX: 38, 44–5, 406.

required developing new crops: English hay to fatten the new breeds of beef cattle bound for Boston; new varieties of apples (Thoreau's specialty) and pears (Emerson's); the new "Concord grape" bred by their neighbor Ephraim Bull from the local wild grapes Thoreau gathered every fall – a huge commercial success that local cranberry growers hoped to emulate. Observing this transition from local subsistence to global commerce meant watching traditional farms fail, the forests fall, and runoff from denuded hills flood the river meadows, destroying the wild native grasslands that had for generations anchored the local ecology. In an irony not lost on Thoreau, his own work as a professional surveyor made him complicit. From his station in town, he kept an eye on the labors of the neighboring farmers, whose life on the land posed a perpetual challenge: was it he, or they, who lived closer to the seasons of nature? In January 1852, as he watched farmers cart manure into the pastures to fertilize spring growth, he admonished himself to do the same. He must farm the white pages, cart the compost of thought from the "barn-yard" of his Journal, plow and plant his furrows of words to flower in poetry, bear the seeds of thought. As he wrote, "The scholar's and the farmer's work are strictly analogous."[4]

Thoreau had become a scholar at Harvard, an education few farmers' sons could afford, made possible by profits from his family's pencil factory. While Harvard in the 1830s offered little in the sciences, it did require a course in natural history taught by the college librarian, Thaddeus Harris. Harris's classroom consisted of dull drills, but outside the classroom he was a talented naturalist whose extracurricular field trips inspired a cadre of young enthusiasts – including Thoreau, who on the eve of his graduation joined with his friends in the class of '37 to found the Harvard Natural History Society. For years afterward, Harris's students kept up a loose network of friends exchanging letters, specimens, and visits; some, including Thoreau and Thomas Wentworth Higginson, became popular nature writers.

Harvard's push to modernize its science curriculum gained speed in 1842, with the hire of the renowned botanist Asa Gray – passing over Harris, the beloved local natural historian, in favor of the cosmopolitan professional specialist. Thoreau's world expanded accordingly, as he kept tabs on both the amateur enthusiasts and, as much as possible, the emerging scientific elite. While he remained lifelong friends with Harris, he also studied Gray's botany manuals with deep interest – so much so that in 1859, Harvard appointed Thoreau to the Examining Committee in Natural History, chaired by Gray himself. In 1847, when Harvard hired the great European zoologist Louis Agassiz – renowned for his theory that glaciers had once covered

---

[4] *Ibid.*, III: 207.

the earth – Thoreau joined Agassiz's collecting network, sending him specimens of fishes, turtles, and mice from Walden Pond. Agassiz became close
friends with Emerson, who watched with amusement as Thoreau pressed
the renowned naturalist into arguments over whether frozen fish could be
revived or how species came to be where they were. Once, when Thoreau
ranted against Agassiz's lapses – "'The ignorant scoundrels have not been in
Concord!'" – Emerson mildly replied, "what were you sent for but to make
this observation?"[5]

Thoreau's daily rounds also included conversations with Concord's farmers, many of whom became his close friends. In January 1852, a number of
them gathered to found the Concord Farmers Club, a weekly seminar and
discussion group. Members were assigned topics, often scientific, to research
and report, and discussions were long and lively. Their goal was to inte-
grate traditional farm practices with the new sciences – geology, chemistry
and soil science, botany and forest management – to create a new, modern
agriculture. Though Thoreau was not a formal member, many of his closest
friends were, and they often drew on his expertise in native plants and the
culture of orchards and forest trees. In time, Thoreau took on a special role
as an intermediary between the local network of farmers, and the regional
network of natural scientists – a service so useful that Emerson thought
every town ought to have a village naturalist, someone who could answer
questions about critters, bugs, and plants – including the management of
cranberry meadows.[6]

Collecting specimens for Agassiz taught Thoreau that even apparently
trivial finds could have value for science. When Jacob Farmer, founder of the
Concord Farmers Club, shot a goshawk, he brought the corpse to Thoreau,
who in turn brought it to Samuel Cabot, curator of birds at the Boston
Society of Natural History (BSNH) – the center of New England science.
From farmer's pest to scientific specimen: the goshawk proved so rare and
valuable that in December 1850, in thanks for his contribution, the BSNH
named Thoreau a lifetime corresponding member. From then on, his trips to
Boston included two stops, one at Harvard's library to visit with Harris, the
other at the BSNH to study the collections and question the members. Word
spread: early in 1853 Thoreau was invited by Spencer F. Baird to join the
American Association for the Advancement of Science (AAAS), the nation's
leading scientific society. Thoreau accepted immediately and returned their
questionnaire, naming his occupation as "Literary and Scientific, Combined

[5] Ralph Waldo Emerson, *Journals and Miscellaneous Notebooks of Ralph Waldo
Emerson*, 16 vols. (Cambridge, MA: Harvard University Press, 1960–1982), XIV: 278.
[6] *Ibid.*, XI: 277.

with Land-Surveying." He remained a member in good standing through 1853, although when it came time to renew, he declined, explaining that he could attend their meetings only if they were held in his "immediate vicinity."[7] Science, for Thoreau, meant actually *meeting* scientists, not passive enrollment but active and immediate participation: questions asked, and answered, person to person.

Yet his role as "correspondent" meant Thoreau never quite belonged to the various constituencies with whom he conversed. On his travels he often struck strangers as "a pedlar of small wares," and in a way they were right: he circulated freely among farmers, local naturalists, and the era's elite professional scientists – not to mention among poets, Transcendentalists, and antislavery activists – peddling to each something of value he'd acquired from the others. To none of them was he quite an insider; his famous refusal to join formal organizations makes his loyalty to the BSNH all the more remarkable. Yet to all of them he was a valued contributor, always bearing gifts – an observation, a specimen, a lecture or essay – and staying just long enough to "take toll" (as he said to Agassiz) in some small way: the loan of a book, the identification of a rare plant or bird or insect, the answer to a question. Thus Thoreau matured into a kind of trader and interdisciplinary diplomat, crossing borders and stitching together fields even as they were fragmenting into specialties guarded by professional rituals and prescribed forms of expertise. Yet having to show his passport daily meant no one – not even Emerson – ever saw the entire Thoreau or quite understood the many-stranded whole he was weaving, like the bird's nests he analyzed in such detail, out of such disparate and carefully chosen materials. Hence even as Thoreau politely informed the AAAS of his scientific specialty – namely, the manners and customs of pre-contact Algonquin Indians – in private he raged that to describe his true interests would make him the "laughing-stock of the scientific community ... inasmuch as they do not believe in a science which deals with the higher law." As he famously added, "The fact is I am a mystic, a transcendentalist, and a natural philosopher to boot."[8]

Thoreau's work as an intermediary among multiple fields meant applying the global concepts of modern science to the most local and immediate of inquiries, untangling networks of relationships until they began to yield fresh insights on a wide range of questions both practical and poetic. Science, to him, was not opposed to what he called "the higher law," but a means to its discovery. Nor was Thoreau alone in this quest. Science in

---

[7] Henry David Thoreau, *Correspondence, Volume 2: 1849–1856* (Princeton: Princeton University Press, forthcoming), 151–3, 181–2.
[8] Thoreau, *Journal*, v: 4.

the early Republic was not a specialty reserved for a professional elite, but a normal part of educated discourse, part of the intellectual commons – indeed, to think and act otherwise was unpatriotic, for in the United States, science was supposed be "democratic" and open to everyone. This national ethic drove the Concord Farmers Club to debate how science could help them be better stewards of the land; in 1826 it inspired Josiah Holbrook to found the Lyceum movement to foster scientific knowledge in towns across the nation, including Concord. Starting in 1828, the Concord Lyceum regularly included scientific topics, including a ten-course series of lectures on chemistry in 1829 that drew a capacity audience. Thoreau was a member from the start, and both he and Emerson became pillars of service. As editor of the *Dial* from 1842 to 1844, Emerson inserted regular updates on scientific events and findings: in his first issue alone, he asked Thoreau to review a stack of state reports on natural history (the result was Thoreau's first major essay, "The Natural History of Massachusetts"); celebrated the return of the United States Exploring Expedition, the most ambitious scientific expedition the United States had ever launched; congratulated Harvard for appointing Asa Gray to the long vacant Chair of Natural History; and chided it for ignoring a meeting of the Association of American Geologists and Naturalists, a meeting that drew naturalists from all over the nation as well as the great British geologist – the founder of the field himself – Charles Lyell.[9] This very society would, in 1848, reorganize as the AAAS.

The exchanges indicated by all this activity were hardly superficial. Lyell was especially important to Emerson, who had first encountered him in 1826 when, as a young minister in the throes of religious doubt, he read a young Lyell proclaiming that all animated beings were gradations on a connected and progressive plan, inhabiting an earth of immeasurable antiquity. Lyell would expand his theories into his landmark work *Principles of Geology* (1830–1833), in which he detailed an earth in constant change, cycling through eons of time that resembled nothing in Genesis – indeed, in his opening pages Lyell compared earth's great cycles with the Hindu Great Year instead, introducing modern geology via ancient Hindu scripture. As Emerson's crisis of faith deepened, he appropriated from Lyell the evidentiary proof he needed to demolish biblical chronology; as Emerson declared in 1831, "The Religion that is afraid of science dishonours God & commits suicide. It acknowledges that it is not equal to the whole of truth, that it legislates, tyrannizes over a village of God's empire but is not the immutable universal law."[10] Five years later he would announce in *Nature* (1836), the

---

[9] [Ralph Waldo Emerson], "Intelligence," *Dial* 3 (1842): 133.
[10] Emerson, *Journals*, III: 239; see also my *Emerson's Life in Science: The Culture of Truth* (Ithaca, NY: Cornell University Press, 2003), 74–98.

book that launched Transcendentalism: to an instructed eye "the universe becomes transparent, and the light of higher laws than its own shines through it."[11] Emerson saw in modern science a new and more solid foundation for modern religious belief, a faith grounded immutably in the "higher laws" of nature as revealed by science. He pursued this faith through the range of the modern sciences – geology, chemistry, zoology, physics – to the end of his life.

Thoreau first encountered Lyell's *Principles of Geology* in Emerson's library, after he had joined the Emerson household as tutor, handyman, and Transcendental apprentice. As Thoreau wrote in 1840, paraphrasing Lyell, geology discovers "the causes of all past change in the present invariable order of the universe"; even the greatest of revolutions are worked by "the light-footed air – the stealthy-paced water – and the subterranean fire," forces easily observed in the course of a daily walk.[12] The principle became foundational to Thoreau's own philosophy, for it opened up the dynamic significance of every object and process, both natural and social, assuring him that the pulse of the universe was beating still. At the end of his life, he still avowed that there was never a sudden re-formation of the world, "but a steady progress according to existing laws" accumulating over an incalculable period. So with the organic world: science knows that all plants "come from seeds, *i.e.* are the result of causes still in operation, however slow and unobserved." To trace the nature and action of each seed, how each particular embryo of life was formed and released into the world, was to trace the evolution of life on the planet and the hope for the world to come.[13]

For Thoreau to reach this point, however, required a break with Emerson. Early in *A Week on the Concord and Merrimack Rivers* (1849) – the book Thoreau went to Walden to write – he had built on Emerson's authority to insult "that old Jewish scheme" of Genesis, insisting instead that "Your scheme must be the frame-work of the universe; all other schemes will soon be ruins." As he continued, "There is more religion in men's science than there is science in their religion."[14] But near the book's close, he added a plea that pushed against Emerson's longing to render the earth "transparent" to reveal the higher law: "May we not *see* God? Are we to be put off and amused in this life, as it were with a mere allegory? Is not Nature, rightly

[11] Ralph Waldo Emerson, *Essays and Lectures* (New York: Library of America, 1983), 25.
[12] Henry David Thoreau, *Journal, Volume 1: 1837–1844* (Princeton: Princeton University Press, 1981), 191.
[13] Thoreau, *Journal*, XIV: 311–12, 334.
[14] Henry David Thoreau, *A Week on the Concord and Merrimack Rivers* (Princeton: Princeton University Press, 1980), 70, 78.

read, that of which she is commonly taken to be the symbol merely?"[15] That there was "a nature behind the ordinary" Thoreau, too, was certain; but at Walden he began to ask this question in a different way. "Why do precisely these objects which we behold make a world? Why has man just these species of animals for his neighbors; as if nothing but a mouse could have filled this crevice?"[16] Agassiz identified the mouse that ate cheese from Thoreau's fingers as "a wild native kind (*Mus leucopus*)," a species he'd never seen before.[17] Such discoveries deepened Thoreau's attention to the organism – even the single, unique individual – in all its numinous specificity. At the same time, his growing studies of natural beings were tracking not single individuals but patterns that were pointing to abstract laws.

In short, while Emerson preferred to wrestle with the power of "higher" laws, Thoreau could never surrender the romance of the irreducible organism – and in this, Thoreau evidences the hallmark of a new science, one he himself helped bring into existence: ecology. As the historian of science Stephen Jay Gould once observed, "Ecologists must live in tension between two approaches to the diversity of life. On the one hand, they are tempted to bask in the irreducibility and glory of it all – exult and record. But, on the other, they acknowledge that science is a search for repeated pattern. Laws and regularities underlie the display." Gould names these two approaches "exultation or explanation," and remarks that while many ecologists treat one or the other with suspicion, the most innovative have loved and practiced both. The tension Gould describes as the dilemma of ecology is the same tension that drew Thoreau away from Emerson into his own unique and characteristic form of transcendental science – one that cherished both nature's "multifarious complexity," on the one hand, and on the other the pattern-seeking generalizations that yielded scientific knowledge.[18]

Only months after publishing *A Week*, Thoreau turned to the scientist who best integrated the two poles of exultation and explanation: Alexander von Humboldt, the polymathic scientist-explorer who had inspired both Lyell and Agassiz, as well as Charles Darwin; whose German example had inspired the formation of the AAAS; and whose work had founded the science that yet another of his disciples would name "ecology." As Thoreau proudly reminded the AAAS in 1853, his own hybrid poetic science would have been welcomed by Humboldt, whose books Thoreau had been reading since 1849. Humboldt was a towering worldwide celebrity, and though

[15] *Ibid.*, 382.
[16] Henry David Thoreau, *Walden* (Princeton: Princeton University Press, 1971), 225.
[17] *Ibid.*, 225.
[18] Stephen Jay Gould, "Exultation and Explanation," in *An Urchin in the Storm: Essays about Books and Ideas* (New York: Norton, 1987), 180–8, 181, 187.

he lacked a single easily named achievement (some historians suggest he invented modern science itself), his image of Mount Chimborazo belted by climate zones – correlating altitude with earth's latitude – became so ubiquitous that Emerson, Melville, and Twain all made casual references to it.[19]

Thoreau, however, went farther, listing plants by altitudinal zones on both Mount Wachusett and Mount Washington – perhaps his most significant contribution to the botany of New England.[20] Humboldt went farther still by investigating the way Chimborazo, as a volcano, built itself over the eons through upthrust and successive eruptions; just as plants composed their own communities, so did mountains and valleys, lakes and oceans, even continents, compose themselves through the geological processes that Lyell explained to the world. Thus Nature was not designed or controlled by divine agency, but was self-organizing and self-creative, unfolding through generative laws one could read in the very earth itself. There was no deeper truth hiding behind or underneath; one need not strike, Ahab-like, through the mask of appearance to reach the real. Reality was right before our eyes, imbricated in nature's historical being, legible to all. This was what Thoreau meant by "the frame-work of the universe": to understand the historicity of nature is to read the mystery of its being. His daily walks were Humboldtian micro-expeditions, setting out by foot or boat with pencil and notebook, keen eyes, and capacious pockets to explore some local place – Beck Stow's Swamp, Hubbard's Woods, Fair Haven Bay – returning to his desk, as he did on August 30, 1856, to spin the most mundane observations into metaphysical quests.

Thus did Thoreau become both "Transcendentalist" *and* "natural philosopher," the era's term for "scientist"; to bring them together he added a third, the "mystic." True, he resisted Agassiz's notion that natural forms embodied Ideas in the mind of God, preferring instead to follow long chains of material causes; as he said, in effect, There is *always* a seed. But therein lies the real mystery: how do the latent energies and designs of self-organizing nature manifest themselves, not in general laws, but in actual lives? – in plant growth and associations, animal behaviors, flooding and erosion, climate and the swings of weather? – not to mention human actions both deliberate and unintended? Thoreau's astonishment at wading into "terrene, titanic matter" so near home echoes the moment on Maine's Mount Katahdin, where he was staggered by the uncanny nature of

---

[19] For extensive documentation and documentation, see my *Passage to Cosmos: Alexander von Humboldt and the Shaping of America* (Chicago: University of Chicago Press), 2009.

[20] Ray Angelo, "Thoreau as Botanist: An Appreciation and a Critique," *Arnoldia* 45.3 (Summer 1985): 13–23, 16, 22.

the fresh and natural surface of the planet Earth ... some star's surface, some hard matter in its home! ... Talk of mysteries! – Think of our life in nature, – daily to be shown matter, to come in contact with it, – rocks, trees, wind on our cheeks! the *solid* earth! the *actual* world! the *common sense!*[21]

This famous passage from "Ktaadn" (1846) voiced Thoreau's exaltation at the mystery of the material, a mystery that permeated everything he wrote thereafter, including *Walden*. That the beings of nature – even matter itself, like the strange ramifying flow of the thawing sand-bank in "Spring" – were self-willed, or "wild," meant that even routine walks could open the gates of sheer astonishment. While Thoreau may have disavowed orthodox religion, in the face of such ultimate mystery his sensibility remained profoundly religious. Thus his long meditation on Beck Stow's Swamp ends in an attitude of worship: "How happens it that we reverence the stones which fall from another planet, and not the stones which belong to this, – another globe, not this, – heavens, and not earth?" Were humanity to become "elevated enough to truly worship stocks and stones," he offers, it would be our very regeneration; in a line that echoes Whitman (whose poetry he greatly admired), "If I could, I would worship the parings of my nails. If he who makes two blades of grass grow where one grew before is a benefactor, he who discovers two gods where there was only known the one (and such a one!) before is a still greater benefactor." Thoreau would "wonder and worship" at every opportunity, just as "a sunflower welcomes the light."[22]

Surprisingly, this vision of mystery was also thoroughly practical. One day late in April 1856, while Thoreau was out surveying, his assistant asked him, Why is it that when a pine woods is cut down, young oaks spring up in their place? Soon Thoreau had an answer: squirrels and birds constantly plant acorns under the shelter of the pines, and every year the seeds sprout into little oaks. Most will annually die, "but when the pines are cleared off, the oaks, etc., having got just the start they want, and now secured favorable conditions, immediately spring up to trees."[23] But this led to more questions: while some of his friends countered that the seeds must have been lying dormant in the ground, others insisted that only spontaneous generation could account for the sudden appearance of species, and few could credit pests and vermin as creative agents planting entire forests. But Thoreau held firm: the principle of succession had to lie in the material agency of the seed and all its associates, including those with feathers

[21] Henry David Thoreau, *Maine Woods* (Princeton: Princeton University Press, 1972), 70–1.
[22] Thoreau, *Journal*, IX: 45–6.
[23] *Ibid.*, VIII: 315, 334–5.

and fur. Whatever transformations one observed in nature, there had to be actual, material agents one could name and observe. Moreover, across the Atlantic Charles Darwin was also tracking the dispersion of seeds, which he called the key to unraveling that "mystery of mysteries," the *origin* of species. As Darwin wrote in *Origin of Species*, "Everyone has heard that when an American forest is cut down, a very different vegetation springs up."[24] The question was, Why?

This was science the way Thoreau liked it, grounded in local observation while addressing some of the day's biggest puzzles. But he didn't see the full implications of his research until New Year's Day, 1860, when Charles Loring Brace brought to Concord the advance copy of *Origin of Species* that Darwin had sent to Brace's uncle, Asa Gray. The four friends – Brace, Franklin Sanborn, Bronson Alcott, and Thoreau – spent the day in excited discussion, reading passages aloud to each other. Soon Thoreau had read it cover to cover, taking extensive notes – making him one of the very first to read Darwin's *Origin of Species* on American soil.[25] Three months later, at a meeting on "Forest Trees," the Concord Farmers Club took up Darwin's remark about American forests. Why was it, wondered Jacob Farmer, that "we find a succession of different trees grow on the same soil. If we cut off pines, oaks will come up. If we cut off oaks, pines will follow."[26] Thoreau's friends must have turned to him for help, for over the next few months he launched a series of field investigations into the question. On September 20, 1860, he presented his findings as a keynote speaker before the Middlesex County Agricultural Society, addressing a large and appreciative audience including local farmers and state dignitaries; thereafter "The Succession of Forest Trees" became the most widely read, during his lifetime, of all Thoreau's writings.

Thoreau knew his latest work had found a real audience. His literary agent, Horace Greeley – publisher of America's largest newspaper, the *New-York Tribune* – rushed "Succession of Forest Trees" into print, then fanned it into a national controversy by publishing his correspondence with Thoreau, arguing over spontaneous generation – a form of creationism that Thoreau staunchly repudiated. All that fall, Thoreau strode out daily into the woods and fields in pursuit of fresh data. For years he'd been gathering material for the book he was calling *Wild Fruits* – in which Beck Stow's cranberries

[24] Charles Darwin, *On the Origin of Species, Facsimile of the First Edition* (Cambridge, MA: Harvard University Press, 1964), 74.

[25] See my *Henry David Thoreau: A Life* (Chicago: University of Chicago Press, 2017), 458–9; Randall Fuller, *The Book That Changed America: How Darwin's Theory of Evolution Ignited a Nation* (New York: Viking, 2017).

[26] Walls, *Thoreau: A Life*, 470–2.

were to have found publication – and now he had enough material for a *second* new book, "The Dispersion of Seeds."[27] Had he lived long enough to complete both books – at the end of November Thoreau contracted a cold that inflamed his tuberculosis, this time fatally – it would be easier to see a fundamental feature of his writing: how closely Thoreau, the poetic/scientific correspondent, worked to connect local farmers with the era's most noted natural scientists, opening fresh theoretical perspectives *and* solving practical questions of ecological succession and forest management. For this was the genius of Transcendentalism, which centered on the ideal of "self-culture" – that is, on the unfolding or "cultivation" of each person's latent capacities. The farmer's literal cultivation of the land was taken, by Thoreau and by his audiences, as both the analogue and the means to higher "culture" of the self and community: a kind of *moral* ecology spread through community collaboration.

Thus, the science of "ecology" turned out to be both thoroughly practical, and loaded with worldly, even metaphysical, consequences. Thoreau anticipated this metaphysical turn at the end of his "Ktaadn" passage, with its urgent call: "*Contact! Contact! Who* are we? *where* are we?"[28] To "contact" means to touch together, to touch *jointly* – that is, what is touched in "contact" touches back. This is not transcendence in the Emersonian sense, nor even immanence in the theological sense, but closer to what the eco-philosopher Timothy Morton calls "subscendence." Whereas in dominant forms of holism the whole is said to be *greater* than the sum of its parts, in subscendence the whole is *smaller* – because each "part," each object, is so fully loaded with its own latent potentialities.[29] In this sense ecological objects are, like brains, books, and Tardises, "bigger on the inside" – the more they are explored, the bigger they get. Whereas holistic environments push apart such conceptual entities as "the farm," "the town," and "wilderness" – or "literature" and "science" – into mutually exclusive categories, Thoreau's ecological environments open up room for the uncanny "wild" in every niche and crevice: wild cranberries growing alongside the European, or wild hairy huckleberries unsuspected, infinite room for biodiversity to flourish within and between the farm and the town.

[27] See Henry David Thoreau, *Wild Fruits: Thoreau's Rediscovered Last Manuscript*, ed. B. P. Dean (New York: Norton, 2000), and Henry David Thoreau, *Faith in a Seed: "The Dispersion of Seeds" and Other Late Natural History Writings*, ed. Bradley P. Dean (Washington, DC: Island Press, 1993).

[28] Thoreau, *Maine Woods*, 71.

[29] Timothy Morton, *Dark Ecology: For a Logic of Future Coexistence* (New York: Columbia University Press, 2016), 114–16.

Thoreau's reading in Darwin not only confirmed all this, but extended it into the social world in a radically different way from the degenerate "Darwinism" that soon dominated the era. The four friends reading Darwin together on New Year's Day, 1860, were all abolitionists, meeting just weeks after John Brown's insurrection and execution. To them, Darwin proved that slavery was an abomination, for his theory of evolution showed the human species was one single family – just as Humboldt had earlier insisted in his bestselling *Cosmos*. It's true that Thoreau focused mostly on scientific applications of Darwin's theory, concentrating on ecological concepts that the impending Civil War might seem to make irrelevant – except that Thoreau himself pushed back hard against this notion. Even his walk to Beck Stow's Swamp was not an escape from politics, but an act of resistance that "drives Kansas out of your head, and actually and permanently occupies the only desirable and free Kansas against all border ruffians."[30] If science opens one's eyes to "higher law," to truth that forges the "framework of the universe," then Thoreau's turn to science was not an escapist indulgence but a higher employment, an "attitude of resistance" that refuses to give ground to his nation's toxic politics. His quest reclaims the wild planet as the only true America: as he famously declared in "Walking," "in Wildness is the preservation of the world." Each day's walk preserves the "holy land," Concord's common fields and woods, from the infidels who desecrate the holiness of creation.

That Thoreau's "Wildness" was a global thought, his way of thinking the planet, is clear from his own language ("planetary matter"); the revolutionary potential of wild thinking becomes still clearer in the writings of another New Englander, George Perkins Marsh, whose landmark *Man and Nature* (1864) anticipated today's horror at the arrival of the Anthropocene by scaling up the implications of human agency in nature all the way from the destruction of local forests and the ravaging of watersheds – themes important to both Humboldt and Thoreau – to the ruination of the very planet itself, what Marsh called man's ruthless war "on all the tribes of animated nature." Humans, that is, were not merely subject to those stealthy agents of Lyell's planetary revolutions – water, wind, and fire – but were themselves, like "every plant, every animal," a "geographical agency" whose smallest of daily acts were accumulating into the greatest of planetary calamities. As Marsh cautioned, "we can never know how wide a circle of disturbance we produce in the harmonies of nature when we throw the smallest pebble into the ocean of organic life." Our present course, he prophesied, would soon

---

[30] Thoreau, *Journal*, IX: 36.

render the earth "an unfit home," its surface so ravaged and its climate so deranged as to threaten the extinction of humanity.[31]

At the end of his short life, Thoreau reasoned that nature's apparent cruelty made sense only on a cosmic scale. Darwin wrestled with the dark implications – if design doesn't govern the progress of nature, then what guarantees the future of humanity? Thoreau's response was fundamentally humanistic: he affirmed his foundational faith in nature's "constant *new* creation," the self-organizing power of natural beings and objects which he saw confirmed, not refuted, by Darwin's theory of evolution.[32] For Thoreau, of course, this deep faith included the human. We, too, are self-willed, hence "wild" and always potentially renewing, never prescribed or limited by the constrictions of custom or the decisions of our ancestors. Even as the Civil War raged all around him, even as he put away his great work unfinished, Thoreau died at peace. It seems uncanny. He knew cruelty too, but finally avowed, as he had at Walden, that joy was the ultimate condition of the universe – joy subtending all, including the joy that could surprise him bare-foot, wading in the sphagnum on a cool fair August afternoon.

[31] George P. Marsh, *Man and Nature, or, Physical Geography as Modified by Human Action* (Cambridge, MA: Harvard University Press, 1965), 36, 39, 52, 91–2, 43.
[32] Thoreau, *Journal*, XIV: 147.

CHRISTOPHER N. PHILLIPS

Coda: War and the Renaissance

While scholars started pushing the temporal boundaries of Matthiessen's early 1850s Renaissance almost immediately, the boundary that has most served to contain the period is the Civil War. As the dividing point between romanticism and realism, the era of Emerson and Hawthorne and that of James and Twain, the war has given us a convenient label – "antebellum" – to mark the Renaissance as a past forever lost to us, a move that says more about our own cultural needs than those of the 1850s, 1860s, and 1870s. As Cody Marrs, Randall Fuller, and others have recently demonstrated, there was significantly more continuity in both individual literary careers and in literary trends more generally than Matthiessen's account has led scholars to assume.[1] While there is little question that the war made a huge difference in the history of American literature and the book trade, as well as in the lives of individual authors, the sharpness of the break between *antebellum* and *postbellum* has become an open question in recent years.

In considering what difference the war made for the authors of the American Renaissance, and for our study of them, we need to remember that while many in the 1850s anticipated the Civil War's approach, almost no one imagined the cataclysm of total war that would ensue. The framework for the anticipated war was provided by the Mexican War, the deeply polarizing campaign of 1846–1848 that made the 1850s United States a consciously *postbellum* nation.[2] Mexico provided a hemispheric historical

[1] See Cody Marrs, *Nineteenth-Century American Literature and the Long Civil War* (New York: Cambridge University Press, 2015); Randall Fuller, *From Battlefields Rising: How the Civil War Transformed American Literature* (New York: Oxford University Press, 2011); Coleman Hutchison, ed., *A History of the American Civil War* (New York: Cambridge University Press, 2016); Christopher Hager and Cody Marrs, "Against 1865: Reperiodizing the Nineteenth Century," *Journal of Nineteenth-Century Americanists* 1.2 (Fall 2013): 259–84.

[2] On the Mexican War's place in American literature, see Robert W. Johannsen, *To the Halls of the Montezumas: The Mexican War in the American Imagination* (New York: Oxford University Press, 1985). Jaime Javier Rodríguez offers an important

backdrop for Manifest Destiny thanks in part to William Hickling Prescott's *History of the Conquest of Mexico* (1843), a work that General Winfield Scott famously claimed to carry in his luggage as he entered victoriously into Mexico City. Adventure novels, memoirs, and poetry patriotic and satirical about the war abounded. One poem in particular offers a glimpse of how closely two American wars came to be associated in the minds of those who lived through the American Renaissance.

Theodore O'Hara's "Bivouac of the Dead" is an elegy with more than one life. O'Hara wrote the poem by 1850 to celebrate the bravery and sacrifice of soldiers from his native Kentucky at the 1847 Battle of Buena Vista. The poem quickly found a recurring place in the ritual of military burials in Kentucky, and following O'Hara's printing of the poem in the *Mobile Register* (which he edited) in 1858, other newspapers and magazines reprinted it, from New Orleans to New York City. It became a favorite of General Montgomery Meigs, Quartermaster for the Army of the Potomac and founder of the first national cemeteries. His choice to display stanzas of O'Hara's poem, without attribution, on cast-iron plaques at Arlington began a trend that would see the poem displayed, always in excerpts and anonymous, from state cemeteries in Mississippi to the imposing national grounds at Shiloh and Gettysburg (Figure C.1). By selecting only the stanzas most generally describing soldiers' valor and the sanctity of their resting place, the poem could speak to audiences across state and sectional lines; it is unknown whether Meigs knew the authorship of the poem or the fact that O'Hara commanded the 12th Alabama during the war, but in the poem's anonymous circulation, O'Hara's role as the origin of this American Renaissance production became irrelevant.[3] Indeed, claiming common literary property was a part of the discourse of union and liberty during the war. Just five days before his assassination, President Lincoln, basking in the glow of victory, greeted a serenading military band from a White House balcony and requested that the band play "Dixie," the Confederacy's unofficial national anthem, claiming that while the South had "attempted to appropriate" the song, "we fairly captured it" with the fall of Richmond; Lincoln joked, "I presented the question to the Attorney General, and he gave it as his

comparative update to Johannsen's work in *The Literatures of the U.S.-Mexican War: Narrative, Time, and Identity* (Austin: University of Texas Press, 2010).
[3] The poem's continued place in national burying grounds stands in contrast to its absence from collections of American poetry, including Civil War-specific collections. A rare modern reprinting in Wade Hall, ed., *The Kentucky Anthology: Two Hundred Years of Writing in the Bluegrass State* (Lexington: University of Kentucky Press, 2005), reinscribes the sectional specificity of the poem.

Figure C.1 Bronze plaque displaying a stanza from Theodore O'Hara's "The Bivouac of the Dead," Gettsyburg National Cemetery, Gettysburg National Military Park. Photograph by the author.

legal opinion that it is our lawful prize."[4] In a war in which property rights, human rights, and national belonging were issues that millions of Americans considered worth fighting and dying for, poetry and other literary forms came to symbolize those issues, even as literature helped to negotiate and manage them.

Literature's role in the war and its aftermath is only beginning to receive sustained scholarly attention among scholars of the American Renaissance. As Randall Fuller has argued, Matthiessen's choice of the war as his literary period's endpoint, along with his avoidance of socially engaged literature in favor of aesthetics and philosophy, helped to cement a narrative of formal experimentation defined by a sharp break between two eras.[5] The chapters

[4] Abraham Lincoln, *Speeches and Writings, 1859–1865*, ed. Don E. Fehrenbacher (New York: Library of America, 1989), 696. On the history of "Dixie" and its Union and Confederate appropriations, see Coleman Hutchison, "Whistling 'Dixie' for the Union (Nation, Anthem, Revision)," *American Literary History* 19.3 (Fall 2007): 603–28.

[5] Randall Fuller, "The 'American Renaissance' After the American Civil War," in *A History of American Civil War Literature*, ed. Coleman Hutchison (New York: Cambridge University Press, 2016), 48–61, 59–60.

in this volume's final section show a major blindspot in this narrative: war, while it certainly affected authors, publishers, and readers, did not mark the demise of many literary careers. Indeed, while Hawthorne and Thoreau both died during the war (of natural causes and far from the front), nearly every author discussed in this volume had a prolific writing career *after* the war, often in new areas or with new styles and topics influenced, though not always directly caused, by the war. Melville completed his turn from fiction to poetry; Whitman revised his entire *Leaves of Grass* project. Longfellow's poetry grew denser and darker as he turned increasingly to translation, while Harper moved from poetry to fiction, work that is more read today than her abolitionist poetry and oratory.

Some writers who came of age during the Renaissance years saw the war as the start of their careers. Louisa May Alcott's harrowing experience as a nurse in a Washington soldier's hospital provided the material for her breakout book, *Hospital Sketches* (1862). Pennsylvania-born poet Margaret Junkin Preston, who longed for literary fame during her first thirty years in the North, had moved to and married in Lexington, Virginia before the war, and found in the death of her brother-in-law, General Thomas "Stonewall" Jackson, an occasion for mourning but also for poetry. Her elegies for Jackson gained a wide audience, making her famous enough to publish an epic poem, *Beechenbrook* (1865), with both Northern and Southern publishers at the close of the war. While she remained in Virginia the rest of her life, Preston enjoyed a long literary career with books published in such prestigious Northern houses as Lippincott in Philadelphia and Houghton Mifflin in Boston. Rebecca Harding Davis, another Virginian (from Wheeling, which would become part of the pro-union state West Virginia), published her groundbreaking short story "Life in the Iron-Mills" in the *Atlantic* the month the war began, enabling her to reverse Preston's migration and settle into Pennsylvania as a professional novelist, married to a Philadelphia newspaper editor. And Emily Dickinson, long anthologized alongside Whitman as a major poet of the American Renaissance, wrote very little before 1860 but produced the bulk of her 1,800 extant poems during the war years, a fact that has recently led scholars to reconsider Dickinson, long thought an ethereal recluse, as a war poet engaged with the newspapers and politics of her time.

As this list suggests, women found remarkable opportunity as authors during and after the war, continuing the trend of women's literary professionalization – and in Dickinson's case, that of the manuscript poetess – in the 1840s and 1850s. The postwar years were more ambivalent for African-American authors, perhaps especially for those who had already gained prominence. While Harper's fiction has already been mentioned, her long poem *Moses* (1869) was an ambitious work in which she sought to declare her independence from her white abolitionist patrons and to puzzle through the question of what was to come after emancipation. While Harper, Douglass, and other black authors knew the battle for African-Americans' equality was only beginning, white abolitionists who had welcomed slave narratives as political ammunition before the war largely lost interest in these stories, as forgetting conflict became many Americans' main political goal in the decade between the war and the national centennial.

The war years were also difficult for Native American writers. While little documentary evidence of George Copway's activities in the 1860s has surfaced, he seems to have spent some time as a Union recruiter and a street healer in the Great Lakes region before his death in Ypsilanti, Michigan in 1869. The Cherokee writer John Rollin Ridge, self-exiled from Indian Territory (now Oklahoma) after his involvement in a blood feud over his father's death, published the first Native American novel, *Joaquin Murieta*, in 1854, and worked as a journalist and poet in California until his death in 1867. Ridge's Western location and his self-image as a fringe figure hampered his reception in the urban East, and it would be nearly a generation until writers such as Zitkála-Šá (Gertrude Bonnin, or Red Bird) would gain attention in American literary centers. Yet the war also launched the first Mexican-American novel, María Amparo Ruiz de Burton's *Who Would Have Thought It?* (1872). A dark satire on the rampant racism and political corruption of the 1860s, Ruiz de Burton's novel drew on her own experience as the wife of a Union officer who moved in influential Washington circles, even as her writing exhibited some of the ascerbic tone and rapid pacing of Fanny Fern's *Ruth Hall* and the moral outrage and continental sweep of Stowe's *Uncle Tom's Cabin*. Ruiz de Burton had seen the American takeover of California first-hand as a teenager, meeting her future husband in the occupying force of her hometown of La Paz. In her career, the full circle of wartime cultural collisions and American Renaissance literary developments coalesced to a degree that has still yet to be fully appreciated.

In his recent study *Why Literary Periods Mattered*, Ted Underwood observes that the boundaries around literary periods – the medieval, romanticism, Victorianism – have persisted from before the invention of the English department to the present day, even as methodologies and theories have come and gone and authors have fallen in and out of fashion. Underwood argues that this persistence is owing to the "prestige of literary culture," the thing that makes it aesthetically special and professionally compelling, being wrapped up in narratives of historical contrast.[6] Only the Renaissance could have broken us out of medieval cul-de-sacs; only Romanticism could overcome the shadow of the classical tradition that bound the eighteenth century. These narratives are convenient but brittle, breaking apart with the pressure of historical investigation. The American Renaissance, posited by a scholar trained in the literature of Shakespeare's time (what we now call the Renaissance, or perhaps the Early Modern period), defined a moment of contrast in American literary history buttressed by the retaining wall of the Civil War, at whose threshold everything purportedly changed. In focusing on that moment of historical difference, this volume participates in the ongoing story of literary periods we tell ourselves, a story whose reference points have proved too compelling to sweep aside with the latest theoretical trend. At the same time, it invites us to rethink what the middle of the nineteenth century really means for American literary history, what lines of continuity and influence link it back into the past and forward into our own time, to wonder why we can't let go of the idea of an American Renaissance – or why it won't let us go.

Balanced on the brink of the period, few writers have dealt as tenaciously with the conundrum of letting go and retaining memory as Emily Dickinson, and it is with one of her newly recognized war poems that this volume closes, imagining a scene of loss and reunion across the disparate locales of Amherst, Maryland, and heaven:

> When I was small, a Woman died –
> Today – her Only Boy
> Went up from the Potomac –
> His face all Victory
>
> To look at her – How slowly
> The Seasons must have turned
> Till Bullets clipt an Angle
> And He passed quickly round –
>
> If pride shall be in Paradise –
> Ourself cannot decide –
> Of their imperial conduct –
> No person testified –

---

[6] Ted Underwood, *Why Literary Periods Mattered: Historical Contrast and the Prestige of English Studies* (Stanford: Stanford University Press, 2013).

Coda

But, proud in Apparition –
That Woman and her Boy
Pass back and forth, before my Brain
As even in the sky –

I'm confident, that Bravoes –
Perpetual break abroad
For Braveries, remote as this
In Yonder Maryland –[7]

[7] Emily Dickinson, *The Poems of Emily Dickinson: Reading Edition*, ed. R. W. Franklin (Cambridge, MA: Belknap/Harvard University Press, 1999), 234–5.

Bercovitch, Sacvan. *The American Jeremiad*. Madison: University of Wisconsin Press, 1978.
  ed. *The Cambridge History of American Literature*. 8 vols. New York: Cambridge University Press, 1994–2005.
  The Puritan Origins of the American Self. New Haven: Yale University Press, 1975.
  Rites of Assent: Transformations in the Symbolic Construction of America. New York: Routledge, 1993.
Bercovitch, Sacvan and Myra Jehlen, eds. *Ideology and Classic American Literature*. New York: Cambridge University Press, 1986.
Blum, Hester, ed. *Turns of Event: Nineteenth-Century Literary Studies in Motion*. Philadelphia: University of Pennsylvania Press, 2016.
Brown, Gillian. *Domestic Individualism: Imagining Self in Nineteenth-Century America*. Berkeley: University of California Press, 1990.
Buell, Lawrence. *The Environmental Imagination: Thoreau, Nature Writing, and the Formation of American Culture*. Cambridge, MA: Harvard University Press, 1995.
  New England Literary Culture: From Revolution Through Renaissance. New York: Cambridge University Press, 1986.
Bush, Harold K. and Brian Yothers, eds. *Above the American Renaissance*. Amherst: University of Massachusetts Press, 2018.
Castiglia, Christopher. *Interior States: Institutional Consciousness and the Inner Life of Democracy in the Antebellum United States*. Durham, NC: Duke University Press, 2008.
Chase, Richard Volney. *The American Novel and Its Tradition*. Garden City: Doubleday, 1957.
Cohen, Michael C. *The Social Lives of Poems in Nineteenth-Century America*. Philadelphia: University of Pennsylvania Press, 2015.
Crain, Patricia. *The Story of A: The Alphabetization of America from the New England Primer to the Scarlet Letter*. Stanford: Stanford University Press, 2000.
Douglas, Ann. *The Feminization of American Culture*. New York: Knopf, 1977.
Fiedler, Leslie A. *Love and Death in the American Novel*. New York: Criterion Books, 1960.
Franchot, Jenny. *Roads to Rome: The Antebellum Encounter with Catholicism*. Berkeley: University of California Press, 1994.

Fuller, Randall. *From Battlefields Rising: How the Civil War Transformed American Literature*. New York: Oxford University Press, 2011.

Grossman, Jay. *Reconstituting the American Renaissance: Emerson, Whitman, and the Politics of Representation*. Durham, NC: Duke University Press, 2003.

Hager, Christopher. *Word by Word: Emancipation and the Act of Writing*. Cambridge, MA: Harvard University Press, 2013.

Kevorkian, Martin. *Writing Beyond Prophecy: Emerson, Hawthorne, and Melville After the American Renaissance*. Baton Rouge: Louisiana State University Press, 2013.

Leverenz, David. *Manhood and the American Renaissance*. Ithaca, NY: Cornell University Press, 1989.

Lewis, R. W. B. *The American Adam: Innocence, Tragedy, and Tradition in the Nineteenth Century*. Chicago: University of Chicago Press, 1955.

Loeffelholz, Mary. *From School to Salon: Reading Nineteenth-Century American Women's Poetry*. Princeton: Princeton University Press, 2004.

Marrs, Cody. *Nineteenth-Century American Literature and the Long Civil War*. New York: Cambridge University Press, 2015.

Marx, Leo. *The Machine in the Garden: Technology and the Pastoral Ideal in America*. New York: Oxford University Press, 1964.

Matthiessen, F. O. *American Renaissance: Art and Expression in the Age of Emerson and Whitman*. New York: Oxford University Press, 1941.

McGill, Meredith. *American Literature and the Culture of Reprinting, 1834–1853*. Philadelphia: University of Pennsylvania Press, 2003.

  ed. *The Traffic in Poems: Nineteenth-Century Poetry and Transatlantic Exchange*. New Brunswick: Rutgers University Press, 2008.

Michaels, Walter Benn and Donald E. Pease, eds. *The American Renaissance Reconsidered*. Baltimore: Johns Hopkins University Press, 1985.

Otter, Samuel. "*American Renaissance* and Us." *Journal of Nineteenth-Century Americanists* 3.2 (Fall 2015): 228–35.

Pattee, Fred Lewis. *The Feminine Fifties*. New York: Appleton-Century, 1940.

Pease, Donald E. *Visionary Compacts: American Renaissance Writings in Cultural Context*. Madison: University of Wisconsin Press, 1987.

Phillips, Christopher N. *Epic in American Culture, Settlement to Reconstruction*. Baltimore: Johns Hopkins University Press, 2012.

Powell, Timothy B. *Ruthless Democracy: A Multicultural Interpretation of the American Renaissance*. Princeton: Princeton University Press, 2000.

Reynolds, David S. *Beneath the American Renaissance: The Subversive Imagination in the Age of Emerson and Melville*. New York: Knopf, 1988.

  Walt Whitman's America: A Cultural Biography. New York: Knopf, 1995.

Rifkin, Mark. *Settler Common Sense: Queerness and Everyday Colonialism in the American Renaissance*. Minneapolis: University of Minnesota Press, 2014.

Sánchez-Eppler, Karen. *Dependent States: The Child's Part in Nineteenth-Century American Culture*. Chicago: University of Chicago Press, 2005.

Slotkin, Richard. *Regeneration Through Violence: The Mythology of the American Frontier, 1600–1860*. Middletown: Wesleyan University Press, 1973.

Sollors, Werner and Greil Marcus, eds. *A New Literary History of America*. Cambridge, MA: Belknap/Harvard University Press, 2009.

Stokes, Claudia. *Writers in Retrospect: The Rise of American Literary History, 1875–1910*. Chapel Hill: University of North Carolina Press, 2006.

Sundquist, Eric J. *To Wake the Nations: Race in the Making of American Literature*. Cambridge, MA: Harvard University Press, 1993.

Tompkins, Jane P. *Sensational Designs: The Cultural Work of American Fiction, 1790–1860*. New York: Oxford University Press, 1985.

Weikle-Mills, Courtney. *Imaginary Citizens: Child Readers and the Limits of American Independence, 1640–1868*. Baltimore: Johns Hopkins University Press, 2013.

INDEX

Cambridge Companions to...

AUTHORS

Lucretius edited by Stuart Gillespie and Philip Hardie

Machiavelli edited by John M. Najemy

David Mamet edited by Christopher Bigsby

Thomas Mann edited by Ritchie Robertson

Christopher Marlowe edited by Patrick Cheney

Andrew Marvell edited by Derek Hirst and Steven N. Zwicker

Herman Melville edited by Robert S. Levine

Arthur Miller edited by Christopher Bigsby (second edition)

Milton edited by Dennis Danielson (second edition)

Molière edited by David Bradby and Andrew Calder

Toni Morrison edited by Justine Tally

Alice Munro edited by David Staines

Nabokov edited by Julian W. Connolly

Eugene O'Neill edited by Michael Manheim

George Orwell edited by John Rodden

Ovid edited by Philip Hardie

Petrarch edited by Albert Russell Ascoli and Unn Falkeid

Harold Pinter edited by Peter Raby (second edition)

Sylvia Plath edited by Jo Gill

Edgar Allan Poe edited by Kevin J. Hayes

Alexander Pope edited by Pat Rogers

Ezra Pound edited by Ira B. Nadel

Proust edited by Richard Bales

Pushkin edited by Andrew Kahn

Rabelais edited by John O'Brien

Rilke edited by Karen Leeder and Robert Vilain

Philip Roth edited by Timothy Parrish

Salman Rushdie edited by Abdulrazak Gurnah

John Ruskin edited by Francis O'Gorman

Shakespeare edited by Margareta de Grazia and Stanley Wells (second edition)

Shakespearean Comedy edited by Alexander Leggatt

Shakespeare and Contemporary Dramatists edited by Ton Hoenselaars

Shakespeare and Popular Culture edited by Robert Shaughnessy

Shakespearean Tragedy edited by Claire McEachern (second edition)

Shakespeare on Film edited by Russell Jackson (second edition)

Shakespeare on Stage edited by Stanley Wells and Sarah Stanton

Shakespeare's First Folio edited by Emma Smith

Shakespeare's History Plays edited by Michael Hattaway

Shakespeare's Last Plays edited by Catherine M. S. Alexander

Shakespeare's Poetry edited by Patrick Cheney

George Bernard Shaw edited by Christopher Innes

Shelley edited by Timothy Morton

Mary Shelley edited by Esther Schor

Sam Shepard edited by Matthew C. Roudané

Spenser edited by Andrew Hadfield

Laurence Sterne edited by Thomas Keymer

Wallace Stevens edited by John N. Serio

Tom Stoppard edited by Katherine E. Kelly

Harriet Beecher Stowe edited by Cindy Weinstein

August Strindberg edited by Michael Robinson

Jonathan Swift edited by Christopher Fox

J. M. Synge edited by P. J. Mathews

Tacitus edited by A. J. Woodman

Henry David Thoreau edited by Joel Myerson

Tolstoy edited by Donna Tussing Orwin

Anthony Trollope edited by Carolyn Dever and Lisa Niles

Mark Twain edited by Forrest G. Robinson

John Updike edited by Stacey Olster

Mario Vargas Llosa edited by Efrain Kristal and John King

Virgil edited by Charles Martindale

Voltaire edited by Nicholas Cronk

Edith Wharton edited by Millicent Bell

Walt Whitman edited by Ezra Greenspan

Oscar Wilde edited by Peter Raby

Tennessee Williams edited by Matthew C. Roudané

August Wilson edited by Christopher Bigsby

Mary Wollstonecraft edited by Claudia L. Johnson

Virginia Woolf edited by Susan Sellers (second edition)

Wordsworth edited by Stephen Gill

W. B. Yeats edited by Marjorie Howes and John Kelly

Xenophon edited by Michael A. Flower

Zola edited by Brian Nelson

Edward Gibbon edited by Karen O'Brien and Brian Young

TOPICS